metaLABprojects

The *metaLABprojects* series provides a platform for emerging currents of experimental scholarship, documenting key moments in the history of networked culture, and promoting critical thinking about the future of institutions of learning. The volumes' eclectic, improvisatory, idea-driven style advances the proposition that design is not merely ornamental, but a means of inquiry in its own right. Accessibly priced and provocatively designed, the series invites readers to take part in reimagining print-based scholarship for the digital age. www.metalab.harvard.edu

Series Editor
Jeffrey T. Schnapp

Advisory Board
Giuliana Bruno (Harvard VES)
Jo Guldi (Brown)
Ian Bogost (Georgia Tech)
Michael Hays (Harvard GSD)
Bruno Latour (Sciences Po, Paris)
Bethany Noviskie (U of Virginia)
Andrew Piper (McGill)
Mark C. Taylor (Columbia)

Art Direction
Daniele Ledda
metaLAB and xycomm (Milan)

T0310964

Chronology

Only a small selection of ancient Egypt's rulers is listed here. All dates are approximate until 664 BCE. The kings who built their pyramids at Giza are highlighted in red.

PREDYNASTIC PERIOD
4500–3100 BCE

Dynasty 0, 3100–2960
    Narmer, 2960

EARLY DYNASTIC PERIOD
2960–2649 BCE

Dynasty 1, 2960–2770

Dynasty 2, 2750–2649

OLD KINGDOM
2649–2100 BCE

Dynasty 3, 2649–2575
    Djoser, 2630–2611

Dynasty 4, 2575–2465
    Snefru, 2575–2551
    Khufu, 2551–2528
    Djedefre, 2528–2520
    Khafre, 2520–2494
    Menkaure, 2490–2472
    Shepseskaf, 2472–2467

Dynasty 5, 2465–2323
    Isesi, 2381–2353
    Unas, 2353–2323

Dynasty 6, 2323–2150
    Teti, 2323–2291
    Pepy II, 2246–2152

Dynasty 7(?), 2150–2143(?)

Dynasty 8, 2143–2100

FIRST INTERMEDIATE PERIOD
2100–2040 BCE

Dynasties 9 and 10, 2140–2040

Dynasty 11 (first part), 2140–2040
    Mentuhotep II, 2061–2040

MIDDLE KINGDOM
2040–1640 BCE

Dynasty 11 (second part), 2040–1991
    Mentuhotep II, 2040–2010

Dynasty 12, 1991–1783
    Senwosret I, 1971–1926
    Senwosret III, 1878–1841

Dynasty 13, 1783–1640

SECOND INTERMEDIATE PERIOD
1640–1550 BCE

Dynasty 14, perhaps contemporary with Dynasty 13 or 15

Dynasty 15 (Greater Hyksos) and Dynasty 16 (Lesser Hyksos), 1640–1540

Dynasty 17, 1640–1550

NEW KINGDOM
1550–1070 BCE

Dynasty 18, 1550–1295
  Thutmose III, 1479–1425
  Hatshepsut, 1473–1458
  Amenhotep II, 1427–1400
  Thutmose IV, 1400–1390
  Amenhotep III, 1390–1352
  Amenhotep IV (Akhenaten),
  1352–1336
  Tutankhamun, 1336–1327

Dynasty 19, 1295–1186
  Seti I, 1294–1279
  Ramesses II, 1279–1213
  Merneptah, 1213–1203

Dynasty 20, 1186–1070
  Ramesses III–XI, 1184–1070

THIRD INTERMEDIATE PERIOD
1070–712 BCE

Dynasty 21, 1070–945

Dynasty 22, 945–712
  Shoshenq I, 945–924
  Osorkon II, 874 –850

Dynasty 23, 818–700

Dynasty 24, 724–712

LATE PERIOD
760–332 BCE

Dynasty 25, 760–660

Dynasty 26, 664–525

Dynasty 27, 525–404

Dynasty 28, 522–399

Dynasty 29, 399–380

Dynasty 30, 380–332

GRAECO-ROMAN PERIOD
332 BCE–364 CE

Macedonian Dynasty
  Alexander the Great, 332–323
Ptolemaic Dynasty, 305–30
  Ptolemy I–XV, 305–30
  Cleopatra VII, 51–30

ROMAN PERIOD
30 BCE–364 CE

BYZANTINE PERIOD
364–476 CE

Introduction

I have always been a cataloguer.
The chaotic state of my desk contradicts
this, but a passion for organizing, cross-
referencing, and establishing patterns
has almost always been a part of my life
and scholarship. As I wandered the
avenues of tombs surrounding the
famous Giza Pyramids for the first time
in 1977, I could not help wondering
how this massive open-air museum
could be "catalogued" for future
generations, and why no center
or institute had tried. This book
describes a small contribution toward
this goal, building on the trials

and triumphs of numerous Egyptological predecessors who gave major portions of their lives to unlocking the site for the world community.

Situated just west of modern Cairo, the Pyramids on the Giza Plateau represent perhaps the most famous archaeological site in the world. The site experienced its first "golden age" as the burial place of three pharaohs of the Egyptian Old Kingdom (Dynasty 4, ca. 2575–2465 BCE). Surrounding the Pyramids are royal temple complexes, queens' pyramids, workers' housing, administrative structures, food-processing centers, and thousands of tombs belonging to royal family members and the elite governing classes.

Giza's second golden age came almost five millennia later. We jump forward in time to the early decades of the twentieth century of our era, when the first modern excavators applied their newly devised archaeological craft to the Giza Plateau. Much of our knowledge of ancient Egyptian civilization we owe to the archaeologists who excavated Giza from 1903 until shortly after the Second World War. Though the Pyramids themselves revealed little in the way of artifacts, the surrounding *mastaba* tombs (Arabic for the modern benches that the tombs' rectangular shapes resemble) of the high officials contained thousands of carved and painted wall scenes and inscriptions, objects of daily life, ritual implements, and diverse types of statuary. The tomb wall scenes capture frozen moments from just about every aspect of life in ancient Egypt. The Giza Plateau is therefore a primary source not just for how the ancient Egyptians died, but for how they lived.

As we now take a twenty-first-century approach to the study of ancient civilizations, we are able to apply powerful new technologies to interpreting the material culture of the past. Conservation and publication have new and wider meanings. Ancient Egypt is poised to come alive as never before, in two, three, and even four dimensions, for all ages and knowledge levels. We can enable expert researchers as well as children to navigate virtually down Giza burial shafts from their own offices or classrooms.

But this approach comes with questions and a potential cost. Are we merely exploiting all these new technologies for their own sake, or truly improving our comprehension and interpretation? How do we transition from the static, black-and-white printed page to the animated image and still call it scholarship? Where is the borderline between academic knowledge and mere entertainment? Should "edutourism" enter our classrooms?

This book offers a brief introduction to the Giza Plateau of the Old Kingdom, (third millennium BCE; Chapter 1) followed by a summary of the history of excavation at the site since 1800. (Chapter 2) It then explores some of the new, primarily digital approaches to organizing and accessing ("cataloguing") the site, highlighting efforts that began in 2000 at the Museum of Fine Arts, Boston, and then moved to Harvard University. (Chapter 3) From here, the next logical step is 3D reconstruction of the site, (Chapter 4) as we slowly work toward a virtual replication of the Giza Necropolis, to allow both general access and targeted research inquiries that were previously impossible, even at the site itself. Case studies and philosophical musings on the nature of visualization in archaeology, a topic that has received increasing attention in recent scholarly literature, round out the volume, (Chapter 5) along with some speculation about emerging technologies and possible next steps. (Chapter 6)

The book is aimed at a fairly wide variety of audiences, and so it may be that no single reader will have equal interest in all the chapters. The book analyzes the early archaeological history of Giza and then carries that analysis into the modern era, asking along the way where these new approaches will lead—to groundbreaking research conclusions, or a new frontier of unregulated archaeological information overload? It is intended both for general readers and for any specialists interested in ancient Egypt and Egyptology, archaeology, anthropology, art history, 3D visualization and other immersive and interactive technologies, and new education strategies.

I have avoided providing either a comprehensive history of the Egyptian Old Kingdom or a detailed discussion of the technologies used to create "Digital Giza." Technical discussions of modeling software, texture mapping, and geographic information system (GIS) applications in archaeology, animation, and immersive digital environments are all available elsewhere. (A few references will be found in the Further Reading and Linkography section at the end of the volume.) Several of these approaches will no doubt fall by the wayside in the coming years; indeed, there are technologies we have already been compelled to abandon since our Giza Project began. (The philosophy behind the technological choices will enjoy, one hopes, a rather longer shelf life.) Instead, this book is an attempt to document a personal journey, taken with the help of countless colleagues, specialists, students, and volunteers, to catalogue portions of this fabulous ancient Egyptian site. Along the way, aspects of modern research methods, digital humanities, and new approaches to teaching and learning are described.

Archaeological standards for visualization are clearly still in flux; Egypt may lie in the east, but our struggles with visual and immersive approaches to ancient data are still in many ways, to use an American term, the "Wild West."

For my mother
Lucy Der Manuelian

Peter
Der Manuelian

Digital Giza
Visualizing
the Pyramids

metaLABprojects

Harvard University Press

Cambridge, Massachusetts, and London, England

2017

Library of Congress Cataloging-in Publication Data

Der Manuelian, Peter, author.
Digital Giza : visualizing the Pyramids / Peter Der Manuelian.
MetaLABprojects.
Cambridge, Massachusetts : Harvard University Press, 2017. |
MetaLABprojects | Includes bibliographical references.
LCCN 2016002080 | ISBN 9780674731233 (alk. paper)
LCSH: Imaging systems in archaeology. | Archaeology—Computer
simulation. | Pyramids of Giza (Egypt) | Virtual reality in archaeology. |
Excavations (Archaeology)—Egypt—Jīzah.
LCC CC79.I44 D47 2017 | DDC 930.1028/3—dc23
LC record available at http://lccn.loc.gov/2016002080

Graphic Design:
xycomm (Milan)
Daniele Ledda
with
Fabrizio Cantoni
Filippo Ferrari
Alessandro Tonelli

Table of Contents

CHAPTER 1

The Giza Necropolis in Time and Space

1.1 Menkaure Pyramid Temple, room 29, looking northeast to the sunlit Khafre pyramid.

The Pyramids have seen empires rise and fall, languages evolve, religions wax and wane, local skirmishes and world wars, and through it all the relentless advance of technological development. As Egypt sorts out the Arab Spring and rejuvenates the country politically and economically, we can assume that worldwide interest in these mountains of stone and their leonine guardian, the Sphinx, will once again result in thousands of visitors every day. (Figs. 1.1, 1.2)

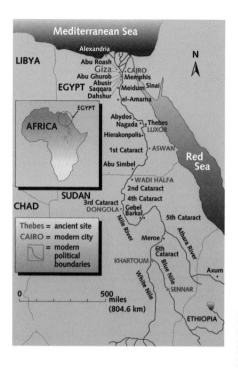

Present politics and tourism statistics aside, we are justified in marveling at how many pairs of eyes have gazed in wonder at the site of Giza over nearly five millennia. More recently we might rephrase that point: How many millions of digital snapshots of Giza are in circulation around the globe? Surely this attention constitutes a form of "immortality" that Khufu (also called Cheops) himself, builder of the Great Pyramid, would have enjoyed. Giza has served as a royal mortuary complex, crowded necropolis, ancient settlement, pilgrimage site, tourist attraction, royal legitimation hub, focus of stylistic renaissance and cultural archaism, getaway destination for modern royalty, meeting place for new-age hippies and "pyramidiots," and commercial and political backdrop for photo ops. Plays, fashion shoots, rock concerts, peace demonstrations, operas, squash tournaments, and even motorcycle jump competitions have all taken place under the placid gaze of the Sphinx. But why does Giza encourage so many different types of endeavors? Archaeology has enhanced the legacy of Giza with a steady stream of discoveries. How did Giza come to symbolize archaeology itself, and when did archaeology turn to Giza as one of its most enduring icons? (Fig. 1.3)

1.2 Map of Egypt, highlighting Giza.

1905–1906

April 4, 1936

Jan. 19, 2011

1.3 Comparison views of the Western Cemetery, looking southeast toward the Great Pyramid. *Top*: 1905–1906; *middle*: 1936; *bottom*: 2011.

Sharia el-Haram, or the "Pyramids Road," ends at the famous Mena House Hotel, where foreign Egyptologists once met to parcel out areas of the site for excavation. (see Chapter 2) Embarking on a hypothetical walking tour of the site, (Fig. 1.4) we ascend a steep and curving incline that has existed for generations, leading up to the Giza Plateau. We stand opposite the north facade of the Great Pyramid, the only facade that is not surrounded by *mastaba* tombs, an Arabic word used for the rectangular superstructures housing the remains of Egypt's elites from the Fourth, Fifth, and Sixth Dynasties. Ancient Egyptians probably took a different route, perhaps entering through the massive gate of the Heit el-Ghurab, or "Wall of the Crow," far to the south. But our horizon is blocked by the 720-foot- (219.5-meter-) long northern side of Khufu's Pyramid, reaching 450 (originally 481, or 146.6 meters) feet up into the sky. The plateau behind it slopes from the northwest to the southeast, averaging about six degrees. Impressive as the pyramid is today, in the third millennium BCE it would have been truly blinding, when its (now removed) fine white limestone casing blocks from the quarries of Tura (across the Nile, south of modern Cairo) were still in place. (Fig. 1.5) Khufu, son of Snefru, the first king of the Fourth Dynasty, selected the site with his architects to be the northernmost royal necropolis to that date, not far from the capital of Memphis. There is evidence of

earlier occupation of the site, but pharaonic eminent domain solved that problem, no doubt with scant objection from the king's subjects. Leveling the limestone bedrock and selecting the quarries for the core blocks, the largest quarry sitting off to the southeast, were Khufu's first priorities. This massive construction project was conceived to ensure the successful afterlife of the deceased pharaoh and renew the cycle of kingship for his successor. But this place was to hold much more than just a mountain of stone for the king's burial. The royal pyramid and its undecorated internal chambers were part of a complex that included two temples, a long connecting causeway between them, small pyramids for queens, a "cult" pyramid for the king, and scores of additional mastaba tombs on all three sides of the giant edifice. Khufu laid these tombs out for family members, elite officials, and court administrators. It was a stunningly ambitious example of urban planning for the dead, and it reveals

1.4 An aerial view of Giza, indicating the direction of a hypothetical walking tour of the Giza Plateau.

1.5 The Great Pyramid "restored."

all the elements of a third millennium BCE complex society and social stratification. Many casual visitors to the site remain oblivious to Khufu's extended achievement—first, because their gaze is fixed on the colossal pyramid before them, the world's tallest structure until the Eiffel Tower eclipsed it in 1889, and, second, because the mastaba fields are generally off-limits or difficult to see behind the queens' pyramids (east). But to walk up and down the well-ordered streets of tombs constitutes a special journey back over nearly five millennia. As battered limestone walls tower over our heads, we pass by the final resting places of inspectors, viziers, scribes, palace attendants, manicurists, judges, priests, and priestesses, many of whom spent portions of their lives in the pharaoh's company. And not just Khufu's company: Giza's tomb owners served many pharaohs, for after Khufu's reign the site remained active, even beyond the end of his ruling house, into the Fifth and Sixth Dynasties. That's when things got messier, and Khufu's orderly streets became choked with smaller subsidiary burials; soon funerary real estate was scarce, and administrative bookkeeping and institutional memory were required to keep burial shafts from crashing into each other underground. Some tombs bear no decoration or identification at all; others are marked by just a tombstone with the deceased's name and title(s), and still others contain one or more decorated chambers, with carved or painted scenes and inscriptions that are encyclopedic testaments not just to Egyptian death, but to all aspects of Egyptian life as well. Even in its ruined and plundered state today, the cemetery is an irreplaceable primary source for studying ancient Egyptian civilization. And while our walk through the cemetery streets may produce only the sound of our feet against the wind-blown sand, we must remember that once this was a bustling, thriving place, filled with administrators, guards, construc-

tion crews, sculptors and painters, offering bearers, priests, family members, and the occasional funeral procession.

East of the Great Pyramid, where Khufu chose to house his family members—and *house* is the correct term, for the Egyptians called the tombs "mansions of eternity"—many of the buildings were later joined together to form long double, or twin, mastabas twice as long as any other tombs at the site. (Fig. 1.6) We wend our way farther east, past the second-largest mastaba in all of Giza, and gain a view of the village of Nazlet es-Samman, just off the edge of the plateau, and separated from it by a series of rock-cut tombs carved into the descending cliff face. It's a breathtaking view eastward toward modern Cairo and the Nile. To our right, that is, south, crouches the great Sphinx, "father of terror" in Arabic, probably belonging to Khufu's son Khafre (Chephren), and guarding his second Giza pyramid. Carved from an outcrop near the eastern edge of the plateau, the Sphinx consists of three separate limestone geological member formations, the healthiest of which is, fortunately, at the head. (Fig. 1.7) Two temples, each with large

1.6 An aerial view of the Eastern Cemetery, looking southeast.

limestone and granite blocks, abut the Sphinx enclosure to the east and southeast, while beside it stretches the long causeway westward up toward the Khafre Valley Temple and Pyramid. We walk up the causeway and see to our right just a single row of mastabas on the south side of Khufu's Pyramid, beneath an unsightly gash in the south facade created by explorers in the nineteenth century. Between the mastabas and the pyramid, two modern structures currently house Khufu's life-size wooden boats, one reassembled and on display, the second currently under restoration from numerous pieces found in its burial pit after 4,500 years.

To the left as we ascend Khafre's causeway lies one of the world's largest and oldest examples of repurposing. The Central Field formed the primary quarry for Khufu's core blocks of limestone, and today it is difficult to imagine just how much of the landscape we no longer see there. But clues and ridges everywhere convey the original height of the area. (Fig. 1.8) In place of the clanging of thousands of chisels and the cacophony of ancient voices, the quarry now stands silent and converted—

1.7 The Sphinx and associated temples, looking southwest.

18

into yet another cemetery. In this case the tombs are partly built and partly carved into the unquarried bedrock, making use of leftover outcrops and cliff walls. Khufu never lived long enough to see this later hodgepodge of irregular structures that evolved in precise opposition to his carefully laid-out streets of tombs to the east and west of his own pyramid.

Khafre's Pyramid, the middle of the three, is instantly recognizable by the white limestone casing blocks that survive toward the top. (Fig. 1.9) Extrapolate downward and imagine the sun's blinding reflection off such blocks, freshly quarried and gleaming white, covering not only Khafre's, but Khufu's Pyramid as well. The image must have shocked and awed the ancient Egyptian populace for miles around. Khafre's entrance is on the north side, as is the case for almost all Old Kingdom pyramids. We continue our walk westward between the two pyramids, remembering that instead of a direct royal succession, another of Khufu's sons, Djedefre, succeeded and buried his father, then moved farther north to construct his own pyramid complex at the site of Abu Roash. It was Khafre who later

1.8 The Central Field quarry, looking west; some of the tops of the limestone bedrock surfaces are indicated in red.

19

returned to continue the Giza tradition. As we pass his pyramid to our left, we see ancient cuttings and grid marks on the limestone floor, and the impressive steep cliff wall that forms an enclosure for his pyramid precinct to the west. To our right, a massive limestone wall protects the largest Giza cemetery of all, the Western Cemetery. (Fig. 1.10) Thousands of cubic tons of limestone blocks, hundreds of mastabas, and countless subterranean burial shafts make up this metropolis of a necropolis. Some of the finest Egyptian wall reliefs and sculptural masterpieces ever to come out of the ground derive from these tombs, and their utilitarian objects, the stone and ceramic vessels, copper razors, and jewelry, fill many a museum. Some of the great architects of the age were buried here, and the largest of all Giza mastabas, dwarfing all but the Pyramids themselves, still guards the secret of the identity of its owner. Lifetimes of academic work of every conceivable nature confront the scholar in this area.

1.9 Nighttime view of the Khafre Pyramid and the Western Cemetery, looking southwest.

Passing by Khafre's pyramid, and walking westwards, almost the length of the Western Cemetery, we feel the terrain

20

rising until we stand at the highest point on the Giza Plateau. Here was the home of one of the longest-running archaeological projects ever undertaken. At "Harvard Camp," the Harvard University–Boston Museum of Fine Arts Expedition worked, ate, and slept for forty-four years. It was little more than a cluster of mud brick huts around a central courtyard, but it offered a commanding view in all directions: two massive pyramids to the east, and a third, smaller one, belonging to King Menkaure, off to the south. These artificial mountains glowed gold and then orange at the end of the day, as the wind picked up and added a special ambience to the place into dusk and then nightfall. Off to the north, the excavators used to gaze upon the Nile and the patches of lush, green fields that flourished thanks to annual inundations that stretched almost to the base of the Plateau. Nowadays the floods are no more, stopped by the Aswan High Dam some 524 miles to the south. One cannot help but be swept away by the and the sheer antiquity of the view, despite the hazy high-rises in the distance. By the end of the Sixth Dynasty (c. 2150 BCE), the scene would have been largely

1.10 An aerial view of the Western Cemetery, looking northwest.

complete from here, with all pyramids and accompanying temples in their "final" form, the quarries much quieter, and the cemeteries filled with mastabas and rock-cut tombs. All that was missing were some New Kingdom additions by Eighteenth and Nineteenth Dynasty pharaohs (c. 1427–1390, 1279–1213 BCE), and much later, some Late Period temples and intrusive burials in the Eastern Cemetery (seventh century BCE).

Walking south from Harvard Camp, behind Khafre's Pyramid, we approach the third and final royal complex, the smaller pyramid of Menkaure (Mycerinus). Tumbled granite blocks all around the base indicate that the lowest third of this pyramid was cased in a material other than the typical limestone. (Fig. 1.11) On the eastern facade we can make out just where the masons left off smoothing the casing blocks. We circle around to the south and come on three queens' pyramids, never quite finished, hugging the southern facade of Menkaure's Pyramid, each with vestiges, now buried, of its own mortuary temple. Directly off the southeast corner of the pyramid lies an L-shaped quarry that supplied the blocks for this pyramid and later served as an additional cemetery for Menkaure's family members and high officials. A settlement and industrial zones lie a bit farther out in the desert. Turning north again, we come to the massive limestone enclosure of the Menkaure Pyramid Temple, connected to yet another causeway, partially washed away by ancient flooding, but once running eastward to the king's (now reburied) valley temple, completed in mud brick by his successor and occupied later in the Old Kingdom as a settlement. On the way to this area, we note one last monumental structure to our left, in the Central Field. Part mastaba, part pyramid, part natural outcrop, and part constructed edifice, this is the tomb complex of Queen Khentkaus, an enigmatic figure of the end of the Fourth Dynasty and beginning of the Fifth. An entire priestly town, with a long row of houses, ex-

tends eastward from the "pyramid" and takes an L-shaped right turn toward the Menkaure Valley Temple; in all, some 900 feet (275 meters) of construction make up Khentkaus's "footprint" at Giza. A system of slopes and ramps in this vicinity, south of the Sphinx, connecting to the ancient harbor, has started to reveal its secrets only in recent years. But when not under excavation, this area, like the Menkaure Valley Temple, lies under the sand just to the north of a central wadi, invisible to our eyes.

Still farther to the southeast we find another excellent vantage point for an overview of the entire necropolis: the Southern Mount overlooks modern Coptic and Muslim cemeteries, built right over portions of the ancient complex, and presents a windy vista of the three Pyramids. On the other side of the mount, a recently discovered cemetery, with additional built mastabas and rock-cut tombs, abuts the limestone ridge. These show an upper elite zone, containing the tombs of necropolis administrators, while the lower zone contains simpler, smaller tombs. The cemetery overlooks the so-called lost city of the Pyramids, an extensive plain full of food-processing areas,

1.11 The Menkaure Pyramid complex, looking southwest.

barracks, corridors, houses, a royal administrative building, and perhaps a port for expeditions to deliver their goods. The Wall of the Crow, which bounds the city to the north, may have served to divert ancient floods coursing through the central wadi. But once again, most of this area is usually hidden from view beneath the sandy overburden.

We have now completed a quick tour of the major zones of the Giza Necropolis known so far, a walk of several hours. But our walk hardly resembles the one an ancient Egyptian would have taken in 2500 BCE. First, the climate in the late third millennium was far moister than it is today, so in addition to the sand cover that we have been trudging over, we should probably imagine some vegetation, and perhaps even landscaping around the royal temple complexes. And second, the Nile has been meandering east and west through much of its existence, and it may have flowed quite close to Giza during part of the Old Kingdom. These are fundamental geomorphological issues that clearly played a role in the Egyptians' selection of Giza in the first place, in the spatial distribution of the mastaba fields, and in the positioning of causeways and temples at the eastern edge of the plateau.

How are we to make sense of this vast, sacred mortuary landscape, and of the architectural decisions at the highest levels of the royal court at Memphis? Alas, we have only rumors from Herodotus, hints of legacy reputations, and precious little else to try to build up a personal picture of any of the three Giza kings. But regardless of the contemporary political and economic development in distant parts of the country, Giza reflects an age of political and economic centralization—all in the person of the king—without which pyramid construction would have been impossible. Once the layout for the Great Pyramid complex was settled, Khufu found his solution for the surrounding mastaba fields: prefabrication. Streets and rows of similarly proportioned tombs, assigned to his family (east) or his officials (west), marked the commencement of the largest funereal zone in Egypt's history up to the Fourth Dynasty. The general construction sequence and direction for both cemeteries is still debated, but a plausible scenario posits the earlier structures farthest away from the pyramid, and successive rows approaching its base. Was this to avoid the chaos—scaffolding, ramps, and limestone block deliveries—surrounding the pyramid itself? For the Eastern Cemetery, this meant beginning at the far eastern edge of the plateau, which moved progressively westward, toward the pyramid. For the Western Cemetery, the construction started in the far west and moved eastward, where the rows closest to Khufu's Pyramid break ranks to form an asymmetrical alignment from one row to the next, perhaps so that entrances to chapels might remain in view. By this time, most of the tomb owners postdated Khufu's reign, and he would not have witnessed the disarray, either of these mastabas near his pyramid's western facade, or of all the smaller, subsidiary tombs that followed in the later Fifth and Sixth Dynasties of the Old Kingdom.

Khafre followed his father's pattern, although the tombs of the Central Field, east of his pyramid, reveal no such prefabricated layout. And while ritual boat pits imitate the Great Pyramid scheme to some extent, no line of three queens' pyramids has yet come to light—merely a cult pyramid on the south side. Menkaure's complex is in many ways the most interesting, not only for its partial granite exterior casing, but also because of its complex series of interior chambers. These include the only example of decoration in any of the three Giza Pyramids, in the form of niched paneling in an antechamber, as well as a ninety-degree turn and sunken staircase leading to burial apartments. Menkaure's officials used almost all the available cemetery zones for their tombs—East Cemetery, West Cemetery,

Central Field, and the Menkaure Quarry Cemetery southeast of the king's pyramid. Moreover, Menkaure's two temples underwent numerous alterations and uses and revealed thousands of artifacts, among them repurposed stone vessels and masterpieces of royal statuary.

Burial equipment at Giza, at least what survives from the "private" (i.e., nonroyal) tombs, shows the finest craftsmanship in the land. Syro-Palestinian import wares are even attested in some tombs, and other grave goods represent the full range, from utilitarian pieces showing the wear and tear of actual use to funerary equipment and even miniature or dummy objects created specifically for the afterlife.

Why did the Egyptians continue to use Giza after the end of Menkaure's reign? Why did so many choose not to move on to the royal pyramid sites of later dynasties, farther to the south, to be near succeeding generations of pharaohs? Some of these officials were employed in the cults of the three Giza kings; others had ancestors here and no doubt wanted to be interred in family complexes. We have no idea how long mortuary cults were kept up by surviving families, but they were theoretically meant to last forever. The result was that Giza's significance continued right through the end of the Old Kingdom. After this era, major activity at the site did not resume again until the Eighteenth Dynasty, when pharaohs such as Amenhotep II and Thutmose IV returned to the site with their horses and chariots and focused their attention on the Sphinx, considerably altering the landscape around it. A second "renaissance" for the site came in the Late Period (seventh century BCE), when elites once more venerated the deities associated with the site, such as "Isis, Mistress of the Pyramids," and added a small temple and numerous burials to the Eastern Cemetery. There is no mistaking their anthropoid coffins for the rectangular Old Kingdom sarcophagi of two thousand years earlier.

Humans have studied Giza for millennia. Is there really that much more to learn? What do scholars still want to know about this sacred landscape and the creative minds behind it? The academic inquiries never stop, and indeed old mysteries are compounded by new ones, as excavations continue and new approaches to Egyptological and archaeological research allow us to ask new questions. Construction methods for the Great Pyramid are just one of the obvious points of debate that remain. But there are also questions about Egyptian society, social stratification, mortuary practices, gender relations, dynastic succession, decoration programs, and the significance of scene distribution in royal and private tombs and temples. We want to know the points of origin of the wood, stones, and clays that make up vessels and statuary, about craftsmanship, art historical development, and the analysis of human skeletal remains. We strive to learn about quarries, labor and project management, language and grammatical development, concepts of kingship, and the roots and evolution of the Egyptian netherworld. Finally, we ask how the Old Kingdom related to later ages; why did Egyptians return to this era thousands of years later with reverence? What role did the Pyramids play for ancient Egyptian society, for Coptic Christianity, for Muslim Egypt, and for imperialist Egyptology of the nineteenth and early twentieth centuries? How was Giza revived and reimagined in later periods, long after the end of the Old Kingdom Pyramid Age? What does this site ultimately mean for modern Egyptian identity today? It was to help answer some of these questions that the Giza Project described in the following chapters was originally conceived.

CHAPTER 2

Archaeological Explorations at Giza from 1800 to the Present

The Explorers, 1800–1840

The beginning of the nineteenth century saw the first organized explorations of the Giza Necropolis.[1] At the turn of the century, the Sphinx was merely a colossal and enigmatic head emerging from the surrounding sand. (Fig. 2.1) Rectangular superstructures poked up here and there among the debris, hinting at untold numbers of buildings east and west of the Great Pyramid.

But the relationships of the royal to the "private" (i.e., non-royal) elements of the site, from tomb to temple, and temple to pyramid, remained completely unexplored. The so-called Central Field, home first to the quarry that produced the blocks for Khufu's Pyramid core, then later numerous rock-cut and built mastaba tombs, lay completely buried. (Fig. 2.2) The most famous antiquities that we have since come to associate with Giza still lay hidden under the sands in 1800: the famous seated statue of King Khafre carved from anorthosite gneiss; the elegant wall paintings in the tomb of Meresankh III; the lifelike painted bust of the vizier Ankh-haf; the tomb of the dwarf Seneb; the unparalleled graywacke pair statue

2.1 The buried Sphinx, looking east, in 1886.

Sept. 13, 1913

May 28, 1938

Oct. 7, 2011

of King Menkaure and presumably a queen; the magnificent funerary boats of Khufu; the powerful, colossal, and corpulent statue of the Great Pyramid's engineer and architect, Hemiunu; and a host of inscriptions—ceremonial, funereal, legal, biographical. In 1800 no one had yet deciphered hieroglyphs. The Nile's annual inundation still reached almost to the base of the Giza Plateau, creating turtlebacks out of the scattered villages in the shadow of the Pyramids. And about nine miles (fifteen kilometers) to the east, Cairo was in transition.

After Napoleon's defeat at the hands of Lord Nelson and the ensuing departure of the French in 1801 owing to Ottoman and British pressure, Mohamed Ali Pasha (1769–1849) initiated a period of modernization and agrarian reform. Thanks to the newly awakened European fascination with ancient Egypt, the race was on between competing powers that sought to stock their home museums with cultural patrimony removed from pharaonic sites up and down the Nile.

2.2 Aerial comparison views of the Central Field and beyond, looking southeast: 1913, 1938, 2011.

In the most lamentable cases they even preferred to destroy a monument rather than watch it fall into the hands of rival collectors. From 1816 onward, the British consul Henry Salt (1780–1827) battled his nemesis, Bernardino Drovetti (1776–1852), the French consul-general from 1802 to 1814.[3] Drovetti's personal collection of 5,268 objects eventually formed the nucleus of the Museo Egizio in Turin.[4] From 1828

Napoleon in Egypt

On July 21, 1798, Napoleon's forces defeated the Mamelukes at the Battle of the Pyramids. (Fig. W1.1) The French general's 150 savants began laying the foundations of a western approach to academic study of the past.[1] The political and military success of Napoleon's campaign is dubious, but the contribution of his savants to a wide range of disciplines, from natural history to Islamic architecture, from floral analysis to ancient Egyptian language, cannot be overestimated. Not least among their finds was the Rosetta Stone, discovered in 1799, the key to the decipherment of hieroglyphs.[2] At Giza the French expedition staff partially cleared and surveyed the Sphinx, along with the Great Pyramid, producing detailed measurements of both the interior chambers and the exterior courses of the Pyramid. Most impressive were the magnificent overview drawings of the Pyramids and surrounding landscape. The illustrations by numerous French artists and surveyors graced volume 5 of the magnificent twenty-three-volume publication series *Description de l'Égypte*.[3] Plate 6 provided one of the earliest contour maps of the entire Giza Plateau, with excellent topography.

One of the few criticisms of the French work at Giza was their attempt to dismantle the top northern courses of the third and westernmost queen's pyramid of the Menkaure complex (pyramid G III-c).

W1.1 Popular print of the Battle of the Pyramids, 1830.

until his death, Giovanni Anastasi (1780–1860) served as the Swedish-Norwegian consul general, selling large collections to the Dutch, the British, and the French. Salt himself worked for short periods at Giza, but he supported the more intensive efforts of the Genoese sea captain and dedicated Anglophile Giovanni Caviglia (1770–1845). Caviglia arrived in Egypt at the end of 1816 and devoted himself to archaeological pursuits for the next two decades, primarily at the Giza Necropolis. Fueled by his deeply religious convictions that the Pyramids held the answers to many of life's spiritual mysteries, his methods overall were far more respectful of the monuments than those of his contemporaries Howard Vyse and Giovanni Belzoni (see below). Caviglia was probably the first of several European explorers to convert the chambers of a rock-cut tomb at Giza into his own personal dwelling. Examining the "well" (actually a pit) inside the Great Pyramid in 1817, Caviglia reached the Pyramid's unfinished subterranean chamber, after much strenuous effort, in 1818. He also explored the lowest of the five stress-relieving chambers situated directly above the so-called king's chamber. (Fig. 2.3) Sadly, Caviglia used dynamite to reach the room.

Turning to the surrounding cemeteries, Salt and Caviglia unearthed numerous mastaba tombs, and they may have been the first to distinguish the individual elements of superstructure and substructure, for each mastaba possessed at least one vertical shaft leading to a burial chamber and sarcophagus. Though it is not possible today to identify every tomb they explored, many are now known, thanks to the discovery—during renovations to the Department of Ancient Egypt and Sudan in the British Museum in 2002—of Salt's mostly unpublished memoir and sketches.[5]

Caviglia's third achievement at Giza consisted of the first systematic clearing of the Sphinx (1816) since Napoleon's men

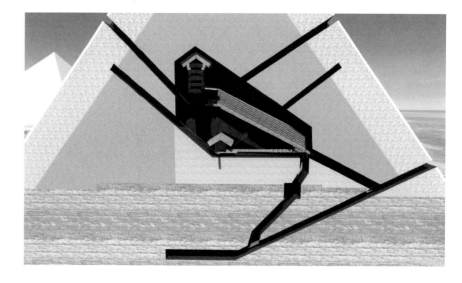

had exposed part of its back. Working in 1818, Caviglia dug a trench 65 feet (20 meters) deep that revealed the statue's northern shoulder. This was the first exposure of a major portion of the Sphinx's body. The clearance work was as perilous as it was frustrating, as high walls of sand threatened to collapse at any moment, and the winds often wiped out the previous day's progress. Caviglia concentrated on the forelegs, unearthing the chapel between the paws and discovering the Dream Stela of Thutmose IV.

Nearby he also found the cobra head from the Sphinx's uraeus and a fragment of its plaited beard. Upon completing his excavations, Caviglia demonstrated a concern—far ahead of his time—for the preservation of his finds. Having noticed local villagers breaking off portions of the Sphinx as amuletic and aphrodisiacal aids, he reburied the statue to preserve it for future generations, despite receiving criticism from some quarters. With Salt's support, Caviglia donated his finds to the British Museum.

2.3 Cutaway section view of the Great Pyramid, showing the king's chamber and five relieving chambers above it.

Thutmose IV

The Dream Stela text of Thutmose IV (Fig. W2.1) relates how the divine Sphinx appeared to the young prince in a dream, promising him the throne in return for clearing the god's body of accumulated debris. Flanking either side of the stela, which was cut by Thutmose IV from a reused granite block originally belonging to Khafre's mortuary complex nearby, are two rectangular slabs, erected by Ramesses II, portraying this Nineteenth Dynasty king presenting offerings to the Sphinx. Both slabs are now in the Louvre.[1]

W2.1 The chapel area between the paws of the Sphinx, looking west.

Less conscientious was Giovanni Battista Belzoni (1778–1823), a former circus strongman who had come to Egypt to sell hydraulic machinery to Mohammed Ali. Turning to archaeology after business failed to materialize, Belzoni also allied himself with Henry Salt. He declined to join Caviglia in his explorations of Khufu's Pyramid—Belzoni never took a backseat to anyone—but instead turned his attentions to Khafre's Pyramid. Belzoni cleared the upper of the two entrances on the pyramid's north side and reached Khafre's burial chamber on March 2, 1818. He was not the first one in; Arabic graffiti indicated the presence of previous visitors, but this did not stop him from adding his own large graffito to the wall of the chamber.[6] The bones of a bull were found in the undecorated sarcophagus, carved from a single block of granite and sunk into the floor.[7]

Two other Englishmen contributed greatly to the pioneering age at Giza. But before their arrival in the 1830s, Egypt and its antiquities were to see major changes. First and foremost, of course, was the decipherment of hieroglyphs in 1822, based on Jean-François Champollion's (1790–1832) brilliant analysis of the Rosetta Stone and other monuments. It is easy to forget that until this singular achievement, none of the explorers mentioned so far could read any of the inscriptions they were unearthing. Now it was as if a window had been thrown open, letting in the fresh breeze of Egyptian history, narrated in the words of the ancients themselves. Forming a joint Franco-Tuscan expedition, Champollion set out for Egypt in 1828 with his student, Ippolito Rosellini (1800–1843), to collect additional hieroglyphic inscriptions. This expedition was financed by Leopold II, grand duke of Tuscany, and the French king Charles X. But Giza seems to have bored Champollion, no doubt because of the dearth of texts—not a single hieroglyph could be found inside the pyramids there. Champollion's shortest letter of all was written at Giza on October 8, 1828, revealing that the scholar was all too ready to sail upstream to Thebes.[8]

A second change in ancient Egyptian affairs came on August 15, 1835, when Mohammed Ali banned the unauthorized removal of antiquities from the country. His decree also designated a building in the Ezbekiah Gardens, Cairo, as a collections storehouse. Unfortunately, Egyptian rulers often dispensed these antiquities to foreign dignitaries as gifts, thereby reducing the collection substantially. But the stage had been set for institutionalizing archaeology in Egypt, as well as preserving its cultural patrimony.

Arriving in Egypt in the same year as Mohammed Ali's antiquities decree, the English army officer Richard William Howard Vyse (1784–1853) teamed up with Caviglia for additional exploration of the Great Pyramid. But after 1836 the relationship began to sour, as Vyse felt that Caviglia was more interested in searching for mummies. Vyse moved on after essentially firing Caviglia on February 13, 1837 (despite the latter's outburst, "You may have the money, but I have the brains"), and subsequently joined forces with the British engineer and anthropologist John Shae Perring (1813–1869). The men camped, as had Caviglia, among the rock-cut tombs in the Eastern Cemetery and set about simultaneous investigation at sites around Giza and elsewhere. Returning to England in 1837, Vyse left the excavations in Perring's hands. The latter published his results in three massive folio volumes, whereas Vyse chose a smaller format for his three-volume publication.[9]

The value of the Vyse and Perring contributions to our understanding of the royal monuments at Giza is undeniable. Recording the numbers of workmen and the daily locations of their excavations, and producing excellent plans, section drawings, and descriptions of their finds, Perring and his team set a new standard for archaeological documentation. Yet, however much we might praise Vyse and Perring, their methods were at times nothing short of horrifying. The men dismantled major portions of the Pyramids and resorted to gunpowder far more than Caviglia had as their most time- and cost-efficient archaeological "tool," blasting their way through pyramids in the search for entrances and burial chambers. At the Khafre Pyramid, dynamite exposed the lower entrance on the north side, as the granite blocking stones were simply blown apart.

Not content to confine themselves to a single location, Vyse and Perring eventually explored all three royal Pyramids, all of Menkaure's subsidiary queens' pyramids, the Sphinx, the great Dynasty 26 shaft west of the Sphinx known as Campbell's tomb, and other locations. On the back of the Sphinx, Vyse drilled straight down using boring rods, in a search for hidden chambers. He eventually abandoned the search at 27 feet (8.2 meters), leaving some of the rods in place, and for once refraining from using dynamite; the cavity was later recleared in 1978, and it revealed a fragment with part of the Sphinx's pleated headdress. In the Great Pyramid, over a period of just a few months, Vyse discovered—again with dynamite—the remaining four stress-relieving chambers positioned above the lowest one, first entered in 1763. These he named after important British personages. As important as this discovery was for the mortuary architecture of the monument, equally valuable was the appearance of the ancient work gang's painted graffiti on the chamber walls, certifying once and for all Khufu's ownership of the pyramid. The most famous graffito, showing the simple form of Khufu's name in a cartouche (oval ring), occurs on the southern gable of Campbell's (topmost) chamber. Vyse also blasted a gash in the southern side of the pyramid's exterior, hoping to find a secondary entrance. The gash is still visible today, and it forms a regrettable but useful "section" view into the core masonry of the structure.

Vyse and Perring are best known for their exploration of the Menkaure Pyramid complex, which, until that time, had received the least attention from these early explorers. Their first approach consisted of tunneling horizontally straight into the pyramid on the north side, using the exposed gash created by Saladin's son Othman in 1196 CE. Bending vertically downward, this "excavation" produced no results, so they refocused their efforts on removing casing stones, based on the locations of the neighboring Khufu and Khafre Pyramid entrances. The entrance appeared on July 28, 1837. Passing through the entrance corridor, which contained an antechamber with palace-facade niching, the only decoration in any of the three Giza Pyramids, they eventually reached the granite-lined burial chamber, which, like Khafre's chamber, showed the Arabic graffiti of previous visitors. Inside remained the king's original stone sarcophagus,[10] while fragments of the lid were scattered in the room immediately above it and connected by a staircase. This upper room also revealed a wooden anthropoid coffin inscribed for Menkaure, but dating stylistically to the Twenty-sixth Dynasty, about two thousand years later. (Fig. 2.4) Human remains were present, too, but radiocarbon dating put them in the Christian period. The wooden coffin and the bones are now in the British Museum,[11] but the stone sarcophagus was lost en route to England when the merchant ship *Beatrice* sank somewhere between Cartagena and Malta on October 13, 1838. As of this writing, efforts to recover the sarcophagus have yet to meet with success, but the sarcophagus represents a critical piece of Giza archaeology.[12]

Vyse and Perring also explored the queens' pyramids just south of Menkaure's Pyramid. Tunneling directly down from the top of pyramid G III-b, the central queen's pyramid, the explorers failed to connect with the subterranean chambers. Eventually, however, they laid bare the entrances to all three pyramids, and none seems to have produced artifacts contemporary with Menkaure's reign.[13] Pyramid G III-a, the easternmost, might originally have served as a cult pyramid; G III-b contained an uninscribed sarcophagus with female human remains inside, and G III-c, whose superstructure had already been partially dismantled by Napoleon's expedition, revealed an unfinished burial chamber. Assigning these pyramids to actual individuals has proved difficult at best. All three have mortuary temple remains on their eastern sides. (see fig. 1.11)

The Early Scholars, 1840–1880

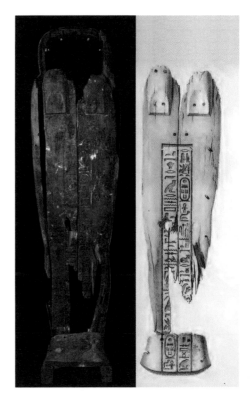

The next significant Giza campaign, the Prussian expedition of Karl Richard Lepsius (1810–1884), represented the end of the era of pioneers and explorers and the start of a new era, one of scientists and archaeologists.[14] Educated at the universities of Leipzig, Göttingen, and Berlin, Lepsius discovered Egyptology in Paris. He was one of the first to wholeheartedly embrace the new grammatical breakthrough of Champollion. In fact, Lepsius is seen by many as a founding father of Egyptology, inheriting the mantle tragically relinquished by Champollion's premature death. After several years studying Egyptian collections in Europe, Lepsius was prepared to direct the

2.4 A Twenty-sixth Dynasty coffin from the Menkaure Pyramid.

largest, best-organized expedition to ancient Egypt and Nubia (modern Sudan) ever assembled up to that time. Working on behalf of Kaiser Friedrich Wilhelm IV, who supported the expedition at the suggestion of Alexander von Humboldt (1769–1859) and Christian Charles Josias Bunsen (1791–1860), Lepsius assembled a team of draftsmen, surveyors, scholars, artists, and craftsmen to accompany him. These men he tasked with producing drawings, casts, squeezes (materials applied to walls to create faithful impressions), and watercolors.

With the decipherment of Egyptian hieroglyphs, Lepsius, unlike members of the Napoleonic expedition of the previous century, could read many of the inscriptions on the monuments he cleared, which represented a quantum leap in terms of epigraphy, historical interpretation, and an archaeological approach to his documentation. In a clever feat of scheduling, Lepsius first visited Giza on the Kaiser's birthday, October 15, 1842, and climbed Khufu's Pyramid in his honor. The team surveyed the surrounding scene and initiated an excavation plan. This marked the beginning of three months of study at the Giza Necropolis. In mid-November the expedition also carved a dedicatory text to the Kaiser on one of the angled blocks over the entrance to the pyramid; the text is still visible today.[15] Around December 20, 1842, two of the expedition members created a striking, almost 360-degree watercolor panoramic view—on multiple overlapping sheets—of the Giza landscape from the top of the pyramid.[16]

Systematic work began on November 11, 1842. Lepsius identified some eighty-seven different tombs, numbering them accordingly. This numbering system is still in use today, although in many cases these tombs have received additional numbers devised by twentieth-century expeditions.

At the Sphinx, Lepsius had to clear the chapel between the paws again to reveal the Thutmose IV stela; he published

Karl Richard Lepsius

Improving on the work of previous expeditions, Lepsius produced both overview and individual plans for the monuments he studied. To round out the picture he was forming of Egyptian history and chronology, he selected specific tombs and temples, protruding from the surface debris, that looked as if they would reward further excavation. One such tomb belonged to an elite official named Merib, whose late Fourth or early Fifth Dynasty limestone chapel Lepsius excavated in the Western Cemetery.[1] The colors were so vibrant on the four chapel walls that Lepsius sought and obtained permission to remove them for shipment to Berlin. Dismantling and packing began in August 1845. But by the time the blocks arrived in Germany, most of the polychromy

had disappeared. Fortunately, watercolors of the decoration had been prepared by Johann Jakob Frey at Giza before the dismantling of the walls.[2] (Fig. W3.1) The chapel is now reconstructed in Berlin's Neues Museum (Inv. Nr. 1107), where for the first time since the Second World War it has joined two other chapels from Saqqara (of Metjen and Manefer), providing spectacular examples of Old Kingdom private mortuary architecture.[3] (Fig. W3.2) Lepsius also shipped many other objects, including reliefs, coffins, ceramics, stone vessels, and even mud sealings, along with an architrave and pillars from the chapel of the mid-Fifth Dynasty official Neferbauptah (Lepsius tomb 15 = G 6010).[4]

W3.1 Modern painting of the tomb of Merib (G 2100-I), chapel, west wall.

W3.2 The chapel of Merib (G 2100-I), reconstructed in the Neues Museum, Berlin.

the first copy of this important text.[17] But he left a final decision on the identification of the Sphinx as either Khufu or Khafre to future archaeologists, who, he believed, would first have to free the Sphinx and neighboring temples completely.

By the time Lepsius departed Giza on February 11, 1843, headed south on his three-year expedition, he had set a new standard for conscientious exploration and documentation of the site. Gone were the days of blasting through pyramids; and though some decorated chapels were dismantled and crated up for shipment to Europe, they were removed with authorization, with care, and with architectural and epigraphic documentation that preserved their archaeological context at Giza.[18] The expedition's epigraphers documented scenes and inscriptions that today are much worse for wear or have disappeared completely. None of this material would have reached world scholarship were it not for the tireless efforts of Lepsius and his successors to publish their massive archive. The twelve-volume oversized folio series *Denkmaeler aus Aegypten und Aethiopien* was published between 1849 and 1856 and contains 894 plates. No other expedition had compiled such a comprehensive record of Egyptian and Nubian monuments, and the improvement in accuracy over previous publications is remarkable. By the middle of the nineteenth century, a host of travelers and scholars had cleared and published large sections of the Giza Necropolis, copied scenes and inscriptions, or otherwise contributed to our knowledge of the site.[19]

A major turning point in Egyptian archaeology and cultural heritage management occurred in 1858, when the Egyptian Viceroy Said Pasha (1822–1863) signed off on the creation of the Service des Antiquités, the French Egyptologist Auguste Mariette (1821–1881) serving as its first director.[20] Mohammed Ali had already banned the unauthorized removal of antiquities in 1835, and he set up a first Egyptian "museum," rather more

of a warehouse, in Ezbekia, in central Cairo. Mariette established the first museum dedicated to Egyptian antiquities in
Bulak, to the west of Cairo. French scholars ran the Service des
Antiquités for nearly a century before Egyptian nationals took
the reins in 1953.

During a first campaign at Giza in 1851, Mariette cleared
the Sphinx completely and discovered the Khafre Valley Temple immediately to the south. Returning four years later, he re-
commenced work in the cemetery east of the Great Pyramid,
near the third and southernmost of Khufu's three queen's
pyramids. Here he cleared the Temple of Isis, "Mistress of the
Pyramid," a New Kingdom–Late Period reconfiguration of the
pyramid G I-c complex, containing the now famous Henutsen
or inventory stela, which actually dates to the Twenty-sixth Dynasty (seventh century BCE), not to the Old Kingdom, as Mariette had supposed.[21] Returning to the Khafre Valley Temple in
1860, Mariette unearthed one of the greatest works of three-di-
mensional sculpture from any period, the seated statue of Khafre, now in the Egyptian Museum, Cairo.[22] (Fig. 2.5) Ironically,
Mariette never realized that the temple was Khafre's, but, rather,
puzzled over whether it was an addition to the Sphinx complex
or vice versa. One of his publications, completed in 1889 by
Gaston Maspero from Mariette's manuscript, included an
eighty-three-page appendix on Giza tombs.[23]

Comprehensive overview plans of Giza were eventually
available from the French mission, from Vyse and Perring
(1837; book published 1849), from the Prussian Expedition
(1842), and from Piazzi Smyth (1864), but in 1878 a new Giza
plan enhanced the corpus.[24] Emile Prisse d'Avennes (1807–
1879) was a Frenchman (of British descent) with consummate
artistic skills, not to mention talents in engineering, languages, and scholarship. In 1858–1860 Prisse mounted a documentary expedition with a small team, and perhaps the most

2.5 The seated statue of Khafre, in a painting by Joseph Lindon Smith.

important result of their work at Giza was their excellent new topographical plan. (Fig. 2.6) Two decades later Prisse published this plan in his *Atlas de l'histoire de l'art égyptien,* which also included plates of the Great Pyramid, the tombs of Snefrukhaf and Mindjedef (Eastern Cemetery, G 7070 and G 7760), and the lost sarcophagus from the burial chamber of Menkaure's pyramid.[25] The travel diary of his assistant, Willem de Famars Testas (1834–1896), contains detailed descriptions of life and work on this arduous journey.[26]

In 1872 the British civil engineer Waynman Dixon (1844–1930), later known for transporting "Cleopatra's needle" to London in 1877 and building bridges between Cairo and Giza, moved temporarily into a rock-cut tomb at the edge of the Eastern Cemetery. He would not be the last to occupy these undecorated chambers. Piazzi Smyth asked Dixon to map the Great Pyramid. Working with his brother John and assistant James Grant, Dixon discovered the airshafts in the queen's chamber by inserting a metal wire in the masonry joints along the south wall. Having chiseled through the wall to find the air shaft, he repeated the process on the north wall, with similar results.[27] The so-called Dixon relics—a small bronze double hook from the south shaft and a granite pound-

er and fragment of wood from the north—were shipped to England, forgotten, and then rediscovered in the British Museum in 1993 (pounder and hook), and in the Marischal Museum, Aberdeen, in 2001 (wood fragment).[28]

Though the Pyramids continued to draw attention, one event regarding private tombs is noteworthy. The German consul in Cairo, Dr. Carl August Reinhardt, purchased a series of decorated mastaba wall reliefs in 1897 from a Bedouin, who reportedly found them in a tomb near the Menkaure Pyramid. Belonging to the Fifth Dynasty "overseer of scribes, and of the

2.6 Plan of the Giza Necropolis, from Prisse d'Avennes, *Histoire de l'art égyptien,* 1878.

pyramid of Menkaure, Iynefret," the reliefs eventually landed in the Grossherzogliche Sammlungen für Altertums- und Völkerkunde in Karlsruhe.[29] This was the second Giza mastaba chapel of five eventually sent to Europe; the first was the chapel of Merib that Lepsius had obtained for the Berlin Museum almost sixty years earlier. (see Window 2.3)

As the nineteenth century drew to a close, awareness of the fragility of Egyptian sites and monuments was reaching new heights, illustrated best perhaps by Mariette's earlier refusal in 1868 to allow Ismail Pasha to simply donate the Bulaq Museum's masterworks, loaned to a Paris exposition, to Empress Eugénie. The flooding of the Bulaq Museum in 1878 resulted in the eventual move to a new location in the old palace at Giza in 1891. Mariette died in 1881, and he was succeeded by Gaston Maspero (1846–1916) as the new director of the Service des Antiquités. During this first (1881–1886) of two terms as director, Maspero introduced the partage system, whereby half of the finds by foreign missions could be given to that mission's country of origin. The system finally discouraged private individuals from excavating. Maspero himself resumed clearance at the Sphinx in 1885–1886, re-excavating what Caviglia and Mariette had already cleared, but no publications survive to document this period.[30] In fact, serious exploration of Giza between 1881 and 1891 all but stopped, with the exception of yet another British national, one who was to usher in the modern era of archaeology.

The Great Expeditions, 1880–1950

The early twentieth century may represent the only period during which excavators in Egypt set the developmental standard worldwide for the emerging field of archaeology.

We owe this to two individuals, the British archaeologist William Matthew Flinders Petrie (1853–1942), and the American George Andrew Reisner (1867–1942). Intrigued as a thirteen-year-old boy by the pyramid mysticism of Piazzi Smyth, Petrie surveyed Stonehenge with his father in 1872 and gained considerable archaeological experience in Britain. At the end of November 1880 he set out for Egypt with the goal of testing some of the pyramidological theories of the day. Giza was the first stop in Petrie's long line of countless field seasons in Egypt, the beginning of an illustrious career spanning seven decades. His typological studies and emphasis on complete documentation, photographic and conservation skills, prolific publication schedule, and tireless energy were nothing short of astounding. He revolutionized our approach to archaeological method and theory, and there are very few major sites or periods in Egyptian history untouched by his contributions.[31] At Giza, Petrie moved into Waynman Dixon's Eastern Cemetery rock-cut tomb on December 21, 1880. He spent his first of two seasons creating triangulations for the pyramids, since the bases were still buried and could not be accurately measured. Petrie stayed at Giza for two six-month seasons between December 1880 and April 1882. His expert assistant was one Ali Gabri, who had worked with Howard Vyse and Piazzi Smyth. Gabri's contributions represent one of the first documented examples of native Egyptian expertise in archaeology, a much-neglected subject that is only now slowly being redressed.[32] Petrie produced the most accurate survey plan of the Pyramids up to that point, publishing it in 1883.[33] He also spent endless hours inside the Khufu Pyramid (noting with alarm the cracks in the king's chamber), usually at night, after all the tourists had departed. He did not write much about the surrounding mastaba fields, but his notebooks reveal that he copied selected inscriptions. Petrie would return to Giza in 1907 but, as we shall see, excavation of the site was largely in the hands of others by that time.

The Western fascination with all things ancient Egyptian was growing in the early twentieth century. In 1900 the Egyptian government designated a series of European inspectors to assist in preserving the archaeological sites, stop the destruction by *sebakhin* (local diggers of ancient mud brick for use as nitrogen-rich modern fertilizer), and prevent illegal excavations. In America, James Henry Breasted (1865–1935) brought the subject to the public through popular lectures and by obtaining the first professorial post in Egyptology at the fledgling University of Chicago. In the spring of 1905 he released *Egypt through the Stereoscope,* a set of one hundred stereograph views created by the firm Underwood and Underwood and enhanced with Breasted's expert commentary. Twelve images of Giza appeared, several taken from the top of the Khufu Pyramid.[34] But not all was moving in a positive direction. An archaeologically inexperienced Royal Brewery owner from Arlington, Berkshire, by the name of Montague Ballard (1851–1936) had obtained permission to dig in the Western Cemetery. He made some remarkable discoveries, including at least ten statues and the famous Fourth Dynasty polychromed slab stela of the "king's daughter," Nefret-iabet (from G 1225), but he kept no records and published no results.[35] Reisner and other scholars protested against such private excavations, which prompted the Service des Antiquités to pass a resolution to issue permits thenceforth solely to accredited representatives of public institutions.

In 1902 the antiquities collections were moved downtown from the Giza museum to the new Egyptian Museum (in Midan Tahrir, "Liberation Square"), where most of the objects are still housed today. One of the last individuals to work at Giza before the era of the great expeditions of the early twentieth century was L. Dow Covington (1862–1935). Born in Kentucky, he first traveled to Egypt in 1899 as an insurance agent for a New York firm, but his dedication to Egyptian archaeology soon put him in contact with Gaston Maspero. Setting up camp at the northeast corner of the Great Pyramid, and enlisting the help of the British archaeologist James E. Quibell (1867–1935), Covington excavated the so-called mastaba mount in 1902–1903, located one mile due south of the Khufu Pyramid. Covington found no fewer than thirty-nine tombs in an arc around the southern zones of Giza, most of them predating the Fourth Dynasty and the construction of the Great Pyramid. Among the more important tombs explored were "Covington's tomb" (also known as "mastaba T"), a large, mud-brick mastaba from the Third Dynasty with palace-facade niching and complex subterranean chambers;[36] and Tomb 11, a rock-cut burial with seals—discovered later by Petrie—inscribed for the Second Dynasty pharaoh Nynetjer. Covington's tomb 3, a well-preserved Third Dynasty stone and mud-brick construction, was investigated in 1981–1982 by an Austrian mission under Karl Kromer, director of the Prehistoric Department in the Natural History Museum of Vienna (see below).[37] Covington's work provided some of our most explicit evidence for the mortuary occupation of Giza before Khufu's organized development of the plateau in the Fourth Dynasty.[38] In addition, Covington recleared the Great Pyramid's air shafts in 1905, improved the ventilation inside, and cleaned the original entrance of debris. In 1909 he located sixteen white limestone casing blocks along the north base of the Khufu Pyramid.[39]

As the numbers of more scientifically minded archaeologists expanded, scholars began to eye the Giza Necropolis as a site ripe for a more serious and comprehensive approach.

When Maspero and the Service des Antiquités finally decided to apportion the Giza Plateau for excavation, several scholars applied for the site. They were told to partition Giza amicably among themselves. George Reisner (Fig. 2.7) had been developing his archaeological skills since 1899 under the patronage of Phoebe Apperson Hearst (1842–1919), mother of the newspaper magnate William Randolph Hearst. After study in Semitic languages at Harvard and in Assyriology and Egyptology in Berlin, Reisner traveled to Cairo in 1897, to join an international commission dedicated to cataloguing objects in the Egyptian Museum. It was there that he met Mrs. Hearst, who provided Reisner with funding for several years to develop scientific methods of excavating and recording. Reisner began his Hearst Expedition at sites in Middle and Upper Egypt, which lasted until 1902, when the Giza concession became available.

The Egyptologist and Copticist Georg Steindorff (1861–1951) was the first student of the great German Egyptologist and philologist Adolf Erman (1854–1937) in Berlin. (Fig. 2.7) After receiving his PhD in Göttingen in 1894, he first became an assistant in the Berlin Museum from 1885 to 1893; he then obtained the professorship of Egyptology in Leipzig in 1904, a post he held until forced to flee to the United States in 1939. His support funds finally came through from a Hildesheim businessman, Wilhelm Pelizaeus (1851–1930), a man destined to have an immense influence on archaeological investigation of the Giza Plateau.

The third scholar interested in Giza was Ernesto Schiaparelli (1856–1928), who studied Egyptology in both Turin and Paris and later became director of the Egyptian Museum in Turin, from 1894 to 1927. (Fig. 2.7) Schiaparelli eventually directed the Italian Archaeological Mission for twelve campaigns at several different sites, beginning in 1903 at Giza.

These three distinguished scholars were told to meet to divide the Giza Plateau: the veranda of the Mena House Hotel, in the shadow of the Great Pyramid, was the setting. Reisner, Ludwig Borchardt (standing in for Georg Steindorff), and Schiaparelli drew strips of paper, representing three east-west portions of the great Western Cemetery, out of Mrs. Reisner's hat. The southernmost strip fell to the Italians, the central strip to the Germans, and the northern one to the Americans. This left the three pyramids and their temple complexes to be apportioned. Reisner noted privately: "I perceived that the Italians were interested in the First Pyramid and the Germans in the Second. I kept my mouth shut and let them wrangle. When they had adjusted the line between the First and Second Pyramid the Italian thinking that I might insist on a ballot resigned to me the northern part of the area east of the First Pyramid, if I would accept the Third Pyramid. I was perfectly willing to have the Third Pyramid but of course accepted his offer."[40] Fig. 2.8 (top) shows the original layout of the concessions: the Italians at Khufu, the Germans at Khafre, and the Americans at Menkaure. The plan would change several times over the ensuing years.[41]

2.7 *Left:* George Reisner at Giza in 1927; *center, seated from left to right:* Selim Hassan, Hermann Junker, and Georg Steindorff; *right:* bust of Ernesto Schiaparelli.

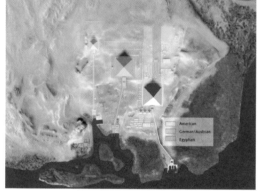

Thus began in 1903 the golden age of Giza exploration. The site had not seen such dedication and activity since the Fourth Dynasty, some 4,500 years ago. A systematic exploration, beginning with tombs in the Western Cemetery, led to the first comprehensive tomb-numbering scheme ("G" for Giza plus a four-digit number, devised by Reisner and still in use today over much of the site), and to the study of matrix relationships and chronological development. Along the way, of course, spectacular finds of every conceivable kind emerged.

Once Reisner was based at his "Hearst Camp" (later "Harvard Camp"), west of the Khafre Pyramid, one of his first orders of business was to establish an area to the north of the Giza Plateau for disposing of his debris dumps. Reisner's test excavations in the Wadi Cemetery, north of the Western Cemetery, began on December 9, 1903, and continued into September 1904.[42] Here he unearthed about seventy-seven modest mud-brick tombs. In one of the earliest examples of stratigraphic analysis, Reisner concluded that the Wadi Cemetery tombs actually predated the Western Cemetery tombs. Moreover, structural debris on top of the Wadi Cemetery tombs seemed to indicate the presence of pre-Khufu tombs on

2.8 Giza concession divisions of 1903 *(top)* and later modifications.

the plateau proper that must have been removed for Khufu's ambitious project for orderly rows of mastabas.[43] After one month of intensive work, he deemed a portion of the area sufficiently examined and commenced in January 1904 with excavation of the Western Cemetery proper, on the plateau, just to the west of the massive tomb G 2000.

The Hearst Expedition appeared to be well on its way to long-term success when, in 1904, Mrs. Hearst informed Reisner that she could not continue to support the dig. This resulted in a scramble for support during the summer of 1905. The negotiations included several individuals, among them Reisner; Albert M. Lythgoe (1868–1934), Reisner's former student, assistant, and first Egyptian curator at the Museum of Fine Arts (MFA), Boston; Harvard University's President Charles Eliot (1834–1926); and MFA officials. The Hearst Expedition became the Harvard University–Boston Museum of Fine Arts Expedition, beginning with the 1905–1906 field season. One of the longest-running excavations ever organized, the HU–MFA Expedition continued until 1947, after working at twenty-three different sites in Egypt and Sudan.

While Reisner's team slowly progressed from west to east in the northern strip of the Western Cemetery, Steindorff began his first campaign nearby in the central strip, working from March 10 to June 14, 1903, and numbering each of his tombs with a "D" ("Deutschland") plus a sequential number.[44] Smaller and later Old Kingdom mastabas filled this part of the cemetery, so coincidentally neither excavator followed the ancient chronological sequence of the site, for the earlier, Khufu-era mastabas lay farther east, closer to the Great Pyramid. Near the easternmost edge of Steindorff's activity, the small mastaba of the Fifth Dynasty "judge and overseer of scribes," Wehemka (D 117), was first unearthed during this field season, and the entire chapel was sent to Hildesheim, after a long delay, in 1925.[45] Steindorff's second season ran from January 1 to April 8, 1905, whereas Reisner had been working steadily since 1903.[46] In 1908, with the financial support of the Stuttgart businessman Ernst von Sieglin (of the company Dr. Thompson's Seifenpulver GmbH), Steindorff's team recleared the large Fifth Dynasty mastaba of Seshemnefer III (G 5170), first found by Mariette.[47] The well-preserved chapel was acquired by von Sieglin and given shortly thereafter to the Eberhard Karls Universität in Tübingen. The painted limestone blocks arrived in Tübingen in late fall 1910 and were presented officially to the university in 1911.[48]

With the support of Ludwig Borchardt, Steindorff conducted some test excavations at the Khafre Valley Temple between February and April 1905. Under the field direction of Uvo Hölscher (1878–1963), the expedition cleared the entire Khafre Pyramid Temple by late March 1909, and between January and April 1910, the Khafre Valley Temple received its first systematic excavation and architectural study.[49]

The Italian mission did not work as systematically, but from the fall of 1903 into the spring of 1904 Schiaparelli laid down test pits in selected areas of the southern strip of the Western Cemetery and also in the Eastern Cemetery. His funds limited, Schiaparelli later chose to focus on the mortuary temple area of Khufu, abutting the east face of the Great Pyramid. His primary interest here was a search for inscribed papyri, but none came forth. The following year, after additional excavations in the Eastern Cemetery, the mission also worked in the Valley of the Queens (Thebes), as well as at el-Ashmunein and Heliopolis. The Italians' Giza concession thereafter was not renewed, being turned over to Reisner and the (by that time) HU–MFA Expedition in 1905. Reisner thus acquired the entire Eastern Cemetery, as well as the southern strip of the Western Cemetery. Nevertheless, many objects from the Italian excavations were dispatched to both the Cairo Museum and the Egyptian Museum in Turin, which has recently reopened after a major renovation. The excavation records include photographs and notes, with a detailed manuscript by Francesco Ballerini (1877–1910), which greatly aided Silvio Curto in compiling the only extensive field report on the Italian mission, some six decades later.[50]

On July 29, 1911, Georg Steindorff and his fellow German Egyptologist Hermann Junker (1877–1962) were among the guests in Hildesheim attending the opening of Wilhelm Pelizaeus's new Egyptian museum. Like Reisner, Junker began his studies far removed from archaeology. By 1907 he had joined the faculty of the University of Vienna, en route to a distinguished Egyptological career—in both Egypt and Nubia—that included the directorship of the German Archaeological Institute in Cairo (1929).[51] In the course of the opening of the Hildesheim Museum, Junker and Steindorff realized that each was more interested in the other's excavation concession: Junker desired an Old Kingdom site, to enrich the collections in Vienna, and Steindorff was ready to head south, for excavations in Nubia, where Junker had been active at Aniba. Permissions to exchange concessions were soon obtained from all sides. Junker completed his season at the Nubian site of Arminna (between the First and Second Cataracts) on January 18, 1912, and four days later began excavations at Giza. In all, Junker worked for seven seasons at Giza, covering 1912–1914 and 1925–1929, with a forced interruption during World War I. The ensuing years, 1929–1962, were spent producing the publication of his fruitful explorations in both the Western Cemetery and the G I-S cemetery immediately south of the Great Pyramid. (Fig. 2.9)

Perhaps Reisner's greatest Giza discovery was the one that occurred in his absence. On February 9, 1925, the HU–MFA

2.9 *Top:* Hermann Junker's expedition at work on tomb G 5340 in the Western Cemetery, looking northwest, 1913–1914 (Junker stands on the tomb of Khufudinefankh in front); *bottom:* Cemetery G 5000, mastaba of Ptahshepses [I], serdab 1 (S 1), statues in situ, looking east, 1913–1914.

George Reisner

The discoveries made by these expeditions are far too numerous to describe here in any great detail, but a few highlights must be mentioned. Among Reisner's earliest finds in the far Western Cemetery mastabas were the so-called slab stelae, often the only decorated portion of Khufu-era mastabas, inserted into an emplacement at the southern end of the east face of the superstructure. Even more perplexing were the "reserve heads," generally thought to act as substitute homes for the deceased's spirit, although interpretations abound for these incomplete images, found almost without exception in disturbed contexts at the bottoms of burial shafts. Reisner found one of the earliest examples of an elaborately dressed female mummy,[1] (tomb G 2220; Fig. W4.1) not to mention historical, ritual, and biographical inscriptions, including stone-carved copies of letters from the king to his loyal and trusted officials. One text even recorded the extraordinary burial for pharaoh's beloved dog.[2] Moving to the Menkaure Pyramid

Temple in 1906–1907, Reisner found fragments of a colossal alabaster statue of Menkaure, which is now in Boston (MFA 09.204). He unearthed Menkaure's Valley Temple, farther to the east, in 1908 and 1910. In one of the earliest triumphs of a modern stratigraphic approach, Reisner discerned the multiple building phases of the temple, begun in stone, completed in mud brick, and then occupied as a settlement later in the Old Kingdom. (see Chapter 5) Mortuary

W4.1 Female mummy as found in situ in a wooden coffin in tomb G 2220, looking south, 1933.

 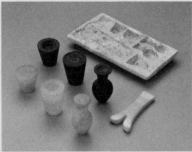

architecture and settlement archaeology were mixed together in a
complex matrix that is only now
being reinvestigated.³ Along with
thousands of stone vessels, ceramics, and other objects of both ritual
and daily life, (Fig. W4.2) the HU–
MFA Expedition discovered some
of the most spectacular royal statuary of any age of dynastic history.

W4.2 Object groups from Giza. *Top left:*
miniature copper items from the tomb of
Impy (G 2381); *top right:* pesesh-kef ritual
implement set; *middle left:* selected stone
vessels; *middle right:* miniature alabaster
vessels from Lepsius 52, shaft S 69; *bottom:*
ceramics.

Here were found the famous pair statue of Menkaure and presumably a queen (less likely his mother or a goddess; MFA 11.1738), four perfect triads showing the king accompanied by the goddess Hathor and one of several nome deities, and fragments of many more statues.[4] (Fig. W4.3)

W4.3 Discovery and Harvard Camp studio photos of the Menkaure dyad.

Expedition photographer Mohammedani Ibrahim accidentally slid his camera tripod into plaster flooring set into the limestone bedrock. This occurred at the northeast corner of the queen's subsidiary pyramid G I-a, for the team had just moved to the Eastern Cemetery the previous year, after a decade of work in Nubia and elsewhere. The slip of the camera tripod revealed that a staircase joined up with one of the deepest shafts ever found, more than 89 feet (27 meters), at the bottom of which lay an unfinished chamber packed with deteriorated remains of a most mysterious burial. Broken ceramics, gold hieroglyphs from decayed but once gilded furniture, jewelry with butterfly inlay patterns, and an alabaster sarcophagus all lay on the floor of what appeared to be a tomb without any superstructure. We owe the reconstruction of this find to Reisner's meticulous and thorough excavation and recording techniques, for the staff spent the better part of two years at the bottom of shaft "G 7000 X," lying on mattresses in the heat and battling the flies in order to draw, describe, photograph, and remove, layer by layer, the thousands of fragments. (Fig. 2.10) Gradually the story came together.

The inscriptions mentioned Queen Hetepheres, mother of Khufu and wife of King Snefru, the first pharaoh of the Fourth Dynasty. The greatest surprise was the sarcophagus itself, tempting the archaeologists with the first intact royal burial of the Old Kingdom. When at last the entire chamber was clear but for the sarcophagus, a party of VIPs descended into the tomb to lift the lid, but to everyone's astonishment, it was completely empty. A canopic chest remained hidden behind a sealed niche; it seemed to contain the remains of the queen's internal organs in a natron solution still in liquid form after nearly 5,000 years. Where was the queen's mummy? Was this a votive burial, cenotaph, a reused chamber, a relocated tomb, or even evidence of foul play? All these arguments have

come into play in efforts to interpret this singular find, and the last word has not yet been written.[52] (Fig. 2.11)

In 1915 Reisner delegated a portion of the northern strip of the Western Cemetery that was filled with smaller, mostly post–Fourth Dynasty tombs to his former assistant, Clarence Fisher (1876–1941), who was awaiting clearance to begin his own expedition at Memphis.[53] Later on, sensational finds in the Eastern Cemetery, where excavations had begun in 1924, included the Sixth Dynasty decorated subterranean chapels of Qar (G 7101) and Idu (G 7102), the elegantly painted chapel of Queen Meresankh III, located beneath her mastaba superstructure (G 7530-sub; see Chapters 4 and 5), with its wide thematic variety of wall scenes, and the massive tomb of Ankh-haf (G 7510), whose exterior

2.10 Noel F. Wheeler excavating underground in the tomb of Hetepheres, G 7000 X, looking north, 1926.

Hermann Junker

In January 1913, during his second season, Junker cleared the Fifth Dynasty mastaba family complex of Kaninisut (G 2155), and by January 27, 1914, he had negotiated for the purchase of its exquisitely carved and painted chapel.[1] The relief blocks arrived in Vienna in July 1914, but owing to the First World War and the constrained financial situation, Kunsthistorisches Museum officials were unable to reconstruct the chapel for another decade. Opening day finally took place on June 17, 1925. (Fig. W5.1)

W5.1 The mastaba of Kaninisut (G 2155). *Top:* packing crates with chapel reliefs, looking north, 1914; *bottom:* chapel, north wall.

mud-brick chapel revealed a lifelike limestone and plaster bust of the deceased.[54]

Junker's excavations began in the middle portion of the Western Cemetery and produced spectacular results as well. One of the largest mastabas at Giza belonged to the architect and engineer Hemiunu (G 4000), son of Nefermaat and Atet and nephew to Khufu. This man, perhaps most responsible for the layout and construction of the Great Pyramid, is famous today for his over-life-size, corpulent, seated limestone statue, arguably the greatest treasure in the Pelizaeus-Museum, Hildesheim (Inv. Nr. 19622).[55] Junker also found the Fifth Dynasty mastaba of Nensedjerkai (G 2100-II), daughter of the same Merib whose decorated chapel Lepsius had removed to Berlin in the 1840s. Her chapel displayed an

2.11 Modern reconstructions of Hetepheres's furniture in the Museum of Fine Arts, Boston: canopy, headrest, chair, curtain box, and bed.

unusual portico with pillars and a round-topped enclosure wall in imitation of domestic architecture.

World War I exiled Junker from Giza for eleven years. In fact, the Egyptian antiquities authorities eventually reclaimed the Central Field, originally part of the German-Austrian concession, possibly owing to rumors of statues to be found in the area.[56] Try as Junker might after the war to reestablish the expedition, British political control of the country, the sale of his equipment, and a general lack of financial support continually thwarted him. It was not until March 1, 1925, that support from Hildesheim, from the Österreichisches Unterrichtsministerium, and from a private donor, allowed Junker to return to the Western Cemetery. It was diplomacy that allowed the expedition to continue: Junker negotiated to retrieve the chapel of the scribe Wehemka (D 117), promised to the city of Hildesheim in 1914 but never shipped because of the war. He obtained permission to proceed with the shipment on May 6, 1925; after just five days, the chapel blocks, packed in thirty-nine crates, landed on May 14 in Alexandria. The expedition continued in 1926 at the far western end of the central strip of the Western Cemetery, clearing an astonishing 18,000 square yards (15,000 square meters) of ground in two months, using at times hundreds of workmen (three hundred in 1927). This area revealed later Old Kingdom sepulchers and the chapel of the now famous dwarf Seneb.[57]

After studying with Ahmed Kamal (1851–1923), one of the great Egyptian Egyptologists, the aspiring young scholar Selim Hassan (1886–1961) furthered his education in Paris and obtained his PhD from the University of Vienna in 1935. (see Fig. 2.7) Serving as professor of Egyptology at the University of Cairo from 1928 to 1936, and then as deputy director of the Service des Antiquités, Hassan trained with Junker for three months in 1928 and then took over the Central Field concession, east of the Khafre Pyramid, that was originally granted to the German-Austrian expedition. This marks the first large-scale expedition by native Egyptian archaeologists at the site, a project that continued for ten years and produced ten exemplary monographs. The first season (1929–1930) focused on seventeen Old Kingdom mastabas surrounding the massive and unusual tomb of the Fifth Dynasty *sem*-priest Rawer (G 8988), which once contained a host of labyrinthine rooms and courtyards, twenty-five *serdabs* (statue chambers), possibly one hundred or more statues, and a famous inscription recording an embarrassing accident during a ritual ceremony involving King Neferirkare of the Fifth Dynasty.[58] Moving west from Rawer, Hassan cleared another twenty or so previously unknown mastabas during his 1930–1931 season, including the tomb of Wepemnefret (G 8882), whose will and testament on the chapel's eastern wall is dedicated to his son Iby.[59] (Fig. 2.12) Additional highlights of Hassan's excavations include the pyramid tomb of Queen Khentkaus; the rock-cut tomb of Debehen, with a biographical text describing a visit by King Menkaure; the controversial mastaba of Queen Khamerernebty II; the Khufu Pyramid Temple; the Sphinx and the New Kingdom Sphinx Temple built by Amenhotep II, with its large stela recounting the king's athletic exploits.[60]

While the major Giza expeditions of the early twentieth century were active, other lone archaeologists concentrated on different Egyptian sites. Three individuals at Giza are particularly noteworthy. One was W. M. F. Petrie, who returned to Giza in 1906–1907 to excavate Predynastic and Archaic Period tombs south of the Pyramids. Second, a Service des Antiquités project to reclear the Sphinx area was initiated by the service's director, Pierre Lacau (1873–1963); Émile Baraize (1874–1952) served as the principal field director. This work began in 1925 and lasted until 1936, when Selim Hassan worked in the area (1936–1938). The French archaeologist Bernard Bruyère (1879–1971) accompanied Baraize at Giza in 1926, and his notebooks are housed today in the Institut Français d'Archéologie Orientale in Cairo.[61] And, finally, Ahmed Fakhry cleared and documented seven rock-cut tombs at the edge of the Eastern Cemetery on and off from 1932 to 1934.[62]

By 1940 methodical excavation had cleared the major portions of the Giza cemetery fields. In fact, aerial photography from about 1930–1940 is generally more useful than recent images, since so much of the site lay exposed and clearly articulated then. Thanks to Baraize, the Sphinx area was free and clear of sand. The mortuary temples surrounding all three pyramids were explored and published, with the exception of Khufu's Valley Temple, which lies off the plateau, underneath the modern town of Nazlet es-Samman. A chronological framework for necropolis development, including mortuary architecture and construction techniques, was by this time firmly in place, and it was up to the individual concessionaires to publish their results. They took somewhat different tacks in their publication strategies. Reisner had delayed his publications to the point where the Service des Antiquités and even the MFA had to implore him to stop digging and start writing. He spent his final years, blind from cataracts, typing and dictating his various Giza manuscripts to his assistants at Harvard Camp. First came his treatment of the Menkaure temples (*Mycerinus*, 1931),[63] followed by what he envisioned as a three-part series: tomb development (preceding Giza and the Fourth Dynasty), the history of the Giza Necropolis, and then the individual Giza mastabas. Reisner's *A History of the Giza Necropolis,* volume 1, is dated 1942, the year of his death, but owing to the Second World War did not actually appear until 1946. This massive tome—whose table of contents alone occupies twenty-two pages—focuses on typologies rather than individual monuments.

Junker's approach was perhaps easier to follow. Although he included interpretive essays in his twelve *Giza* volumes (1929–1955), most of his publications progressed tomb-by-tomb, chapter-by-chapter. Junker's focus was on the reliefs and inscriptions, the mortuary architecture, and the dating of the mastabas. He included far fewer objects or expedition photos in his volumes than did Reisner, but he did produce valuable indexes in his twelfth and final volume, published in 1955.

Selim Hassan followed Junker's lead in the tomb-by-tomb approach, but he included several volumes dedicated to specific topics, such as the funerary boats of Khafre, the development of false doors and offering lists, the Sphinx, and even a manual for proper excavation methods. Hassan produced ten *Excavations at Giza* volumes (1932–1960), and the final one also contained indexes of tomb owners and their administrative titles. Taken together, the Reisner, Junker, and Hassan publications make up the major collection of Giza excavation reports, and though their methodology may seem out of date in some respects today, they have yet to be equaled in the sheer breadth and depth of material covered. They also contain arguably the best overview

2.12 The will of Wepemnefret, from G 8882, painting by Joseph Lindon Smith.

plans of the site.[64] The three publication series form the basis for any substantial research of the Giza Necropolis, and indeed of Egyptian Old Kingdom society in general.

Following the "big three" expeditions (American, German-Austrian, and Egyptian), the decade 1940–1950 was a relatively quiet one. The HU–MFA Expedition limped along with a reduced crew after the Second World War and Reisner's death, until colleagues from Boston could safely travel to Egypt again in 1947, at which point they opted to close the dig and send the expedition records home. But in 1948 a committee met at the Club of Odd Volumes on Boston's Beacon Hill to establish the American Research Center in Egypt (ARCE), based essentially on the model of the Harvard Camp concept. To this day ARCE remains the principal umbrella organization for supporting American archaeological projects in Egypt (www.arce.org).

The Modern Era, 1950–1980

The next project worthy of note was a second Egyptian mission. Abdel Moneim Abu-Bakr (1907–1976) trained with Vladimir Golenischeff (1856–1947) in Cairo and Kurt Sethe (1869–1934) in Berlin, then joined the University of Alexandria (1939) and subsequently Cairo University (1954) as professor and then dean. In 1945 Abu-Bakr found a water-filled shaft inside a tunnel running underneath the Khafre causeway from north to south. Later dubbed the "Osiris shaft" by the Egyptian archaeologist Zahi Hawass, the shaft had long been used as a swimming pool and source of water for local villagers.[65] Abu-Bakr moved farther south in the winter of 1945–1946 to excavate the Twenty-sixth Dynasty tomb of Tjery (seventh century BCE), less than two miles (about three kilometers) south of Khufu's Pyramid.[66] The following season (1946–1947) he unearthed an additional seven Late Period tombs to the west of that of Tjery, each with superstructures of limestone, unusual entrances, and common access to about twenty-two shafts.[67] Abu-Bakr also commenced work on what ultimately became his primary area of excavation, at the northwest corner of the former American concession in the far Western Cemetery. His first season lasted from December 15, 1949, to May 25, 1950, and focused on two sections: the first, next to the great mastaba G 2000, and the second, 550 yards (500 meters) farther west. Abu-Bakr described the results of his first season, but he never published his additional work in the area, which continued all the way to 1975, and today most of his excavation records appear to have been lost.[68] This marks the last large-scale excavation work to take place in the Western Cemetery to date, although several smaller missions have been active in recent years.

The decade of the 1960s saw relatively little substantial archaeological progress at Giza. Georges Goyon explored the causeway and ramps associated with Khufu's pyramid,[69] and in 1960, during the clearance of the remains of the small satellite pyramid G II-a, at the south base of the Khafre Pyramid, Abdel Hafez Abd el-'Al found a sealed passage.[70] In the ensuing decade attention refocused on Giza in a wide array of approaches. Hans Goedicke, from Johns Hopkins University, and a colleague conducted excavations south of the Khafre Valley Temple and south of the Wall of the Crow, but no publication has yet appeared. Abdel-Aziz Saleh of Cairo University began searching for boat pits at the Menkaure Pyramid complex in 1971–1972, but instead turned up an industrial settlement area near the southeast rim of the pyramid's quarry.[71] Saleh excavated a thick embankment, houses, store-

The Boats of Khufu

While Abu-Bakr was excavating in the far Western Cemetery in 1950, the Egyptian Antiquities Organization architect Kamal el-Mallakh (1918–1987) was supervising routine clearance work on the south side of the Great Pyramid. Assisted by Mohamed Zaki Nour, Zaki Iskander, and Salah Osman, el-Mallakh found two long boat pits between the Pyramid itself and the row of G I-South mastabas excavated by Junker in 1928–1929. The pits were covered with massive lime-stone slabs, forty on one and forty-one on the other. On May 26, 1954, the eastern pit was found to contain a dismantled boat—in 1,224 individual pieces—made of Lebanese cedar.[1] Equally important, masons' marks mentioning the name of Khufu's successor, Djede-fre, indicated that the latter was involved in Khufu's burial and was hardly the dynastic usurper originally presumed by earlier Giza archaeologists. Though politics eventually forced el-Mallakh to turn to a

W6.1 *Left*: south side of the Great Pyramid, looking north, showing the Khufu Boat Museum (indicated by the arrow) and, to its left, a temporary structure over the ancient boat pit, in which conservation work on the second boat has been undertaken;

career in journalism, the Egyptian master conservator Hagg Ahmed Youssef (1912–1999), who had earlier assisted Reisner in conserving the furniture of Queen Hetepheres from tomb G 7000 X, took on the task of reconstructing the first boat, which occupied most of his time from 1958 to 1968. This triumph of conservation, reconstructed at 142 feet (43.3 meters) long, stands in a small museum constructed right over the pit itself; it opened to the public on March 6, 1982. The second boat, not as well preserved, was examined by a combined Egyptian and US National Geographic team in 1987, and at this writing (2016) is being prepared for reconstruction by the Egyptian Ministry of State for Antiquities and Sakuji Yoshimura of Waseda University, Tokyo. When the boats might move to the planned Grand Egyptian Museum, just north of the Giza Plateau, remains to be determined. (Fig. W6.1)

right: two views of the Khufu boat in the museum.

rooms, and ovens and even located large alabaster workshop fragments strewn about the landscape.

As another example of archaeological research on settlements rather than on tombs, the Austrian archaeologist Karl Kromer (1924–2003) excavated from 1971 to 1975 near the Southern Mount, south of the Menkaure Valley Temple area. Here he found a large debris dump, possibly representing a dismantled and destroyed settlement, in the geological Maadi Formation, which lies south of the Central Wadi.[72]

In 1971 William Kelly Simpson (1928–), the Egyptian Department curator at the Museum of Fine Arts, Boston, and professor at Yale University, decided to initiate the third part of Reisner's desired publication series, the Giza mastabas. That year, as part of the Pennsylvania-Yale Expedition, in collaboration with the Museum of Fine Arts, Boston, Simpson's team returned to Giza to complete the epigraphic documentation on the unique tomb of Queen Meresankh III (G 7530-sub), a key member of the Fourth Dynasty royal family whose unusual subterranean painted chapel remains one of the marvels at Giza today. Meresankh's tomb formed the first volume of the new Giza Mastabas Series, written by Simpson and the former HU–MFA Expedition member and retired MFA curator Dows Dunham (1890–1984).[73] After completing three more volumes through the 1970s and 1980s, Simpson turned the Giza Mastabas Series over to colleagues.[74] Epigraphic missions, directed variously by Kent Weeks, Edward Brovarski, Ann Macy Roth, and Peter Der Manuelian, have returned to Giza intermittently through the interceding decades to the present day. Other epigraphic missions to Giza in the 1970s included one led by the UCLA Egyptologist Alexander Badawy, who spent two seasons (1973–1974) in the Eastern and Western Cemeteries, documenting tombs that belonged to the HU–MFA Expedition concession.[75]

Site Management and Interdisciplinary Archaeology, 1980–2015

Before the end of the 1970s, the Sphinx too received renewed attention. In 1978 the Giza inspector Zahi Hawass and the American archaeologist Mark Lehner explored the statue's northeast corner, and in the following year Lehner commenced the first systematic survey and archaeological description of the monument, eventually mapping each individual stone. Lehner, who received his PhD in Egyptology from Yale University in 1990 with a dissertation on the Sphinx, formed the Giza Plateau Mapping Project as part of his nonprofit organization, Ancient Egypt Research Associates, or AERA (1985–), which has now devoted several decades to exploring the site of Giza.[76] In 1984–1985, with the assistance of a surveyor, David Goodman, Lehner established the first control network over the entire Giza Plateau.[77] Other Giza work during the 1980s included a search for the Valley Temple of Khufu, in the course of the American British Consultants (AMBRIC) Greater Cairo Wastewater Project in the Giza zone, which provided sewage modifications in the town of Nazlet es-Samman (Zahi Hawass, Hishmat Messiha); geophysical measurements inside the chambers of the Great Pyramid (Gilles Dormion and Jean-Patrice Goidin; Sakuji Yoshimura); salvage excavations southeast of Giza at Kafr el-Gebel (Zahi Hawass); additional epigraphic campaigns in the Western Cemetery cluster of mastabas belonging to administrators bearing the title *khentiu-she,* perhaps meaning "palace attendants" (Ann Macy Roth); and excavations at Flinders Petrie's so-called workmen's barracks west of the Khafre Pyramid, which turned out instead to be structures for craft production and storage (Mark Lehner and Nicholas Conard).[78] Zahi Hawass, by this time chief inspector for the Giza Plateau, initiated his site management plan in 1987, the first modern attempt to consider Giza in toto, with a strategy intended to preserve the site and balance the competing needs of access, tourism, scholarship, and preservation. Concerns about rising water tables around the Giza Plateau and interest in geophysical studies, with attention to the geomorphology and the ancient landscape, including the proximity of the Nile in antiquity, have all grown from the 1980s to the present day.[79]

From December 1988 to January 1989, Mark Lehner moved his excavations to his "Area A," the zone south of the Wall of the Crow (Arabic *Heit el-Ghurab*), 440 yards (400 meters) south of the Sphinx. In contrast to earlier scholars who were concerned primarily with tomb and temple excavations at Giza, Lehner was more interested in the economic and social implications of the Fourth Dynasty monuments. How were the pyramid builders organized? Where were they housed, fed, and managed? Lehner's interdisciplinary approach to his "lost city of the Pyramids" excavations has revealed massive amounts of invaluable data on ancient settlement, housing, diet, social organization, administration, and architecture. Additional excavation following the eventual relocation of a nearby soccer field and sports club may reveal clues to royal administrative structures that housed the management of this specialized city, one that seems to have been abandoned once the royal pyramid sites moved to other locations in the later Old Kingdom. This zone represents the largest exposed area of Old Kingdom settlement anywhere in Egypt, and it has provided the largest corpus yet uncovered of human and animal bones, seal impressions, ceramics, plant remains, and other finds. Most recent hypotheses suggest the use of the area as a port zone for expeditions to offload goods from both the south and the north.[80] The AERA expedition has expanded its exploration of this area, including additional investigations of the Wall of the Crow itself, the nearby Khentkaus pyramid town and its relationship to the Menkaure Valley Temple, and the ramps and access points relating to the ancient harbor fronting the Giza Plateau.[81] (Fig. 2.13)

As Lehner's team was exploring how the pyramid builders lived, a tourist's minor horseback-riding accident led Zahi Hawass to discover a "new" cemetery of tombs on the ridge just west of Lehner's lost city of the Pyramids.[82] Mortuary architecture here shows some fascinating deviations from the standard forms elsewhere in the Giza Necropolis, and the tombs produced a large number of statuettes as well. What Hawass has termed the artisans', or upper, cemetery consists of elaborate, elite stone mastabas constructed high up on the cliff face, with causeways and multiple shafts, whereas a more modest workmen's cemetery appears at the foot of the ridge. This lower cemetery contained, as of 2003, sixty larger and six hundred smaller structures.[83]

Hawass was also active in other parts of the Giza Plateau. Among his many discoveries, excavations in the Western Cemetery (HU–MFA Expedition concession) revealed more than seventy tombs, several apparently dedicated to disabled individuals, among them the tomb of the dwarf Perniankhu (1989–1990); the second tomb of the overseer of ka-priests, Kapunisut Kai (G 1741, also the owner of tomb G 4651), with its exquisitely painted chapel and statue (1990); the satellite pyramid of Khufu, found just off the southeast corner of the Great Pyramid (1991); a fragmentary, discarded colossal pair statue, perhaps of Ramesses II and a solar deity, carved from a reused granite block, at the southeast corner of the Menkaure Pyramid (1996); and an excavation of the "Osiris shaft" Late Period tomb (1999).[84]

Interest in the air shafts in the king's and queen's chambers of Khufu's Pyramid grew during the 1990s, spawning a series of technological experiments in these passages, which are much too narrow for human access. In 1992 the German engineer Rudolf Gantenbrink created a wheeled, remote-controlled robot dubbed Upuaut ("Opener of the Ways"). This device explored the air shafts leading off the King's Chamber with a small mounted camera. A repeat performance took place in 1993 with Upuaut II in the southern shaft of the Queen's Chamber. This robot reached 213 feet (65 meters), to what appeared to be a small stone door set with metal pins. In 2002 a US company called iRobot designed a new robot, the Pyramid Rover, equipped with a drill to penetrate this door, upon which a small chamber blocked by a large stone was revealed. Not until 2010 did the next joint international-Egyptian phase begin, this time with a robot named Djedi (after an ancient Egyptian sage), designed by Robert Richardson of the University of Leeds, UK, with the collaboration of the 3D modeling company Dassault Systèmes, Paris. (see Chapter 4) A bending micro-snake camera sent back images from beyond the stone blocking the door that showed red ochre mason's marks.[85]

Progress in the mastaba fields continued in the final decade of the twentieth century. In the mid-1990s a great archival discovery in Germany was made of the Steindorff plans and sections from the original German concession in the central strip of the Western Cemetery. These were edited and published by Alfred Grimm.[86] And the Egyptian Egyptologist Naguib Kanawati, from Macquarie University, Sydney, undertook the epigraphic documentation of two tombs excavated by the HU–MFA Expedition (Seshemnefer I and II, G 4940 and G 5080 = 2200, respectively), and two more by the German-Austrian Expedition (Kaiemankh, G 4561; Seshathetep/Heti, G 5150).[87]

From March 2 to May 2, 2002, a German Archaeological

Institute expedition directed by Günter Dreyer excavated some late Old Kingdom rock-cut tombs in the so-called Khafre Quarry Cemetery, west of the Khafre Pyramid. An architrave found in this area led to a new rock-cut tomb, with burial chamber and limestone sarcophagus, belonging to a previously unknown Sixth Dynasty vizier named Irienakhti (QC 1). The expedition documented additional rock-cut tombs in the quarry wall, some known to Mariette and Lepsius, others revealed for the first time.[88]

From 2000 to 2009 a joint Cairo University–Brown University expedition directed by Tohfa Handoussa and Edward Brovarski reexamined the Abu-Bakr cemetery (northwestern section of the far Western Cemetery), with the goal of documenting the mastaba tombs that still remained unpublished, and to make their wall decoration available to the scholarly

2.13 Ancient Egypt Research Associates (AERA) 2012 excavations of the Silo Building Complex and the Fourth Dynasty Khentkaus I basin, with the pyramids of Menkaure, the tomb of Khentkaus I, and the pyramid of Khafre in the background, looking northwest.

community. Fifteen mastabas were recorded, and the Egyptian Egyptologist Ali Radwan intends to join the codirectors in publishing the results. An unusual feature of this area is the so-called hyena den, published by the expedition staff member Stephen Phillips, of the University of Pennsylvania.[89]

On the other side of the Khufu Pyramid, in the Eastern Cemetery, Eleonora Kormysheva of the Institute of Oriental Studies, Russian State University for Humanities, Moscow, started work in 1998 with the reclearance of the Fifth Dynasty rock-cut tomb of Khafre-ankh (G 7948), known as Lepsius 75 since 1842, and excavated by Reisner's HU–MFA Expedition in the 1930s. The Russian expedition has continued in this area of rock-cut tombs along the eastern edge of the Eastern Cemetery, and additional monographs have followed the publication of Khafre-ankh's tomb.[90]

This cursory survey of exploration of the Giza Necropolis reveals not only the daunting nature of the archaeological matrix on the site, but also the difficulty of keeping abreast of wide-ranging scholarly research. Despite the Egyptian Revolution of 2011, archaeological activity at Giza continues apace. Mark Lehner's AERA organization has mounted unique archaeological field school sessions for the upcoming generation of Egyptian antiquities officials, many of whom are now directing their own Ministry of State for Antiquities excavations at Giza and other sites. Ann Macy Roth has been excavating minor, later Old Kingdom mastabas in portions of the Western Cemetery traditionally overlooked by scholars more interested in elaborately decorated tombs.[91] Recent SCA excavations are revealing the extent of Thutmose IV's additions to the area east of the Sphinx and Khafre Valley Temple, as well as additional Old Kingdom private tombs in the vicinity of the Menkaure causeway. International teams have used infrared thermography and directed cosmic-particle detectors (muon radiography imaging) at the Khufu Pyramid in the hopes of detecting hitherto unknown chambers or cavities. And special exhibitions featuring or including Giza continue to fascinate museum visitors the world over.[92] Nevertheless, the ever-accumulating volume of data has become unwieldy, and no single scholar can command expertise in the many disciplines required for contemporary archaeological research at Giza.[93] (Even the identity of the Sphinx has once more come under lively debate.)[94] Some potential solutions to coping with the information overload are described in the following chapters.

CHAPTER 3

From Stone to Silicon: Translating the Medium

The jaw drops. This is often the reaction of visiting scholars who arrived at the Department of Ancient Egyptian, Near Eastern, and Nubian Art (now called Art of the Ancient World) at the Museum of Fine Arts, Boston, to study the excavation archives of the Harvard University–Boston Museum of Fine Arts Expedition. George Reisner died at the Pyramids on June 6, 1942, exactly two years before D-Day, and was buried in the American Cemetery in Old Cairo a few days later.[1] The archives, however, remained stranded at Harvard Camp, on the Giza Plateau behind the Khafre Pyramid, for an additional five years. Only after World War II hostilities had ceased could MFA curators Dows Dunham (1890–1984) and William Stevenson Smith (1907–1969) venture to Egypt from Boston to assess the situation. Should the expedition continue? Should Harvard Camp become the nucleus of some sort of American field school or archaeological institute in Cairo? Or was it simply time to disband and go home?

After much deliberation, the latter decision was reached, and more than forty years of excavations came to a close in early spring of 1947.[2] Dunham packed and shipped ninety-two cases from Harvard Camp. Fifteen of these contained Sudanese (ancient Nubian) objects that went to Khartoum; the rest headed for Boston via Port Said. There were twenty-three cases of Reisner's detective fiction library, all of which ended up in the Harvard Library, as specified in Reisner's will; eighteen cases containing the remaining 16,000 photographic glass plate negatives (two cases went to Philadelphia, to become part of the University of Pennsylvania Museum's photo archive; thousands had been sent earlier to Boston); five cases of antiquities; thirty-one cases containing the scientific library, office records, and five cases of personal effects.

All this material eventually cleared customs and reached the Museum of Fine Arts, Boston, before the end of June 1947. Ever since, Egyptian Department curators have faced a mountain of documentation, attempting to organize, house, catalogue, conserve, and publish as much of it as possible. There were the extremely fragile glass plate negatives, 21,000 of them for Giza alone (45,000 total for all twenty-three sites); thousands of pages of diaries, notes, and manuscripts; plans and section drawings large and small, some healthy and indestructible, others brittle and crumbling; oversize ledgers containing object information; photo records and diaries describing almost every day on the site—who dug where and how deeply, and what was discovered. And of course, most important, approximately 30,000 Giza antiquities, which had been steadily arriving at the MFA, and to a lesser extent at Harvard's Peabody Museum of Archaeology and Anthropology, over many decades. By 1947 the MFA and the Metropolitan Museum of Art possessed without doubt the largest and finest Egyptian collections in the United States. In the MFA's case, it was all due to Reisner's unceasing devotion to unearthing Egyptian history by way of its material culture. Moreover, the MFA collection represented only half the finds. Under Antiquities Service law, the partage system called for a fifty-fifty division of objects discovered—between the Egyptian Museum, Cairo, and the excavating institution. Thus, it was often the case that when two statues turned up in a single tomb, one went to Cairo and the other to Boston.

Information Overload

Each successive Egyptian Department curator took a turn at ascending the hill of data amassed at the MFA. Dows Dunham created an accession card system, using three five-by-seven-inch index cards for every object, filed in drawers by number, by location, and by description (such as "amulet" or "sarcophagus"). At the beginning of 1956, he decided to retire early to devote his time to publishing the tremendous backlog of Nubian material. As Dunham put together a number of exemplary volumes, William Stevenson Smith took over the curatorship. Smith himself had published several books on the Giza excavations, including his *History of Egyptian Sculpture and Painting in the Old Kingdom* (1946, 2nd ed. 1949), and, with Reisner as co-author, *A History of the Giza Necropolis,* vol. 2, *The Tomb of Hetep-heres, the Mother of Cheops* (1955). When Smith died prematurely, in 1969, he was succeeded by William Kelly Simpson, who somehow managed to take on this added responsibility while retaining his professorship of Egyptology at Yale University and driving a weekly "triangle" between Boston, New Haven, and his home in Katonah, New York, for seventeen years (1970–1987; see Chapter 2). Simpson returned to Giza to initiate the tomb-by-tomb publication series that Reisner had envisaged but never produced. Publishing four volumes of a new Giza Mastabas Series between 1974 and 1980, Simpson laboriously waded through the wealth of material to find the relevant photos, notes, and drawings for the tombs in question, supplemented by his own epigraphic expeditions that returned to Giza to create new facsimile line drawings of scenes and inscriptions. These were funded by PL480 Title I money, by which the US Government supplied Egypt with wheat in exchange for Egyptian currency that had to be spent in Egypt. Back home in Boston, Simpson had the advantage, as Egyptian Department curator, of leisurely browsing, sifting, and hunting through the HU–MFA Archives until the sought-after documents surfaced.

Visiting scholars had no such luck. While the study of the Giza excavations continued, the difficult access to the data resulted in important material missed, and projects and dissertations put on hold or rendered impossible by the herculean task of locating relevant items. Giza scholarship had benefited from Reisner's meticulous approach, but it was now suffocating under the sheer weight of the material he had created. Moreover, after so many decades, the data began to suffer a fate similar to that of the antiquities themselves: deterioration. Brittle maps and plans became brittler; the emulsion on glass plate negatives, never fixed long enough in their original chemical baths in the field, began to separate or discolor. All-important identification numbers started to fade or become separated from the objects they identified.

It grew clear that cultural heritage is often a question of format; as one medium gives way to another, the survival of the data left behind is thrown into jeopardy. The ancient Egyptians had committed their legacy largely to stone. Not a bad move, all things considered. Millennia later, at the beginning of the twentieth century, along came the great expeditions to usher in the dawn of archaeological method. These expeditions converted that ancient legacy to paper, glass, and later film. Our generation has sought to transform the medium once again, this time to electronic form as ones and zeroes. There are arguments to be made for the advantages of all three systems. Some are more portable; others contain higher-quality information, and still others trade sustainability for convenience. In the case of the Giza material, this encapsulation of a moment from ancient Egypt, frozen onto glass plates, notebooks, graph paper, and diary pages, was not only fairly inaccessible, but desperately in need of a conversion and an upgrade.

A New Approach

Fast forward to the year 2000. The Museums and Conservation division of the Andrew W. Mellon Foundation in New York decided to devote some resources to digital heritage projects. The program officer, at that time the indefatigable Angelica Zander Rudenstine, approached several museums in search of groundbreaking pilot projects. Nancy Allen, formerly the Susan Morse Hilles Director of the MFA's Information Resources Department, knew about the plight of the

Art of the Ancient World Department's expedition negatives and contacted me for a possible proposal. Two conceivable pathways lay before us. One was to digitize the entire collection of 45,000 glass plate negatives from all twenty-three archaeological sites excavated by Reisner and the HU–MFA Expedition. There was no downside to this strategy, and at this writing the scanning of all remaining (non-Giza) plates is close to completion.

The second option, however, represented the more interesting experiment. Why not try to capture the *entire* range of data, not just the photographs, from a single site? This might produce a research tool with possibilities for search and retrieval across media that would constitute an entirely new—for the year 2000, at least—type of "publication" in Egyptological, archaeological, and art historical scholarship. This was an example of "digital humanities" before the term existed. Those "frozen moments" from ancient Egypt, so carefully documented by Reisner's expedition, now had the opportunity to survive in a new medium, and what's more, one available to the entire world via the Internet. Gone would be the days of specialized curatorial permissions required for access, of limited, supervised hours over an impossibly short stretch of days granted by a stingy travel grant or research budget. The most important elements of the Giza expedition data would go online, and in a cross-referenced fashion that could provide for research along any one of a number of paths, from any one of a number of starting points. A welcome byproduct was the liberation of the MFA curators from many basic but time-consuming Giza inquiries, so that they could focus on their many other responsibilities.

The proposal that went to the Mellon Foundation in the summer of 2000 highlighted the threefold nature of converting the Giza archives to electronic form:

First, it is our aim that "The Giza Archives Project" enhance the study of Egyptian civilization during the Old Kingdom, or Pyramid Age, in a way that is not always possible at the site of Giza itself. Some tombs and artifacts at Giza are now reburied, denuded, or otherwise inaccessible; they are sometimes better preserved in their documented state sixty to ninety years ago in the Harvard–MFA Expedition archives. Second, we expect that online posting of the Expedition records will allow scholars unprecedented access to our archaeological materials. This includes scholars who are unable to visit the site of Giza, or the portions of the site crucial to their research, as well as those actually working at the site and needing supplemental documentation no longer accessible or available. Third, the Giza Archives Project would ideally do far more than provide simple access to a body of expedition records and images online. Our goal is to serve as a robust scholarly research tool. It should theoretically be able to answer research questions that today cannot even be posed because of the overwhelming number of archival documents, the impractical search requirements and the limited time constraints under which most scholars work.

Three documentation categories became the primary focus of an initial four-year, $750,000 Mellon Foundation grant. The first of these consisted of 21,000 glass plate expedition negatives (in three sizes: 8 × 10, 5 × 7, and 4 × 5 inches [20 × 25, 12.7 × 17.8, and 10.2 × 12.7 centimeters, respectively]). Far and away the largest and most valuable historic Giza photo archive in existence, these images capture elements of ancient Egyptian culture, and the twentieth-century archaeological process, that are available nowhere else. (Fig. 3.1) Reisner and his primarily Egyptian photography team had to decide in each case which size glass plate was most appropriate for the

scene at hand, and further had to devise a way to safely ship the entire collection (45,000 for all HU–MFA sites) back to the United States. Egyptian Department staff then mounted prints of many of the negatives, arranged in gray archival boxes by tomb number, along with the many thousands of pages of manuscripts and other documents. Accompanying the plates themselves were five bound Photographic Register volumes recording for each photograph the negative number, the site, a brief description, the date, and the photographer, totaling approximately 1,500 pages for all twenty-three HU–MFA Expedition sites. Two examples illustrate how these images increase in value over time. One then-and-now comparison shows engaged statuary in the subterranean chapel of

3.1 Large-format camera setup in the burial chamber of Hetepheres, G 7000 X, 1926.

Meresankh, (Fig. 3.2) and the other reveals that all the painted decoration has disappeared from the granite sarcophagus of Akhethetep, now in the Brooklyn Museum of Art. (Fig. 3.3)

The second category of items to be processed included twelve bound volumes of Expedition Diaries containing narrative accounts and sketches of daily excavation progress at Giza (approximately 3,150 pages). Some were handwritten, some typewritten, and though all are in English, we met with a more welcome Arabic-language surprise halfway through the course of our work (see below).

The third documentation category provided the collections "database" of its time: thirty bound Object Register ledgers recording, for each object excavated, the registration number, description, a sketch, material, measurements, date of entry, provenance, and remarks such as photographic number details (approximately 2,380 pages containing 19,764 object records). Extremely fragile today, these ledgers remained in storage, as researchers refer to bound printouts made from microfilms of the originals. (Fig. 3.4)

After outsourcing the scanning of the previously existing microfilms of the Object Registers, we prepared to hire

3.2 Then-and-now comparison of the north wall engaged statuary in room C of the chapel of Meresankh (G 7530-sub). *Top:* 1930; *bottom:* 1999.

data entry and word processing consultants to convert handwritten entries into database records and text files.[3] In addition, we added a modest number of archaeological drawings (plans, sections, figural renderings of scenes and inscriptions) to this list. Finally, we scanned Reisner's three primary published tomes on the Giza Necropolis, eight volumes in the Giza Mastabas Series by W. K. Simpson and his successors, and relevant scholarly articles in the *Bulletin of the Museum of Fine Arts, Boston* and other journals (where copyright permissions allowed).

The process of aggregating and cross-referencing such diverse media was relatively new territory for Egyptology back in 2000. Evaluations and decisions were required for everything from sizes, formats, and image resolutions necessary for scholarly research to whether to rotate landscape illustrations to their proper orientations in PDF files. Most critical to the success of the concept, however, was the integration of the data. By creating a multimedia repository for scholarly research, we were hoping to virtually "reconstruct" the ancient environment of the Giza Necropolis.

3.3 Then-and-now comparison of the sarcophagus of Akhethetep (G 7650), showing the disappearance of painted decoration. *Top:* 1929; *bottom:* 2008.

1190

No. 33-2-	DESCRIPTION	MATERIAL	MEAS.	DATE	PROVENANCE	REMARKS
191.	Model alabaster jar with mark in ink on bottom	Alabaster	H. = 4 cms D. = 2.2 »	Feb. 25th	Debris of chamber of G 2340 A	C 13413
192.	6 model offering dishes with marks in ink on bottom	Alabaster	D. = 3.5-5.2 cm H. = 1.1-1.5 »	Feb. 23rd	"	C 13412
193.	7 frags. of two lids of canopic jars, one incomplete and one nearly complete	Limestone	D. = 16.6-17.9 cm H. = 2.8 »	Feb. 23rd	"	C 13412
194.	Door lintel, broken into two pieces.	Limestone	L. = 187 cms W. = 40 » T. = 20 » D.=4.3; H=3	Feb. 24th Feb. 23rd	From top of mastaba G 2342	Photo A 7055 Mark preparing with plate
195.	Basket full of thin twigs	Wood, twigs	L. = 30 cm D. = 2.5-2.8 »	Feb. 25th	Around skeleton in chamber of G 2340 A	
196.	Bones of human skeleton	Bones	—	Feb. 25th	Debris of chamber of G 2342 U	Box 159
197.	Bones of human skeleton.	Bones	—	Feb. 25th	Debris of chamber of G 2349 Z	161
198.	Frag. of flint with very sharp edges	Flint	L. = 6.3 cms W. = 3. T. = 0.9	Feb. 25th	Debris of chamber of G 2356 A	Photos A 7043/44
199.	Flint knife	Flint	L. = 11.5 cms W. = 2.9 » T. = 0.6 »	"	"	"
200.	Flint	Flint	L. = 8.8 cms W. = 5.8 » T. = 1.4 »	"	"	"

3.4 HU–MFA Expedition Object Register, volume 25, page 1190, handwritten by Hansmartin Handrick.

90

All Things to All People?

For scholars with varying research goals (archaeological, historical, philological, architectural, sociological, or art historical), we strove to create different access portals to the data. Maximum ease of entry was also critical for other types of website visitors, from the amateur Egypt fan to the specialists in fields outside Egyptology. Suddenly, once the material was out in the public domain, we could no longer hide behind our typically obtuse scholarly jargon. All Egyptologists know what *JEA* means, but without cumbersome concordances how would anyone else know that this was the *Journal of Egyptian Archaeology* and not, say, the *Journal of Etymological Antonyms* if we did not provide such abbreviations in full? Familiar territory for the specialist had to be "translated" to reach the masses. And how would one deal with non-English speakers? Funds were certainly lacking to create multilanguage versions of the entire website. An English speaker might search for King Khufu, but our German colleagues preferred Cheops, and the French Khéops. The Pyramids site itself is known by such variant spellings as Giza, Ghizeh, Gizeh, and even Jizah, not to mention the spelling in Arabic script. Our databases had to be equipped with alternative spellings wherever possible. This issue applied for ID systems, too; a statue of the tomb owner first received one field number upon removal from the ground, but a completely different one upon entering its new life in a museum collection. For example, in the field Reisner used object numbering systems such as 36-4-53 (1936 being the year, April being the month, and 53 being the object number for that month), whereas the subsequent MFA accession number might be 37.638 (1937 being the year of acquisition, and 638 being object number for that year). The Egyptian Museum in

Cairo used a completely different system, of course, for its *Journal d'Entrée* and subsequent *Catalogue Général*.

The range of search entry portals for the planned Giza website included three different approaches:

Quick Search: A general catch-all keyword text field box, not unlike Google's home page, familiar to everyone, that searches across the majority of database fields. Example search terms might include "pair statue," tomb "G 7110," "Sphinx," "Lord Cromer," "limestone," "furniture," "sarcophagus," "1925," and so on. The advantage was that users with no previous knowledge could search for any and all terms. The disadvantage was that the returned results could be unparsed and overwhelming. For example, a search for museum object number 12.125 might also return any items simply bearing the number "125" in any context ("125 workmen at the site today").

Advanced Search: This page was meant to contain the following sublevel search categories: Tombs and Monuments, Finds, Photos, Diaries, Plans and Drawings, Published Documents, Unpublished Documents, and People (ancient and modern). Each section would have its own search results page customized to the particular type of data sought. Criteria would be built into the system in a number of combinations, for example:

- all items related to the Giza tomb of the high official Nefer (photos, maps, finds, diary entries)
- all photos taken in the Western Cemetery before 1910
- all Excavation Diary pages mentioning Gaston Maspero, head of the Antiquities Service
- all published references to statue "X" from tomb "Y"
- all views of the Great Pyramid looking east

Visual Search: We aimed to base a graphical portal into the site on a zoomable aerial photograph of all Giza. Since there was no one single year or day when all Giza tombs lay discovered and exposed to best viewing advantage from the air, this photograph was a montage of images taken in 1936 and 1999. The user would zoom in to an individual cemetery, a single tomb, or a temple by clicking on the appropriate buttons embedded in the actual photograph or line drawing. Eventually he or she could arrive at an individual structure, with options for viewing a host of documents related to that structure, including excavation photos, discovery images, corresponding field diary pages describing the discovery, and modern color studio images of the finds. Fortunately, this geographical approach was assisted first by the orderly layout of the mastaba tombs by Khufu into rows of streets and avenues, and second by Reisner's four-digit numbering system for all the large mastabas (with rounded numbers such as "G 2140"), as well as all the later intrusive and smaller sepulchers between and around them (with intercalary numbers such as "G 2147"). We had the rudimentary beginnings of a coordinate system, thanks to the HU–MFA Expedition, and a poor man's approach to "Google Street View" two years before Google launched this feature.

Workflows

A staff of two Egyptologists supervised four dedicated data entry contractors converting the Photo Registers, Object Registers, and Expedition Diaries to electronic form. An imaging company was brought in-house and provided with a small studio in the MFA basement for copy-stand camera work. One challenge that required efficient organization was the sifting through glass plate negatives for images of Giza among the twenty-two other HU–MFA Expedition sites. For example, negative A4881 might display ceramics found in a Giza tomb, but negative A4882, the next negative in sequence in the storage cabinet, might show human remains from a Nubian grave in Sudan. Moreover, there was an "old series" and a "new series," since Reisner switched designations with the change of his sponsorship from the University of California (Hearst Expedition) to Harvard and the MFA. We therefore faced the constant possibility of two different images with the same number, old series A100 and new series A100. The creation of the Photo Registers database, including information for all 45,000 expedition negatives from all twenty-three sites, allowed for searches (by series) for Giza negatives only. Students could then use these lists to pull glass plates from the appropriate cabinets for the digital scanning team. Once they brought a glass plate to the nearby studio, our digital photographers illuminated it by a strobe from below. The photographers (Marisa Privitera and Francisco Robledo) worked in two successive shifts, from 9:00 AM to 11:00 PM. Each one processed 75 plates per shift, totaling 150 plate scans per day. The entire 21,000-negative process took less than one year, from April 2001 through February 2002.

In the first month of the project, twelve individuals had come aboard. By the end of its first year of operation, the Giza

Archives Project had generated so much interest that we were able to attract students, interns, docents, and other volunteers in unprecedented numbers. Some nine hundred hours of volunteer labor were donated to the Giza Archives Project between July 1, 2000, and June 30, 2001, and the numbers only grew in succeeding years. The work also provided the opportunity for both undergraduate and graduate students from Tufts University (where I was teaching at the time) to contribute to the project, in many cases for course credit. By the end of the project, in 2011, five hundred people, from all walks of life and with all manner of skill sets, had contributed their time and expertise. As one of the earliest examples of crowdsourcing, almost exclusively based at the Museum of Fine Arts, this success allowed us to expand far beyond our original project goals.

The Giza Archives Project also offered employment opportunities to a series of younger Egyptologists, both pre-PhD and postdoctoral, no small feat in a field with a dearth of paying positions. They all contributed their unique talents to various aspects of the work; in roughly chronological order of employment they were Heidi Saleh, Heather Evans, Christine End, Nicholas Picardo, Rachel Aronin, and Jeremy Kisala. Besides the project director, however, only one Egyptologist remained with the project over an entire decade, from 2000 to 2010. Our senior research associate, Diane Victoria Flores, left an indelible mark on all our efforts. With her unrelenting devotion to accuracy and quality control, and her laserlike focus on ferreting out the legions of discrepancies hidden in the excavation data, she, more than any other colleague, corrected the numerous mistakes of the original expedition staff and accounted for the high-value product that is available online today. What Egyptological and archaeological scholarship owes to Dr. Flores cannot be overstated.

With such exemplary support, not to mention large numbers of undergraduate and graduate students, we were able over the course of the entire grant period to expand our ambitions and digitize all manner of supplementary Giza documents in the MFA Archives. These included post-expedition-era images such as the MFA's professional studio photographs of Giza objects; thousands of 35-millimeter color slides taken by curatorial department staff since the 1960s; several thousand large-scale Giza maps and plans, as well as individual burial shaft plans and section drawings; 5,000 unpublished Reisner manuscript pages; paintings by expedition artists and draftsmen; (Fig. 3.5) boxes full of copies of hieroglyphic inscriptions; flat files full of epigraphic facsimile drawings of tomb wall scenes and texts; preliminary reports; and a host of other items. Managing all these paper archives became a full-time challenge in itself, and so we were very fortunate to gain the services of Catherine Pate, first as a volunteer in 2002, and thereafter as a professional archivist. She oversaw the reorganization, proper storage, and creation of finding lists for a host of diverse expedition materials, as well as organizing the digital file structures of our servers and managing much of the staff. She also supervised our growing team of weekly museum associates, women without whose dedication to all manner of operations the museum would probably have ground to a halt. The museum associates summarized the original expedition correspondence and associated documents, which in turn fueled my own interest in George Reisner and the history of the HU–MFA Expedition. As a direct outgrowth of the Giza Archives Project, and the work of the museum associates, I now hope to produce a biography of Reisner's life and career.[4]

As our personnel changed and grew, so did our locations around the museum. Owing to the retirements of certain administrators, and experimentation with best practices, the

Giza Archives Project operated over the course of its decade-long tenure at the MFA under three different departments: Information Resources under Nancy Allen (2000–2001); Libraries and Archives under Maureen Melton (2002–2004); and, finally, Conservation and Collections Management under Arthur Beale, followed by his successor, Matthew Siegel (2004–2011). Each of these department heads supported the work in every way, and each has my gratitude. Because the MFA was embarking on an ambitious expansion plan that included the new American Wing, our office locations changed as well. Despite the sometimes turbulent side effects of working near a construction zone, museum management sought at every turn to keep the Giza workflow operating with maximum efficiency.

A proof-of-concept demo website was launched in April 2001, and a scholarly board of advisers convened. In 2002 we contacted a group of forty-five Egyptologists from around the world who specialized in the Old Kingdom or were knowledgeable about information technologies (or both). We wanted to sample their research preferences for Giza Project material. Many provided extremely useful guidance on the types of

3.5 Modern painting by Norman de Garis Davies of jousting in the papyrus marsh, from the east wall of the chapel of Sekhemka (G 1029).

data that should be searchable and cross-referenced. Their research questions pointed to two major preferences:

1) the desire to research the entire ancient site of Giza, cutting across all excavations; this demonstrated the artificiality (for scholarship) of searches limited to the areas excavated by the HU–MFA Expedition (even though it was the largest of all areas excavated by a single expedition);

2) the desire for specific Egyptological data (example: provide a list all Egyptians buried at Giza bearing a particular hieroglyphic administrative title) that could be provided only by expanding the project beyond basic scanning to customized Egyptological database work, beyond the simple digitizing of primary sources for basic accessibility, as laid out in our first grant proposal.

Here is a sample of our Egyptological colleagues' research questions and requests:

- Show all the tombs where the owner has the title is *jrj-Xt-nswt* ("keeper of the king's property"), giving the area of the mastaba and the area of the chapel.
- Which tombs was Reisner working in during the first half of 1939?
- Can I measure dimensions electronically off your plans?
- Show all tombs with imported Syro-Palestinian vessels.
- Provide a list of tombs of all individuals who were priests in the royal mortuary cult.
- Provide a list of all intact burials at Giza.
- Provide a list of all tombs in which offering bearers representing funerary estates are shown.

- Show all the stone mastabas or rock-cut tombs with more than one inner room for the chapel.
- Show information about all offering tables and libation basins found in situ in the Western Cemetery.
- Show drawings or sketches of all lintels with family scenes.
- Show all photos of modern individuals such as Georg Steindorff (Egyptologist), Friedrich Koch (photographer), or Egyptian excavation crews, daily life, and so on.
- Show all photos taken by a specific photographer.
- Provide bibliography and literature for a specific tomb, object, and the like.
- Show all images and information regarding unfinished statues from the royal pyramid complexes.
- Show all images and information regarding tombs in the Central Field (Egyptian excavations) with representations of the tomb owner decorating the pillars.
- Show all information for statues of females (no groups, single statues only).
- Show the manuscripts by Reisner that discuss questions of tomb typology.
- On the plan of Giza Plateau, show the position of all non-royal tombs that cover an area larger than, for example, 700 square yards (600 square meters).
- Show all available material (including diaries) connected with a specific statue found in situ (or with all statues found in situ).
- Show records and documents about the division of finds from 1912 to 1914.
- Show all photos of statues and fragments of statues from the mastaba of Ba-ba-ef (G 5230) and give information about where they are now (Boston, Vienna, Cairo, or elsewhere).

- Provide a list of all the pottery found in the tomb of Queen Hetepheres (G 7000 X).
- Show all information on tombs in the Western Cemetery that were excavated in cooperation between Reisner and Steindorff or Reisner and Junker.
- Search for mention of certain excavation visitors, such as Theodore Roosevelt, Queen Elisabeth of Belgium, and Wilhelm Pelizaeus (funder of German excavations).

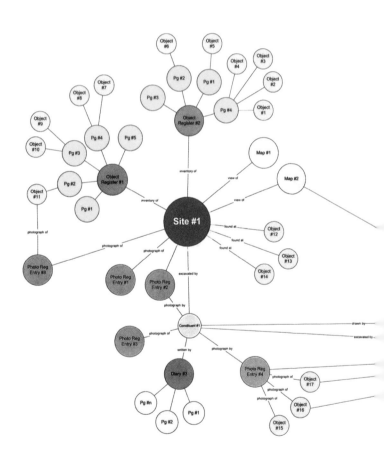

Web Launch: Giza Goes Live

Most of the primary source item databases were frozen by April 2004 and batch-uploaded into The Museum System (TMS), a popular proprietary collections management system operated by Gallery Systems of New York. This integration phase was crucial. (Fig. 3.6) We faced complex mapping of data fields from preliminary databases, such as Filemaker, into TMS, resizing of images and creation of derivatives for thumbnail, preview, study, and other formats, and cross-linking

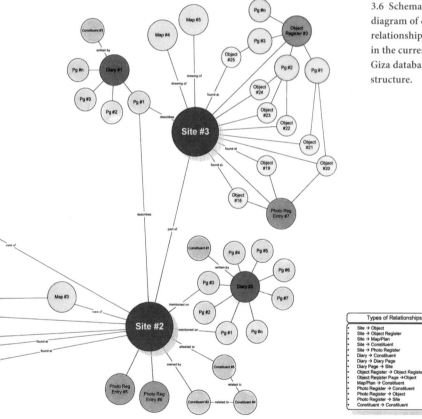

3.6 Schematic diagram of data relationships used in the current Giza database structure.

between the Giza TMS database and the MFA's primary TMS collections database (called Artemis). The MFA system focused solely on its own collections of art objects, whereas the Giza database focused on archaeology, provenance, and archival documentation; but the two overlapped in critical ways when it came to the Egyptian antiquities themselves.

We then applied for and received a second Mellon grant of $545,000 for three additional years, 2004–2007, moving from the Mellon Foundation's Museums and Conservation Program, under Angelica Zander Rudenstine's leadership, to the Scholarly Communications Program, under Donald Waters's direction, with the eventual assistance of Helen Cullyer. The first year of our second grant cycle saw the long-awaited public iteration of all our efforts—the Giza website (www.giza pyramids.org)—first launched in 2005. It was initially hosted by Gallery Systems in New York and moved to the MFA's own servers in 2010. Our efforts were successful largely because of programmers and database managers from the MFA's Conservation and Collections Management Department. Linda Pulliam, Kay Satomi, Jeff Steward, and (after Steward's departure for Harvard) Kenneth Leibe consulted, coded, debugged, encouraged, and consoled through each stage of the data entry and website construction process. Jeff Steward in particular also built the bridges so that our Giza data (archaeological) would link seamlessly in-house with the MFA's own collections management system (art historical). For example, where the museum's Artemis database housed the excellent professional studio color photography of a particular statue, our system contained the discovery photos portraying the site where it was originally found and the diary entries describing the event.

3.7 Statue of Khui-en-khufu lying in shaft D of G 2407, 1936.

The most useful element of the new Giza website lay in its ability to aggregate all relevant documents and media for a given tomb, temple, pyramid, or other site, and the user could arrive at this aggregate page in a variety of ways. We can follow this paradigm in some detail using the example of the Fifth Dynasty standing statue of the high official Khui-en-khufu from tomb G 2407, shaft D. The overview plan of this so-called Cemetery en Echelon (named for the skewed rows of mastaba tombs west of the Khufu Pyramid) reveals the entire tomb and surrounding context. Excavation glass plate images show the statue in situ on April 19, 1936, lying on its side in the pit. (Fig. 3.7) The diary entry, which was translated from the original Arabic account, describes the statue found underneath a broken limestone lintel:

> English diary entry for Sunday, April 18, 1936:
> G 2407 D: It is north of the serdab which is north of shaft
> C. Lined with dubsh [= debris, rubble]. On west, big stone,

the same as a roof in shaft. Down 90 cm. Limestone debris and dubsh. Found in the beginning of the shaft: big door lintel [36-4-56] inscribed in relief and hav[ing] a cartouche with the name "Khufu," broken into two fragments. After photograph[ing] the door lintel we removed it from the pit; and underneath the lintel door we found—statue [36-4-53], standing, half size, broken in two pieces above knee. Named Khufuw-khenui [= Khui-en-khufu]; tip of right thumb and handkerchief broken off. Seated statuette [36-4-52], tip nose and part over left eye and tip of middle toe chipped off. Lower part of right hand, corner of base broken off. Name Ka-m-Iset [Ka-em-iset]. The statue and the statuette are both photographed and removed to camp. Not reached the rock in shaft. Chamber not yet reached.

No. 36-4-	DESCRIPTION	MATERIAL	MEAS.	DATE	PROVENANCE	REMARKS
53.	Standing statue (c. half life size) of Khufu-khenui broken into two pieces through knees, but otherwise complete; name written horizontally on top of base in front of feet, titles above that in front of left foot. Little color of body preserved, [illegible] right thumb, knob of handkerchief in right hand, small part of inner left calf and chip of lower right corner of base broken off. Short wig, pleated apron (golden) over white skirt, belt with buckle.	Limestone	H. – 83.5 cm W. – 28.0 cm Th. – 34.0 "	April 19 – W of base – L of base	From G 2407 D	A 7566/7. B 8695: 2. C 828: MFA 37. [illegible]
			WSS, HESP, BMFA Vol.	P. 75 XXXVI,	No. 214, pp 26, 27, 29	
54.	Small frags of plaster with traces of hieroglyphs painted in red, black and yellow.	Plaster		April 20	From top of middle G 2407	
55.	Two pieces of copper (fibula?)	Copper		" 20	"	

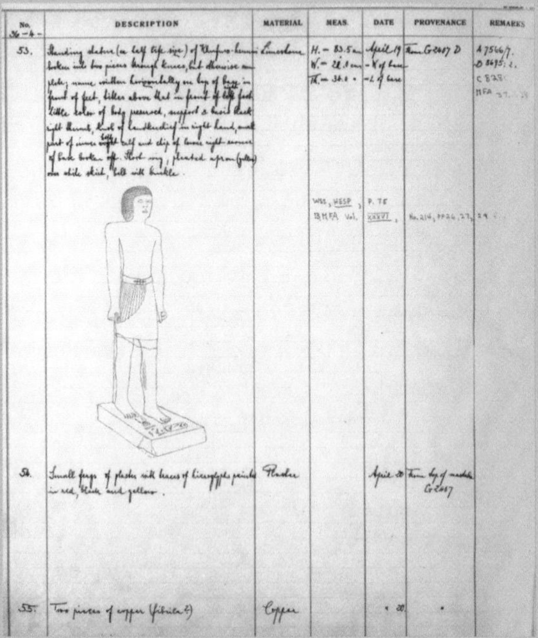

3.8 HU–MFA Expedition Object Register, volume 28, page1354.

The expedition staff subsequently removed the statue to Harvard Camp, gave it the field number 36-4-53 (meaning in April 1936 this was object number 53 to be inventoried), and entered it into the Object Register book with a sketch and relevant metadata. (Fig. 3.8) Just a few days later, on April 24, an expedition photographer, Mohammedani Ibrahim, took documentary photographs on glass plate negatives in the Harvard Camp photo studio against a black backcloth. (Fig. 3.9) Meanwhile, the draftsmen prepared a plan and section drawing of the shaft, and eventually Reisner wrote up the tomb and the find in his (still unpublished) manuscript for additional volumes of the *History of the Giza Necropolis* series. The Egyptian Antiquities Service gave the statue of Khui-en-khufu to the MFA, while another statue from the same pit (36-4-52),

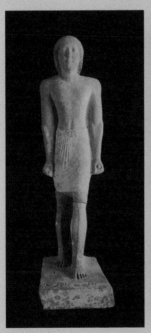

3.9 Harvard Camp studio photographs of the statue of Khui-en-khufu (MFA 37.638), 1936.

belonging to Ka-em-iset, headed for the Egyptian Museum, Cairo (Journal d'Entrée 67571). Before it was shipped, packing lists from 1937 recorded Khui-en-khufu's statue, in both text and photograph. After its arrival in Boston, the MFA registrars gave the statue the accession number of 37.638 on August 1, 1937 (meaning that in 1937 this was the 638th object accessioned by the museum). Reisner first published the piece the following year in the *Bulletin of the Museum of Fine Arts* for April 1938.[5] Finally, in recent years MFA studio photographers produced an excellent color studio image of the statue. (Fig. 3.10) All these items appear, along with additional documentation, in the amalgamated search results page for either the tomb (G 2407), the statue (MFA 37.638), or even simply the name of Khui-en-khufu in various spellings. (Fig. 3.11)

3.10 MFA studio photograph of the statue of Khuien-khufu.

Museum of Fine Arts Boston   The Giza Archives

GIZA LIBRARY	SEARCH THE ARCHIVES	MY GIZA RESEARCH	NEWS	CONTACT

Search ⭘

8 query results for "g 2407" > 1 Tombs & Monuments > Western Cemetery   Result 1 of 1

Show search form

< Previous   page... 1   Next >

⊞ view images   ⊟ view list   ▣ view 1 item at a time

Enlarge Image

· **All related photos are below**
For other items, use links at right

Western Cemetery: G 2407

Stone-built mastaba

PorterMoss Date: Late Dynasty V

Excavator: George Andrew Reisner
American, 1867–1942

Attested: Kaemiset (in G 2407)

Tomb Owner: Khuienkhufu (G 2407)

Shafts: G 2407 Serdab; G 2407 A; G 2407 A2; G 2407 B; G 2407 C; G 2407 D; G 2407 E; G 2407 F; G 2407 U; G 2407 V; G 2407 W; G 2407 W2; G 2407 X; G 2407 X2; G 2407 Y; G 2407 Z

Selected bibliographical references:
Lehmann, Katja. Der Serdab in den Privatgräbern des Alten Reiches 1-3. Ph.D. Dissertation, Universität Heidelberg, 2000, Kat. G139.

Manuelian, Peter Der. "An Approach to Archaeological Information Management: The Giza Archives Project." In Filip Coppens, ed. Abusir and Saqqara in the year 2001. Proceedings of the Symposium (Prague, September 25th-27th, 2001). Archiv Orientální 70, No. 3 (August 2002). Prague: Oriental Institute, Academy of Sciences of the Czech Republic, pp. 324, 327-328, 334-335, figs. 2, 3, pls. 9,10.

Porter, Bertha, and Rosalind L.B. Moss. Topographical Bibliography of Ancient Egyptian Hieroglyphic Texts, Reliefs, and Paintings 3: Memphis (Abû Rawâsh to Dahshûr). Oxford: The Clarendon Press, 1931. 2nd edition. 3: Memphis, Part 1 (Abû Rawâsh to Abûsîr), revised and augmented by Jaromír Málek. Oxford: The Clarendon Press, 1974, pp. 92-93.

Reisner, George A. "Note on Objects Assigned to the Museum by the Egyptian Government." Bulletin of the Museum of Fine Arts, Boston 36, No. 214 (April 1938), pp. 26-27.

Publications (PDFs) in Giza Archives Library:
Lehmann, Katja. Der Serdab in den Privatgräbern des Alten Reiches 1. Text. Ph.D. Dissertation, Universität Heidelberg, 2000.

Lehmann, Katja. Der Serdab in den Privatgräbern des Alten Reiches 2. Abbildungen. Ph.D. Dissertation, Universität Heidelberg, 2000.

Lehmann, Katja. Der Serdab in den Privatgräbern des Alten Reiches 3. Katalog. Ph.D. Dissertation, Universität Heidelberg, 2000.

Porter, Bertha, and Rosalind L.B. Moss. Topographical Bibliography of Ancient Egyptian Hieroglyphic Texts, Reliefs, and Paintings 3: Memphis (Abû Rawâsh to Dahshûr). Oxford: The Clarendon Press, 1931. 2nd edition. 3: Memphis, Part 1 (Abû Rawâsh to Abûsîr), revised and augmented by Jaromír Málek. Oxford: The Clarendon Press, 1974.

Reisner, George A. "Note on Objects Assigned to the Museum by the Egyptian Government." Bulletin of the Museum of Fine Arts, Boston 36, No. 214 (April 1938), pp. 26-32.

See Related Items...

FINDS
25 Finds

DIARIES
18 Diary Pages

PEOPLE
1 Modern Person

PEOPLE
2 Ancient People

PHOTOS
46 Photos

DRAWINGS
33 Plans and Drawings

PUBLISHED
5 Published Documents

UNPUBLISHED
51 Unpublished Documents

3.11 The Giza website amalgamated tomb record for G 2407.

107

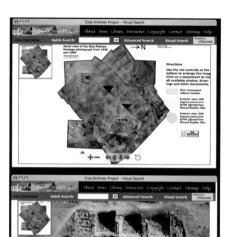

We were able to realize most of the features described above in the planning stages for the first Giza grant, including the Visual Search page. Its two features provided maximum access to Giza while requiring no specialized Egyptological or computer-programming knowledge. First, almost every tomb became a red "button" containing the tomb's number that flashed when the mouse cursor rolled over it. Clicking on the tomb compiled for the user the same aggregate list of all available relevant data, in identical fashion to a typed query for the same tomb. The second feature on the Visual Search page consisted of round, pulsating yellow and blue buttons placed all over the site. These represented nearly 1,300 different standpoints; a click on each one took the user down to ground level at that location showing a 360-degree "Quicktime Virtual Reality" (QTVR) panorama. These interactive "movies," which I had created at Giza in several short field seasons in 2005 and 2006, (Figs. 3.12–3.13) allowed the user to view the immediately surrounding landscape and provided a sense of distance and relative sizes of contiguous monuments that no ordinary 2D photograph could match. Yellow dots represented outdoor (exterior) locations, while blue dots took the user inside a decorated chapel, pyramid, or rock-cut chamber. (One of my more enduring personal Giza memories consists of scrambling into the burial chamber of King Menkaure to protect my QTVR camera rig from the outburst of a sudden, heavy rainstorm. It was the first time I had

3.12 The Giza website Visual Search page.

ever used a royal pyramid as an umbrella.) Now, a decade later, we await the implementation of more sophisticated tools to improve on this original immersive tour of the Giza Plateau, especially since Apple has ceased to support its QTVR software.

As the website matured in design and functionality, we added a feature aimed primarily at scholars. The MET, or Multilingual Egyptological Thesaurus, is a controlled vocabulary covering almost every aspect of the field, from classification of objects and wall decoration to locations of all the world's Egyptian collections. For our Giza data, users had no way to search images for content, such as scenes of musicians, viticulture, craftsmanship, or even female figures holding specific ritual objects. Searchable image captions could hardly account for every scene detail represented on tomb chapel walls, so we added MET descriptors as attribute items linked to the media record for each image. There were fifteen different descriptive thesaurus sections in the MET thesaurus: (1) present location; (2) category; (3) provenance; (4) dating; (5) material; (6) technique; (7) state of preservation; (8) description; (9) language; (10) writing; (11) category of text; (12) text content; (13) divine names; (14) royal names; and (15) acquisition. Once these MET links were posted online, students of Egyptology could search images by content; those seeking scenes of fishing boats on the Nile could gather—and eventually save—their search results in personal collections. Located under the "Advanced Search for Photos" heading, this feature proved extremely labor-intensive to produce, for each

3.13 *Left:* QTVR camera rig in the chapel of Meresankh (G 7530-sub), 2004. *Right:* the resulting panoramic image, before unwrapping by means of software.

image required item-by-item linking with each attested thesaurus item. The Visual Search feature was also buried too deep in the website's navigational structure to be noticed by more than the most intrepid web explorers. We plan to redesign the interface in future iterations of the website.

Another, much more successful feature implemented some years into the project was the integration of the bibliography module in the cross-referenced database system. The "Digital Giza Library" began as a static page where text-searchable (through optical character recognition, or OCR) PDF versions of Giza-themed Egyptological monographs and journal articles were posted in one long alphabetical list for selected downloading. We later reformatted the library to behave as an integral element in online search results. In other words, by giving each bibliography item its own record in our bibliography module, and then linking that record to all relevant items in other modules, the downloadable PDF literature files would appear alongside photos, diary entries, and drawings. This necessitated critical reading of the scholarly content and the creation of authority lists parsing all personal and place names, tomb and object numbers for linking to site, object, and constituent module records.

Seeking to include all possible figural drawings of tomb wall decoration from our vast archives, we supplemented basic scanning of old one-to-one line drawings with what I came to call "digital epigraphy." A major documentation priority, as an interpreted supplement to photography, (see chapter 5, on objectivity and "trained judgment") Egyptological epigraphy is the production of facsimile line drawings of scenes—carved, painted, or both—and inscriptions on tomb and temple walls and other artifacts. This process has a long tradition in the field, from tracing directly off the wall to drawing on photographic enlargements (the "Chicago House method"). Our approach converted the process to digital formats, using high-resolution photographs that are then traced on-screen using commercial vector-based software.[6] The advantages of this method over traditional work with pen and ink on paper include a simplified editing process; the ability to weather unexpected changes of scale or line width for publication; and repurposing for 3D reconstructions, color restorations, or hieroglyphic paleographies. The use of vintage photography, such as the HU–MFA Expedition's glass plate negatives, as the epigraphic base for digital tracing often provided much more surviving detail than is visible either in modern-day photography or on the Giza tomb wall itself today. (Fig. 3.14)

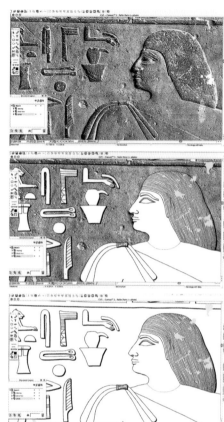

3.14 Digital epigraphy, showing the onscreen tracing process, from top to bottom; this example is from the chapel of Nefer (G 2110).

As we further aimed at increasing accessibility to Giza Plateau scholarship, we tried to extend the logic of Reisner's tomb-numbering system to areas outside the original HU–MFA Expedition concession. The Central Field, excavated primarily by Selim Hassan, is the largest zone requiring such structured tomb numbers. With the blessing of the (then) Supreme Council of Antiquities, we labeled this as the G 8000 Cemetery. The G 9000 Cemetery is now the area just to the north of Khafre's causeway. Other zones that would benefit from four-digit number assignments include, but are not limited to, the tombs in the far Western Cemetery, excavated first by Abdel Moneim Abu-Bakr and later by the Cairo University–Brown University Expedition; those to the northwest of the Khentkaus complex, cleared by Wahiba Saleh in the 1990s; and the rock-cut tombs at the eastern edge of the Eastern Cemetery, currently under investigation by the Russian Archaeological Mission.

"Giza Central"?

Though the MFA's Giza holdings represent important finds from the areas assigned to the HU–MFA dig concession, several other expeditions made spectacular discoveries as well. For example, five decorated tomb chapels, removed by their excavators from Giza, are now on view in museums of Europe (Berlin, Hildesheim, Karlsruhe, Tübingen, and Vienna). From any single institution's point of view, the site of Giza always "stops" as soon as one steps beyond the bounds of that institution's individual excavation concession. From the scholar's point of view, however, the "next tomb over" signifies equal relevance regardless of which institution excavated it and where the derivative material might currently be housed. Up to the present, this unilateral, even "isolationist," approach to documentation between museums and institutes has presented a stumbling block that hinders research. What good is it to know everything possible about tomb G 4140, while its adjacent tomb, G 4150, remains a cipher simply because the German-Austrian, not the American, expedition did the excavating?

It soon became clear—and as our scholarly colleagues had indirectly intimated early on in the project's history—that the value of the MFA's Giza Archives Project website would substantially increase should it one day grow into "Giza Central," that is, a one-stop source for information from all the major excavation archives and museum collections, past, present, and even future. Such a corpus would provide answers to research questions that we cannot pose because of the current logistical obstacles to archaeological and historical inquiry. It would enhance and optimize the publication process of individual monuments and serve as a centralized clearinghouse for all information concerning the Giza Pyramids. Just as the Acropolis, Pompeii, and the terra-cotta army of China have their own study centers, it was time that one was established for Giza, even if it did not consist of bricks and mortar.

Results from the major early twentieth-century excavations are spread today over nine primary Giza collections located in Berkeley, Berlin, Boston, Cairo, Hildesheim, Leipzig, Philadelphia, Turin, and Vienna. In addition, a few thousand objects from Giza have also found their way through indirect or private channels into other museums great and small, the most important of which are the Metropolitan Museum of Art, the British Museum, the Ägyptisches Museum in Berlin, and the Louvre. Since no collection possessed more diverse types of data than that of the HU–MFA Expedition in Boston, that city was the logical base from which to attack the larger international integration problems. Challenges involving the foreign collections included the creation of some common standards, inspired by the ancient layout of Giza itself, that could be applied to the diverse numbering systems of the various institutions. Foreign collections management systems also tended to use German, French, or Arabic, an added challenge. Most of the institutions readily saw the advantage to contributing to a "Giza International Archive," but they were unable to participate without assistance in the form of funding, personnel, and equipment. For this reason I traveled to all the major Giza collections of Europe during the summer of 2006.

Amid the Italian, Austrian, and German frenzy for the World Cup (headquartered in Berlin that summer), I was able to persuade all the institutions to join our efforts.[7] Thanks to a supplemental Mellon Foundation grant of $306,000 (2007–2008), we subsidized the contributions of our new European and American partners. It is hard to overemphasize the significance and kindness of the Egyptologists and other authorities who provided photographs, object information, manuscript scans, and other forms of documentation, often at considerable cost in time and labor.[8] The international collaboration could not have run any more smoothly.

The Giza website thereafter underwent numerous redesigns, and tweaks as well as new features and fundamental improvements continued to enhance functionality between 2005 and 2011. Portions of the non–HU–MFA material slowly began to appear online. Instructional videos, satellite imagery, a news blog, and a "My Collections" feature that saved and retrieved user-generated assemblages were just some of the enhancements. The research community took note as well; awards included mention as one of *Archaeology Magazine*'s "favorite websites" (2007); an ABC-CLIO online history award (honorable mention; 2007),[9] the Philip M. Hamer and Elizabeth Hamer Kegan Award for promoting the knowledge and use of collections (2010),[10] and an IDG Computerworld Honors Program laureate, Training and Education category (2011).[11] Our analytics pages tracked users from 139 countries, and tens of thousands of hits. The secretary general of the Egyptian Supreme Council of Antiquities and vice minister of culture, Zahi Hawass, wrote an article about the website on his official blog, stating: "Visitors to museums, or tourists at Giza will one day have access to all the information that was once accessible only to scholars in libraries. I believe the Giza Archives Project provides a unique model for archaeological site management, preservation, and access, and I hope that similar projects and websites will follow this example for other sites, in Egypt and elsewhere." We were also able to secure a final Mellon Foundation grant of $714,000 to cover the years 2008 through 2011, along with an additional $500,000 to go toward a three-to-one matching challenge for endowment and sustainability beyond the final grant period.

Numerous publications have benefited from information made available by the Giza website. Some dealt with narrowly focused Egyptological research queries that nevertheless bore greater implications for understanding Egyptian culture. For example, Juan Carlos Moreno García collected instances of a particular hieroglyphic mortuary title to determine the contexts in which it appears and thus its deeper connotations. He concluded that holders of this title had duties not only within the funerary sphere but also of a broader ritual and administrative nature.[12] On the basis of archival photos and unpublished notes from earlier excavations, Stéphane Pasquali was able to suggest the probable location of a temple south of the Sphinx and built more than a millennium later by a son of Ramesses the Great (1279–1213 BCE). This discovery speaks to issues of cultural memory, that is, how Giza was reused and reinvented in later periods, long after the end of its original flourishing in the third millennium BCE.[13]

Other studies have posed broader Egyptological questions that may be explored by the different types of data available in the Giza Project's holdings. May Farouk's 2010 Berlin PhD dissertation studied spatial relationships between tombs in one particular cemetery at Giza using GIS. She relied heavily on the detailed maps and site data available on the website, which allowed for large-scale analysis to address wide-ranging questions of tomb and cemetery development, state involvement, and the relative status of tomb owners.[14] Florence

Friedman produced a comparative art historical study of one of the greatest masterpieces of Egyptian sculpture, the Menkaure dyad (MFA 11.1738), using photos and Excavation Diary notes to argue that the unidentified woman standing beside the king must be his mother (rather than his wife or a goddess) and addressing important aspects of royal iconography and representations of female power in ancient Egypt.[15] Antje Spiekermann traced the convoluted history of tomb G 2005 at Giza, which was excavated three times (and not always well) by three different expeditions, to demonstrate how early, nonscientific archaeology could confuse or even destroy original archaeological contexts.[16] In addition, Spiekermann made frequent use of the website in the creation of a German counterpart project, based in Hildesheim, that focused on Georg Steindorff's excavations at Giza.[17]

Still other authors have studied Giza Project data to formulate and address research topics in humanities fields far outside Egyptology. Wendy Doyon, in a forthcoming PhD dissertation for the University of Pennsylvania, has examined the lives of native Egyptian workmen employed by Western Egyptologists of the late nineteenth and early twentieth centuries, whose experiences are recorded in Expedition Diaries, allowing her to address aspects of social history, labor, and the ethics of archaeology over the past two centuries. Benjamin Stangl's 2010 Vienna master's thesis employed a 3D computer model of a decorated tomb at Giza as a case study for simulating interactive virtual spaces in the digital humanities, citing the Giza Project as "both a reference and a related visualization project."[18] Erica Pastore's 2008 SUNY Buffalo master's thesis in arts management examined the configuration of the original Giza website itself (rather than its Egyptological content) in a detailed investigation and evaluation of a number of art museum websites and online archives. Pastore argued that these "virtual museum spaces" more or less successfully reflect the evolving public mission of American art museums and the increase of public access and visitor empowerment as primary goals within the museum community.[19] In their chapter "Archaeological Information Systems," Iman Kulitz and Peter Ferschin lauded the Giza Project as one of only a "few projects [that] store all kinds of documents in databases and make the information accessible via internet."[20] Other major online academic resources, such as the UCLA Encyclopedia of Egyptology, make use of the scholarly Giza website content as well.[21]

Diaries Lost and Found

The story of an unexpected addition to the Giza dataset bears recounting before we close this chapter. To gain more insight into the workings of the original HU–MFA Expedition, I had long been seeking descendants of George Reisner's Egyptian foremen. In January 2006, during one of my field seasons at Giza, my Egyptian Inspectorate colleagues Mohamed Shiha and Mansour Boreik and I located a descendant in Cairo. Mr. Hassan Diraz, then in his seventies, remembered frolicking as a boy at Harvard Camp for years, while his father, Mohamed Said Diraz, ran most of the critical aspects of the expedition. Although the MFA curator and expedition member Dows Dunham had shipped all the archives home to Boston in 1947, the Diraz family had preserved seventy-two Arabic-language Expedition Diaries of the Harvard–MFA Expedition, of which forty-two concerned the work at Giza (about four thousand pages). These volumes had been faithfully recorded over decades primarily by Mr. Diraz's father and his grandfather Said Ahmed Said Diraz. After successful negotiations with the Diraz family, I obtained permission from the Egyptian

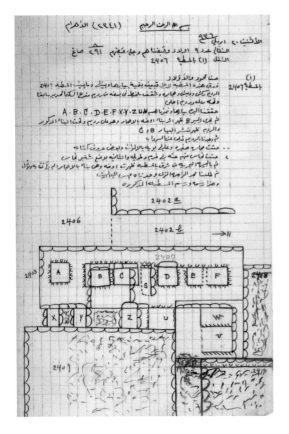

Supreme Council of Antiquities in October 2006 to acquire the diaries and ship them to Boston for digitization and preservation. (Copies of the resulting digital files were to be sent back to Cairo.) The books arrived in Boston in December 2006 and were scanned and translated over the succeeding years.[22] As an example of the original Arabic entries, fig. 3.15 shows the entry for the tomb of Khui-en-khufu, described above.

Lessons Learned

3.15 HU–MFA Expedition Arabic Diary, book 29, written by Duwy Mahmoud, page 2341, with the description of tomb G 2407 (Khui-en-khufu).

In late 2010 my place of employment changed from the Museum of Fine Arts, Boston, to Harvard University. This shift presented a unique opportunity to access the other half of the HU–MFA Expedition, allowing me to "close the circle," view the expedition from the Harvard side, and add archival documents and object information from the university's holdings. The Giza Project regrouped at Harvard in late 2011. The milestone of ten years of Giza work at the Museum of Fine Arts, Boston, and more than $3 million in Mellon Foundation support provided an apt moment to reflect on the triumphs, as well as the shortcomings and disappointments, and to sum up some lessons learned, not only for our own future work, but for other large-scale digital information management projects, particularly in the realm of archaeology.[23] (Fig. 3.16) Overall, and despite some of the missteps that will dog any large-scale documentation initiative, the decade-long approach to Giza archaeological data management succeeded in breathing new life into old archives and has supported researchers worldwide, particularly those requiring comprehensive access to the Giza dataset. It is gratifying to read of similar efforts espoused for archaeological sites as far away from the Pyramids as Mexico.[24] A summary of some our lessons learned closes this chapter.

1. We regretted that the grant was for scholarly access in the digital realm only, and it could not provide for physical rehousing of some of the most fragile archival materials.

2. We have noted that funds did not suffice to cover scanning all 45,000 glass plate expedition negatives, diaries, and Object Registers from the other twenty-two HU–MFA sites beyond Giza. The HU–MFA Expedition was a single unit and in many ways should be considered as such. Moreover, on the subject of scanning, our image resolution was too low, and we were not permitted to keep the sixteen-bit negative scans. But this is criticism in hindsight; there will always be better scanners and cameras, higher resolutions and sharper lenses. I expect that new technologies will be revolutionary, not just evolutionary. Imagine, for example, a scanner that

3.16 *Top:* some of the MFA museum associates who contributed years of work to the Giza Archives Project. *Bottom:* MFA Deputy Director Katie Getchell addresses project staff, volunteers, and Art of the Ancient World curators at the project's final party, June 28, 2011, concluding ten years of work.

could extrapolate 3D reconstruction data automatically from a 2D image. This might necessitate scanning the original expedition glass plates again, no matter what resolution had previously been used. This is yet another argument for physical conservation and preservation measures marching hand in hand with digital conservation project grants; should the glass plates not survive, there will be no going back.

3. The project's mandate focused solely on scholarship, not on educational materials for K–12 or older students. In retrospect, attention to casting a wider net with more popular appeal would have been useful, not only to extend the educational range of the work, but to further raise awareness and perhaps improve the possibility of future funding. At the beginning of the grant period (2000), social media were not widespread, and so plans for web pages that explained pyramid construction theories, the concepts of pharaonic kingship, or general Egyptian mortuary practices would have represented a useful component to the project. Now, in 2016, we are still striving to fulfill this obligation to an underserved portion of our international constituency.

4. As far as file-naming conventions are concerned, we learned that wherever possible, numbering schemes already in existence should be retained in the digital realm. To do otherwise tends to introduce unnecessary, additional levels of complexity and force the creation of burdensome concordances. A case in point is the 21,000 glass plate negatives that already had their own unique negative numbers designated by plate size (e.g., A125, B4001, C17723) given by the original HU–MFA Expedition. Our scanning company insisted on using its own meaningless numbering system for image file names. Our workflow progressed much more smoothly

on all fronts after we changed course and renamed all 21,000 images according to their original negative numbers.

5. Debate over vended (i.e., proprietary) software applications versus those developed in-house (or with open-source software) will probably continue, and each case demands its own set of solutions. We were fortunate at the MFA to be able to work with powerful proprietary solutions and yet also to have the expertise within our institution to customize them as necessary to meet our very Giza-specific needs.[25] The complex nature of the Giza material presented a unique set of cross-referencing challenges that were met through a combination of standardization and innovation. These issues become particularly acute when US federal funding is at stake, for it often prohibits the use of proprietary solutions.

6. We learned to keep all original documents and paper versions at hand, at least for the duration of active data entry. There are always omitted pages, cropped-off areas, image montaging questions, or original expedition numbering discrepancies that can be resolved only by returning to the original documents. The concept of "deep-sixing" or completely retiring original archives after they have been converted to electronic form is something of a fallacy, although immediate access certainly becomes a lower priority. It is critically important to link the original physical object with its newly created digital surrogate, usually by writing the name of the digital file on the physical object whenever possible and keeping an updated database record of the physical server location(s) of the scanned items. This will aid in subsequent verification, provenance, error correction, and so on.

7. With data migration issues, we learned that when compiling and organizing records for batch uploading into Structured Query Language (SQL) collections management systems, it is important first to consider (a) that the form of the data aligns with formatting in the corresponding destination fields; and (b) how the formatting of the data affects the ordering of web output (e.g., display order of records in list views) and the resulting experience for the website user. Failing to take these factors into account may require substantial reworking of data before batch uploading.

8. Data management plans are critical to long-term maintenance and preservation. Digitization projects should include a plan for the indefinite care of the resulting digital assets. Without such care, permanent maintenance, migration, and upgrades, the asset will ultimately degrade to the point of uselessness, which would probably constitute an irreplaceable intellectual and financial loss.

9. Reliance on commercial software can be risky. If software is redesigned or abandoned by the manufacturer, one could be left with unusable, broken data. This occurred in our case with Apple's revisions to its QTVR software, which caused browser crashes with all 1,300 QTVR panoramas on the Giza website. Similarly, iPhones and iPads, which came into existence after the Giza Archives Project was well under way, at this writing still do not accommodate Flash-dependent web content. As most of the interactivity on the Giza website (such as the "Zoomify" enlargeable pages) was Flash-based, this means that these images and pages are simply not viewable on such portable devices. As iPads and other smart devices increasingly become part of the field archaeologist's equipment, Flash-based content is at a seri-

ous disadvantage. The solution—for now—is a complete re-write in HTML5.

10. The Giza Archives Project could not have accomplished either its originally mandated or its bevy of additional tasks—such as the creation of the international Giza repository—without the army of volunteers who read, scanned, culled, processed, and reviewed thousands and thousands of records. Volunteers were a huge asset but simultaneously created a large management burden because of their varying skill sets. Matching volunteers to projects that they were suited for, designing workflows, training and supervising them, and reviewing and editing their work was often extremely time-consuming. Any digital undertaking that will rely on the services of volunteers must include built-in time and personnel for management as well as the integration of all the data they generate into the larger project.

11. "If you build it, they will come." Once a body of records is made public, people will find new and creative applications for them. Being prepared to serve the users and collaborate with them on new uses for the dataset is critical for long-term success.

CHAPTER 4

Giza 3D: The Real-Time Immersive Experience

Three-quarters of the way through the ten-year Giza Archives Project, it became clear that our data "grooming" and navigability enhancements would never reach their final destination. (Nor should they, as new technologies and new research approaches are part and parcel of archaeological investigation.) Administrators rarely want to hear the word "Never" in answer to the question "When will you be finished?"

GIZA LIBRARY   SEARCH THE ARCHIVES   MY GIZA RESEARCH   NEWS   CONTACT

Search ⊙

3,841 Results in Tombs & Monuments
Click here to refine your search if more than one tomb is listed

3,105 Results in Diary Pages
Harvard-MFA Expedition diary pages

37,199 Results in Photos
Includes images from 1901 to the present (black-and-white and color)

15,006 Results in Plans & Drawings
Tomb and site plans/sections; drawings of objects, wall reliefs, and inscriptions

22,022 Results in Finds
Ancient Giza object data

547 Results in Published Documentation
Includes books and articles (text searchable PDF files)

3,977 Results in People
Ancient Egyptians and modern individuals related to Giza

5,351 Results in Unpublished Documentation
Includes manuscripts, notes, and other documents

Be that as it may, by 2008 major portions of the site of Giza were digitally under control: primary and secondary sources (excavation photographs, plans and drawings, object information, diary accounts, manuscripts, and publications) were all in process at one stage or another. SQL databases, and the Giza website that fed from them, were allowing for aggregated search results on scales that no individual researcher could previously have gathered. The archival "backlog" for Giza, at least as far back as the birth of responsible archaeological method (roughly 1900), had been successfully converted to electronic form in a way that would inform current and future generations. (Fig. 4.1)

Despite this new integration, however, the data still remained largely static and free-floating. The great Giza expeditions of the early twentieth century had no standardized data points to align their surveys to, no Google Earth–type latitude and longitude geo-references to tie all the information together

4.1 A screenshot of the Giza website records totals as of February 1, 2016 (wwwgiza pyramids.org).

spatially. And comprehensive visualization of the site, beyond standard 2D photography, had yet to be attempted. As the first decade of the twenty-first century drew to a close, several archaeological projects were already experimenting with virtual reality reconstructions of ancient sites, in varying levels of complexity and detail, but these were based mostly on modern archaeological data; very few possessed the massive archaeological archive from a century ago that could be converted to digital formats for visualization. The Giza data were, by contrast, ripe for such a holistic combination of old and new. The old was getting "done"; it remained to define the new.

The French Connection

In 2008 our team became aware of an intriguing theory positing internal ramps as the construction method used in the Fourth Dynasty for the Great Pyramid at Giza. Put forward by the French architect Jean-Pierre Houdin, the theory had captured the attention of the French 3D modeling software company Dassault Systèmes, which "provides businesses and people with virtual universes to imagine sustainable innovations."[1] The company's "Passion for Innovation" sponsorship program, later expanded to the Passion for Innovation Institute, took on the challenge of visualizing Houdin's interpretations and animations in 3D, using their own proprietary virtual environment. Whether the argument for internal ramps will be vindicated will be determined in the future. For our purposes, we saw a potential for visualizing Giza in new and exciting ways, tailoring our archival data to the 3D environment, providing innovative research options, and reaching new audiences. My Egyptological colleague Bob Brier facilitated a meeting for me at his home in New York on July 25, 2008, with

Mehdi Tayoubi, Dassault Systèmes's Passion for Innovation Institute director and vice president for Experiential Strategy. Common interests in Giza were obvious, and so negotiations commenced between Dassault Systèmes and the Museum of Fine Arts, Boston, for a sponsorship agreement of the Giza Archives Project. One priority consisted of clearly demarcating the two projects, Houdin's theory on the one hand, and the larger documentation and research goals of the Giza Archives Project on the other, especially in the face of some academic resistance to Houdin's interpretations. By 2009 licensing software and some financial support were in place, and the Giza team took on a new priority, the virtual reconstruction of portions of the Giza Necropolis in 3D. Although this new immersive and experiential development was a worthy archaeological goal in itself, we saw yet another potential portal, or user interface, to the deeper archaeological data. Moreover, following Johanna Drucker, we felt that such visualizations of Giza could fulfill two roles: as "*representations* of information already known and those that are *knowledge generators* capable of creating new information through their use."[2] Our goals were academic and comprehensive, but we had to find the right balance to coexist with this new assistance from the corporate world, whose own goals, beyond an admirable philanthropic focus on contributing to world knowledge, leaned toward the marketing of their powerful software tools. What company would not relish an association with Giza, the most famous archaeological site in the world? But most for-profit businesses would prefer to associate their products with pyramids, temples, art masterpieces, and the Sphinx, not with sequences of empty, unused burial shafts, anonymous, undecorated tombs, or any of the other mundane elements that constitute archaeological completeness. For our part, it was clear that we could not rely on Mellon Foundation funding indefinitely; the foundation's generosity had already extended over four grants totaling more than $3 million and covering an entire decade. Similarly, start-up projects that subsequently generated ongoing sustainability costs could not expect to be absorbed automatically into the home institution's operating budget; the Museum of Fine Arts was already contending with more than its fair share of needs and priorities.

At the same time that the Dassault Systèmes negotiations were taking place, another opportunity for collaboration presented itself. In 2008 I was asked to give a Giza presentation for the scientists at the oil services company Schlumberger at their Schlumberger-Doll Research Center in Cambridge, Massachusetts.[3] Here the mutual interest was in subsurface Giza, both natural and man-made. This line of research is critical for understanding the development of the necropolis, but is so much more difficult to study than the superstructures and landscape aboveground. Schlumberger had access to the tools and expertise required to look miles underground; we were interested in perhaps fifty yards (fifty meters) underground at most. Thirteen research scientists from the Cambridge labs visited the MFA on November 17, 2008, to discuss possible collaboration.[4] As it happened, several of the Schlumberger team, in particular Michael Oristaglio and Jakob Haldorsen, had already experimented with remote sensing by the northern front paw of the Sphinx at Giza, so the mutual interest was already in place.[5] For the Giza Project, the chance at a comprehensive approach to the geomorphology of the Giza Plateau, and an eventual 3D model reconstruction of what lies below the Giza Necropolis, would be most welcome. We were convinced that by using seismic (sound wave), electromagnetic, and gravity sensors, modern geophysics could enhance archaeological work on the Giza Plateau. We felt that magnetic and electromagnetic (EM) methods, such as magnetometry, resistivity, EM induction, and ground-penetrating radar (GPR), were the best candidates for rapid surveys of our Giza flyover zone. Our aim was to link our Giza data to such a subsurface model. For the Schlumberger scientists, the attraction lay in contributing to a high-profile project that would test some new approaches and reflect favorably on their relations with both the Egyptian government and the MFA. Our planning meetings with Schlumberger representatives, particularly with Michael Oristaglio, the geophysicist Andreas Laake, and Schlumberger-Doll's managing director, Tarek Habashy, continued over the following years, and plans for remote sensing flyovers at Giza, covering two square miles (five square kilometers), began to take shape, in collaboration with the Egyptian National Authority for Remote Sensing and Space Sciences (NARSS); Farouk el-Baz, director of the Center for Remote Sensing at Boston University; and Aeroquest International, a remote-sensing company based in Ontario. We are particularly grateful to Andreas Laake, of WesternGeco, for his contributions to this phase of the work.[6] (Fig. 4.2) Just as final plans were taking shape, however, the Egyptian Revolution of January 2011 erupted, putting Giza flyover plans on hold indefinitely, although the cooperation with Dassault Systèmes continued to move forward.

Thanks to the perseverance of Mehdi Tayoubi at Dassault Systèmes and Debra Lakind, director of Business Development and Strategic Partnerships at the MFA, the sponsorship agreement with Dassault Systèmes was signed with CEO Bernard Charlès in Paris on February 24, 2010. Although several Giza mastabas had already started to come to life as 3D models the previous year, 2010 marked our first attempts to build a photo-realistic computer model of the entire Giza Plateau. As we worked on both sides of the Atlantic, between Boston and Paris, we benefited tremendously from a century of archaeological

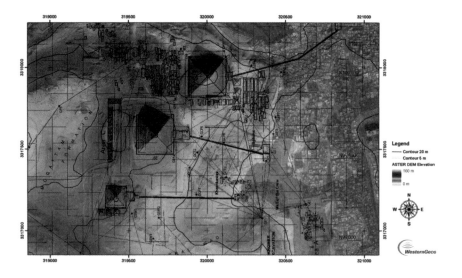

4.2 Topographic map of the Giza Plateau overlaid with the archaeological map produced by Ancient Egypt Research Associates showing potential flooding extent (in blue) during the Fourth Dynasty.

material to work from, in contrast to so many documentary TV show projects, which had perhaps larger budgets and higher production values in simulating Giza, but nowhere near the level of accuracy. From the start our approach was a mixture of archaeological fidelity and artwork, a true digital humanities project, to bring the site alive and allow for new modes of research. By fall of 2010 my move from the Museum of Fine Arts, Boston, to Harvard University provided an added motivation for creating pedagogical tools for the classroom and not just for the casual museum visitor.

A combination of satellite imagery, digital elevation models, 1978 Egyptian Ministry of Housing and Reconstruction topographic maps, contour data for Giza topography generously provided by Mark Lehner and Ancient Egypt Research Associates (AERA), and the HU–MFA and other expedition plans of the various cemetery zones all combined to provide

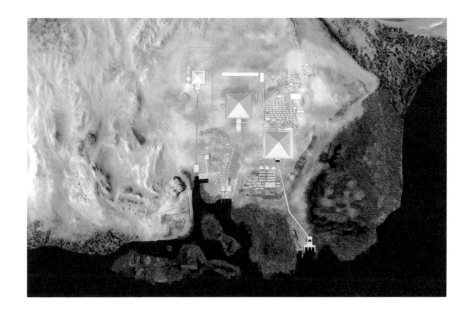

the framework for our Giza Plateau model. We are particularly grateful to AERA for fruitful discussions and collaboration over several years, and especially for the kind provision of mapping data created by Peggy Sanders, Mark Lehner, Ana Tavares, Farrah Brown, Rebekah Miracle, Camilla Mazzucato, David Goodman, Glen Dash, and others. Understanding the geomorphology of Giza, with its various limestone member formations, (see Chapter 1) was critical before the digital construction of any funerary structures could be localized. (Fig. 4.3) We also had to reposition the course of the Nile much closer to Giza, as the river has meandered far to the east in the intervening millennia, to the point where today it is nowhere near the site.[7] The choices the ancient Egyptians made, where to build causeways and harbors, where to place pyramids and commence with the surrounding cemeteries, were all influenced by a landscape that is only partially preserved and

4.3 Aerial view render from the Giza Plateau model. (West is at top.)

131

understood today. Giza has been anything but static over the past five thousand years.

An immediate challenge in trying to reproduce the Fourth Dynasty appearance of the site was the virtual removal of modern elements that had altered the landscape: excavation dump heaps, expedition dig houses, walls, asphalt roads, nearby modern Muslim and Christian cemeteries, rest houses, and other intrusive structures. Eventually, we were ready to implement a first test area for modeling—a cluster of related mastabas from Dynasties 4 through 6. West of his own pyramid, Khufu, second pharaoh of the Fourth Dynasty, had laid out scores of mastaba tombs for the elite members of society. Specific clusters of tombs seemed to form architectural and archaeological units, prompting the modern division of the Giza Necropolis into discrete "nucleus cemeteries." The tombs chosen for 3D modeling were in the cemetery once numbered by Reisner as G 2100, one of the six nucleus cemeteries at Giza. My own interest in Old Kingdom mortuary development at Giza had led me to explore the distinguishing features of such a grouping of tombs and tomb owners: relative chronology and individual artistic styles, common administrative titles, possible familial connections to the king, and the relationship of the earlier, major mastabas to the subsequent, minor burials surrounding them. More than a century had elapsed since 1906, when the HU–MFA Expedition had first excavated the fourteen major mastabas and about sixty-two smaller subsidiary tombs of Cemetery G 2100. Moreover, the southern edge of the cemetery fell within the excavation concession granted to the German-Austrian expedition under Georg Steindorff and later Hermann Junker, on behalf of their institutions in Leipzig, Hildesheim, and Vienna.

Since 1993 I had been reexamining this cemetery, studying the excavations between 1842 and 1940, and gathering documentation on the derivative objects now in museums in Berlin, Birmingham, Boston, Cairo, Copenhagen, Hildesheim, Paris, Philadelphia, Rome, and Vienna. Examples included the Boston "reserve head" of Nefer (mastaba G 2110), and his chapel reliefs, spread today across three continents; one of the best-preserved and oldest female mummies (G 2220); and two complete chapels removed to Europe—the chapel of Merib in Berlin (G 2100-I), and of Kaninisut I in Vienna (G 2155).[8] The chapel of Merib was long known only from Lepsius's illustrations from the 1840s, so I had commissioned new color photography in Berlin. Each of the monuments presented different challenges, which we shall review in the following chapter. Here I provide a brief summary of our workflow.

It was easy to create a basic 3D skeletal framework for the structures on the Giza Plateau. After all, few forms are simpler to model than a pyramid—no Corinthian columns or detailed moldings to worry about. And the mastaba tombs themselves were basic rectangles, with sloping exterior walls and offering niches, or perhaps just a few chapel rooms. Modeling based on digital archaeology, however, presented an entirely different set of challenges. There were various types of casing stones used on the mastabas: some tombs showed small blocks set back vertically a few centimeters from one course to the next; others had massive boulders towering over each other; and still others used casing stones with perfectly smoothed, sloping exteriors. (Fig. 4.4) Representing the actual look and feel of even the few major mastabas in Cemetery G 2100 required much more serious effort. Fortunately, we had the documentation, both old and new. The old documentation of course derived from Lepsius's, Junker's, and Reisner's expeditions. For our digital technical artists, color, texture, and modern image views from all sides and angles became critical. Fortunately, I had exhaustively documented this portion of the Western Cemetery

during several field seasons' work, the longest one during November 1993. In addition to the original excavators' plans and section drawings, there was therefore color imagery of the north, south, east, and west exterior mastaba walls for each tomb, as well as interior views of the decorated and undecorated chapels. We converted digitized tomb plans and sections to vector formats, imported them into 3D rendering software, and dressed them with various texture maps to lend a photorealistic appearance. (Fig. 4.5) The resulting computer models could be superimposed on-screen over the original excavation plans and sections for purposes of quality control.

As word spread of the progress we were making with our construction of Giza 3D, several sister institutions requested

4.4 Sample casing stone types at Giza. The red-and-white stick (lower right) indicates one meter.

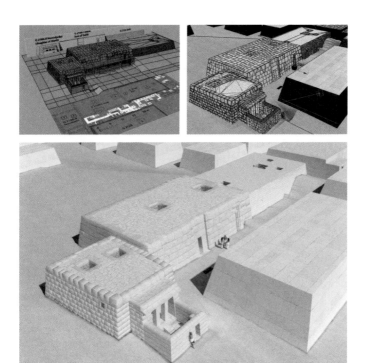

the use of our models for display in their special exhibitions. The Pelizaeus-Museum in Hildesheim, Germany, used the Giza Plateau model in the exhibition "Giza—Am Fuß der großen Pyramiden," from April 16 to August 21, 2011.[9] And the Oriental Institute Museum, Chicago, followed suit with its show "Picturing the Past: Imaging and Imagining the Ancient Middle East," from February 7 to September 2, 2012.[10] A third major event was a special Giza exhibition at the Kunsthistorisches Museum, Vienna: "Giza: Im Schatten der Pyramiden," which ran from January 22 to May 20, 2013.

4.5 *Top:* wireframe computer images for reconstructing the G 2100 family complex, looking northwest, based on original HU–MFA and German-Austrian Expedition plans and survey data from 1936. *Bottom:* the rendered computer model.

Family Matters

Much of our early experimentation focused on a contiguous family cluster of three tombs with an interesting history. The earliest (G 2100) was the most enigmatic: one of the original Khufu-era mastabas from Dynasty 4, it showed small exterior casing blocks, no interior chapel but merely an emplacement for a rectangular tombstone, known as a slab stela, toward the southern end of the east exterior wall. Although such carved and inscribed slab stelae were intact in other mastabas, this emplacement had been robbed long before Reisner's team arrived in 1906. The original tomb owner's identity would have remained unknown but for other clues both above and below ground. Immediately to the south was a second mastaba (G 2100-I), this time with massive casing blocks that enveloped—and hence postdated—the south exterior face of the first mastaba. Unlike the latter, however, this second tomb contained a fully carved and painted interior stone chapel, along with an exterior architrave and facade representations of the tomb owner, a Fifth Dynasty official named Merib, who served as an army general and administrator of the fleet, among other duties. By the time the HU–MFA Expedition staff reached this mastaba chapel in 1906, only a gaping hole greeted them, and no trace of this decoration remained; it was all in Berlin. In 1842 the Prussian expedition led by Lepsius (see Chapter 2) had removed the entire chapel; by the time of its arrival in Berlin, all the color had faded from the walls. Thanks to Lepsius's artists, however, paintings made before the chapel's removal will eventually allow us to restore the pigments digitally to our 3D computer model. In fact, one of the earliest examples of "Giza virtual reality" was a painted plaster reproduction of the chapel walls that was on display in (East) Berlin's Egyptian (Bode-) Museum before the fall of the Berlin Wall. Created by the

Egyptologist curators Karl-Heinz Priese and Caris-Beatrice Arnst, and colleagues from Berlin's *Gipsformerei* (plaster cast workshop), the chapel reproduction is at this writing on long-term loan to the Stadtmuseum Naumburg, birthplace of Karl Richard Lepsius himself. Merib's actual chapel reopened to the public with the renovation of the Ägyptisches Museum on the Berlin Museum Island in 2009 (the "Neues Museum").[11] Although no wife was portrayed, Merib's figure stands on several walls accompanied by his mother, Sedit. Bones discovered by the HU–MFA Expedition in the burial chamber beneath mastaba G 2100, next door, belonged to a woman who died in her thirties. It is most likely, then, that Sedit, the mother of Merib, was the owner of this earlier mastaba.

Sedit's burial chamber presented an interesting opportunity. Plunging 35 feet (10.7 meters) beneath the superstructure, the burial shaft connects to a small corridor leading southward to the burial chamber. Most Giza burial chambers follow this layout, and the earliest ones, dated to Khufu's reign, often show walls lined with beautifully cut and shaped limestone blocks. (In later reigns things got sloppier, and walls were left rough and unlined.) The primary burial shafts in this part of the cemetery also show in plan view a unique T-shape, designed to allow a portcullis or blocking stone to slide down within two grooves and seal the corridor off from the shaft, to thwart robbers. The HU–MFA Expedition reached Sedit's—unfortunately plundered—chamber in 1906; no one has been there since, and today the shaft is full of sand again. But in 1906 the expedition mapped every fallen blocking stone, scattered bone, miniature alabaster dish, and fragment of wood from the (missing) coffin. This allowed us to reconstruct, for the first time and in color, the original appearance of the chamber. (Fig. 4.6) In addition, the virtual environment of our computer model lets the viewer "magically dissolve" through the walls out of the chamber

4.6 Sequence showing the computer modeling process, from an excavation photograph of the burial chamber of G 2100 A to a wireframe, to the final, rendered image.

and into the surrounding limestone bedrock. (Fig. 4.7) Rotating one's point of view around the entire chamber, the connected corridor, and the shaft presents a unique perspective on the construction of Sedit's subterranean apartment. Extrapolating to the hundreds of neighboring burial shafts and chambers, we continue to dream of one day completing what I call the "tomb's-eye view" of Giza, a vantage point no mere mortal could ever attain. (Fig. 4.8) The physical proximities and relationships of one shaft to another—with the z-axis, namely, the depth, included—would tell us much about the chronological development of the entire necropolis and the duration of the many mortuary cults on the surface. Sedit's burial chamber provided an example of reconstructing not the ancient Fourth Dynasty appearance—although we reconstructed that later, too (see Chapter 5)—but the modern, 1906 appearance of the monument.

The final tomb in the Cemetery G 2100 family cluster lies farthest to the south and belongs to Merib's daughter, Nensedjerkai. Her mastaba contains a picturesque columned portico and courtyard surrounded by round-topped walls, in imitation of a villa. (see Fig. 4.5) The tomb also straddles the east-west division line between the American and German-Austrian excavation concessions; Hermann Junker, not George Reisner, excavated Nensedjerkai's tomb in 1912. Each tomb of this family cluster presented unique archi-

tectural features, superstructures and substructures, and a historical continuity that we needed to represent in our computer model. With data provided by both the American and the German-Austrian expeditions, all three mastabas slowly came to life. In the chapels, color photography of the carved wall reliefs was mapped onto the virtual chapel walls. In Merib's case, it was the new 2009 photography of the individual carved blocks in Berlin that were montaged together and "repatriated" onto his chapel walls in our 3D model. A future project consists of restoring the colors on the basis of the 1842 watercolors created by the Prussian expedition under Lepsius.

We also mapped recent color photography onto the computer model of chapel G 2155, the tomb of Kaninisut, a Fifth Dynasty "controller of the palace," and "master of secrets of the robing room." Junker had sent this chapel to Vienna in 1914. One of the finest examples of raised relief carving in the cemetery west of the Great Pyramid, Kaninisut's chapel remains one

4.7 A 3D reconstruction of G 2100 A, looking southeast, showing the portcullis stone in the shaft, corridor blocking, and burial chamber.

of the treasures of the Kunsthistorisches Museum's spectacular Giza collection.[12]

Polychrome Perfection

4.8 A 3D reconstruction of the burial shaft arrangement for the G 2100 family complex, looking east toward the Khufu Pyramid.

We took a very different approach on the eastern side of the Khufu Pyramid. On April 23, 1927, the last day of the dig season, the HU–MFA Expedition cleared an unusual subterranean chapel belonging to Queen Meresankh III (G 7530-sub), a granddaughter of Khufu, the daughter of his eldest son, Kawab, who disappeared from history before ever taking the throne. This multichambered rock-cut chapel contained pillars, engaged statuary, a vast repertoire of wall scenes and inscriptions, and a burial chamber with an inscribed sarcophagus. Kawab appears on the east wall and, nearby, Meresankh is seen in a papyrus skiff with her mother, Hetepheres II. Most impressive of all was the state of preservation of the colors. This allowed our Giza technical artists Rus Gant and David Hopkins to "restore" the chapel to its original Fourth Dynasty appearance, a very different visualization experience from texture-mapping modern photography onto the tomb walls. Using the surviving original pigments as a guide, we digitally "hand-painted" individual polychromed inscriptions over the epigraphic line drawings produced by the HU–MFA Expedition, and then texture-mapped them onto the walls. (Fig. 4.9) An additional challenge was the rendering of the engaged statuary in the chapel, and decisions had to be made about how far to restore missing and damaged areas of the decoration. (see also Chapter 5) But the tomb provided a useful template for us, since it preserved so much interesting architecture aboveground and contained a burial shaft below,

with an unusual, west-facing burial chamber that housed the inscribed stone sarcophagus (now in the Egyptian Museum, Cairo) and some canopic jars, meant to hold Meresankh's internal organs.[13] Superimposed plans and sections from the original HU–MFA Expedition reveal the sub- and superstructure relationships, as well as providing good quality-control benchmarks for our 3D model. (Fig. 4.10) Our simulation also gave us insights into Egyptian religion and architecture; I will return to this point in the next chapter.

4.9 The north wall of Meresankh's chapel room A, in 1927 *(top)*, in 1999 *(middle)*, and in a 3D model rendering *(bottom)*.

Just Add Humans

4.10 A 3D model
of the chapel
of Meresankh
(G 7530-sub)
with the original
excavators' plans
and sections
aligned for
comparison.

Though 3D reconstructions can provide derivative still images for traditional print publications, a truly immersive experience involves real-time, user-controlled navigation and, where appropriate, animation. For Giza, animation could mean the gentle flow of the nearby canals and the Nile, vegetation rustling in the wind, migratory birds flying overhead, stray animals wandering through adjacent settlements, or, of course, most important, human activity. Since Giza was such a highly significant location for Egyptian ritual, our colleagues at Dassault Systèmes expressed an interest in re-creating ceremonial activity, in this case inside our newly built virtual Khufu Pyramid complex. Each royal mortuary complex in the Old Kingdom included the royal pyramid and a mortuary temple on the east side of the structure that connected to a long causeway leading eastward to a "valley temple." This last item probably fronted a harbor to the river or a canal. Additional structures included queens' pyramids and a so-called cult pyramid for aspects of the royal spirit. As an experiment, we chose to create the "opening of the mouth" ceremony, whereby the deceased, mummified pharaoh is ritually reanimated with magical implements held to the mouth, accompanied by priestly utterances of appropriate spells. Our ritual took place in the courtyard of Khufu's Pyramid Temple, today just a ruin with basalt flooring on the pyramid's east side. Several challenges arose with this ritual, (see Chapter 5 for a fuller discussion) but the overall effect seemed pedagogically useful to lend visualized purpose to the royal complex.

The Enigmatic Queen

Pedagogy and research also factored heavily into our reconstruction of one of the most important discoveries made at Giza. The 1925 chance find of the extremely deep burial shaft of Queen Hetepheres, wife of Pharaoh Snefru and mother of Khufu, was described in Chapter 2. Descending some 89 feet (27 meters) underground, the unfinished chamber was filled with fragmentary furniture, broken ceramics, bits of jewelry, cosmetic items, an empty alabaster sarcophagus, and other objects, all in a perilous state of multilayered deterioration. Since this tomb had been well documented by the HU–MFA Expedition, (Fig. 4.11) we decided to take advantage of the countless photographs, object notes, measurements, and sketches to reconstruct the original appearance of the tomb in the Fourth Dynasty. In this case, the reconstruction consisted of objects rather than carved and painted tomb wall scenes, for the rough-cut chamber was not even symmetrical, let alone finished or decorated. Several pieces, but by no means all,

4.11 *Top:* Harvard students study the 1925 appearance of the burial chamber of Hetepheres (G 7000 X). *Bottom:* a 3D model of the same burial chamber.

of the queen's elaborate wooden and gilded furniture had been reconstructed in modern wood by both the Egyptian Museum, Cairo, and the Museum of Fine Arts, Boston, but the reconstructions failed to convey the archaeological context of the discovery. The 3D computer model of the tomb gave users for the first time a sense of the awesome depth of the chamber and the layout of the burial equipment, whose orientation and positioning actually bore numerous clues to the historical decipherment of the situation. To date we have not fashioned every one of the several hundred fragmentary items found in the tomb, but enough of its contents has been assembled to convey its original appearance in the Fourth Dynasty. The model, and particularly the reconstructed chairs, boxes, bed with bedroom canopy, and curtain box all provide an excellent starting point for the study of Old Kingdom furniture and woodworking and inlay techniques. (Fig. 4.12)

Khafre and the Sphinx

Returning to the surface, some of our larger projects involved the 3D construction of all three Giza royal pyramid complexes. Better preserved than Khufu's mortuary structures are the temples of his second successor, Khafre, along with the

4.12 3D model of Hetepheres's furniture.

addition of the Sphinx and Sphinx Temple just north of the Khafre Valley Temple. Recent publications have suggested the Sphinx represents other pharaohs, such as Khufu or his successor, Djedefre, rather than Khafre himself, but the archaeological evidence continues to favor Khafre, primarily in the construction sequence of the two aforementioned temples.[14] The massive limestone and granite blocks, architraves, and pillars, the near total lack of contemporary inscriptional material, and the myriad emplacements in the floor of both the valley and Sphinx temples emphasize the critical ritual significance of this easternmost portion of the Giza Plateau. Questions arise concerning the location of the canal or harbor farther east, the approach to the Sphinx monument, and its original color scheme. (see Chapter 5) The statue emplacements, bare rectangular spaces in the temple floors, often positioned up against pillars or walls, present intriguing clues to the original number and size of the royal statues of Khafre. Some would argue that this was the first Old Kingdom pharaoh to indulge in statuary manufacture on a massive scale. Others feel that Khafre's predecessor, Khufu, was likewise prolific, but that his poorly preserved temples failed to reveal his rich statuary program. The flexibility of our visualizations allowed us to experiment with the emplacements and how they might have been filled. (see Chapter 5)

A Complex Complex for Menkaure

We might end this brief tour of our 3D structures on the digital Giza Plateau with the last and smallest of the three pyramids, belonging to the penultimate king of the Fourth Dynasty, Menkaure (Mycerinus).[15] The Menkaure Pyramid complex—particularly the Menkaure Valley Temple—was by far the most involved project we have faced. The pyramid is the only one to contain any decoration in its interior chambers (in the form of wall niching). In addition, there were three smaller queens' pyramids off to the south, some of them unfinished, and to the east the pyramid temple, connected to the valley temple farther east by a long causeway. (see Fig. 1.11) Reisner had accepted the Menkaure complex as part of the American concession, while the Italians had "won" Khufu, and the Germans Khafre. Thanks to Reisner's work, the largest amount of modern documentation survives for Menkaure's complex. One small example demonstrates that Reisner was already thinking ahead of his time. He ordered his Egyptian photographer Said Ahmed Said to climb one-third of the way up the Menkaure Pyramid each day and capture the progress of the clearance of the pyramid temple.

The resulting "time-lapse movie" of daily still images from the end of 1906 into the first months of 1907 is unique in early archaeological photographic documentation. (Fig. 4.13)

The most intriguing structure for purposes of visualization was the Menkaure Valley Temple. This building was never fully exposed by the expedition, as Reisner backfilled some portions of it while he continued to clear others. It has lain completely reburied since about 1910, with the exception of some recent reclearance by Mark Lehner and his AERA expeditions.[16] Menkaure intended to complete this temple in stone, but he probably died prematurely; his son, Shepseskaf, finished what he could in mud brick. (Fig. 4.14) The temple fell out of use, then was revived, probably in the Fifth Dynasty, becoming part mortuary cult station and part settlement, in which dwellings, storage bins, and other structures choked the large, open courtyard, and porticos were altered and even the entrance approaches changed. Wadi floods and a "second temple" (Reisner's term), along with additional phases of settlement structures, continued into the Sixth Dynasty. The phasing of this temple, that is, the chronological decipherment of its many forms and stages, is still under study. (Chapter 5) The immersive 3D computer model allows us to superimpose one phase on

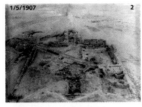

4.13 "Time-lapse" sequence of the excavation of the Menkaure Pyramid Temple, 1906–1907, taken from one-third of the distance up the east face of the Menkaure Pyramid.

another, or on the historical maps and plans, in an attempt to understand the construction sequence better. The addition of human animated characters also lends a sense of scale, while defining some of the activities that such an inhabited temple courtyard would have witnessed.

As an experiment in recontextualization of objects, we built the famous pair statue of Menkaure and a queen (possibly Khamerernebty II, or his mother, or a goddess; see Fig. W2.4.3 and, with very mixed results, Fig. 6.8) and placed it in the area it was originally found (discovered on January 18, 1910). Reisner called this "a robber's hole," however, and so the statue's original position remains open to debate. Following recent scholarship that has assembled additional statue fragments, we created a second, smaller pair statue and colorized both according to similarly painted statuary from the Old Kingdom.[17] The pair statue is just one of a large number of royal statues found in the Men-

4.14 Excavation of the Menkaure Valley Temple, 1910. *Top:* looking southeast; *middle:* looking west; *bottom:* looking north.

kaure temples; it is supplemented by thousands of stone vessels, ceramics, objects of daily life, and even a few tantalizing but fragmentary royal stelae with important historical and economic inscriptions. The reconstruction and virtual "repatriation" of these many thousands of objects to their original findspots still awaits.

Going Live

Although the Giza website, with its hundreds of thousands of legacy data files, had served the online community since 2005, (see Chapter 3) the 3D models did not debut for the public until spring 2012. A second website, this one hosted by Dassault Systèmes, (http://giza.3ds.com) delivered a more accessible approach to Giza for the lay public, with a scrolling, animated front page outlining Giza's significance and a listing of some members of the project team, based in Boston, Paris, and Casablanca. (Fig. 4.15) After the user clicks on the "play" button, the rotating Giza Plateau model appears, serving as a floating "table of contents," with a menu containing all the monuments available. For each monument, users have the choice of a preset guided and narrated tour, free navigation (using a mouse or arrow keys), historic discovery and excavation photos ("Object Gallery" and "Photo Gallery"), or images from our "Construction Process." A link to the rich data on gizapyramids.org was hard-wired experimentally, but our longer-term goal is to incorporate the features of both websites into an amalgamated Giza website at Harvard. In the meantime, users also have the option of clicking the "gear" icon to switch their personal computer display or television into 3D mode. (either anaglyph or 3DTV; Fig. 4.16) At this writing, PCs fare better than Macs with the Dassault Systèmes Giza website and free plugin, but that, we hope, is but a temporary issue.

4.15 The Giza 3D website homepage.

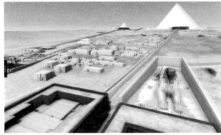

A special event commemorating the launch of the Giza 3D website and the collaboration between Dassault Systèmes and the Museum of Fine Arts, Boston, took place at the MFA on May 8, 2012. After presentations and a live demo of the website, the hundreds of participants tested Giza 3D on touch tables and interactive monitors throughout the museum's glass-enclosed courtyard beside the newly constructed Art of the Americas Wing. (Fig. 4.17) Between mid-May and June 19, 2012, worldwide press coverage of the website was assembled in a 583-page PDF file, one story per page, in numerous languages. (Fig. 4.18) A second press event took place at the Théâtre Marigny in Paris on July 11, 2012.

By late 2012 the Giza 3D website had garnered 450,000 hits worldwide. At this writing it has now been translated into thirteen languages in order to reach a global audience. (And an introductory video on YouTube has registered nearly 93,000 viewings to date).[18] A second launch, with the addition of several tombs and royal temples, plus the reconstructed Sphinx, took place in conjunction with a keynote speech and participation at the Digital Heritage International Conference in Marseille (October 28–November 1, 2013).[19] A number of other papers and keynote speeches by Giza Project staff have presented the work to diverse audiences, both scholarly and technological.[20]

4.16 Two screenshots from http://giza.3ds.com, one in 2D, one in 3D.

Beyond providing excellent pedagogical tools for almost any age group, the Giza 3D models have begun to illuminate many research pathways, some traditional, some new. A few examples follow:

How did the various cemetery clusters develop chronologically, both internally and in the context of the entire Giza Plateau? Our plateau model allows for juxtapositions and comparisons, both above and below ground, providing a clearer matrix of relationships among individual structures.

How do genealogical and other relationships between tomb owners effect the historical reconstruction of the Old Kingdom, the first flourishing of ancient Egyptian statehood? New views of tomb wall scenes and inscriptions in

their archaeological context present the ancient names, administrative titles, and lineages to help us link families, duties, and historical events together. Connections are revealed that would be missed by studying single tombs in isolation.

What is Giza's contribution to the overall development and metamorphosis of Egyptian art? Dynasties 4 through 6, when many of the Giza monuments were built, include unique stages in the decorative program of funerary chapels, sculptural forms, and modes of artistic expression. Our 3D rendering of the Giza Plateau provides immersive exploration of the art of this period.

4.17 The Giza 3D launch event at the Museum of Fine Arts, Boston, May 8, 2012.

What were the politics and socioeconomics of space and place at Giza, and how are they represented? What constituted status, and how was it conveyed? We can now highlight class structures in 3D at multiple levels of ancient Egyptian society, from the workers who quarried the stone and constructed the pyramids and tombs to the artisans who decorated these monuments, to pharaoh himself, accompanied by his courtiers and officials.

The visualization of the Giza Plateau, and the progress made thus far in detailed fabrication of selected royal mortuary complexes, sculptures, vessels, and private tombs, with both sub- and superstructures, has exposed a wide variety of opportunities as well as challenges to reconstructing this most important archaeological site. Stepping back to view the larger context, we must analyze the influence of our work on research, teaching, and our own efforts to reach a more diverse audience worldwide. Some of these philosophical issues as applied to Digital Giza are considered in the next chapter.

After some consultation, both Harvard University and the Museum of Fine Arts, Boston, saw fit to revive once again the historic collaboration of the HU–MFA Expedition. This new form of partnership takes place at present primarily in the virtual realm, rather than in the field at Giza, but it nevertheless represents a pooling of archival sources that strengthens both individual collections as well as the overall Giza repository for the world community. In December 2013 representatives from both institutions signed a collaborative agreement planning for a new Giza website at Harvard University that would integrate all the materials described in this chapter and in Chapter 3.[21] This arrangement is consistent with the original 1905 letter and spirit of the first collaboration protocol that Harvard and the MFA signed, whereby the artworks excavated and apportioned to the expedition were

designated for the MFA, while the rights to the archives and to publication belonged to Harvard, an arrangement that was never subsequently altered. As we come to define the new Giza website, currently in preparation, as a "publication" in the broadest sense of the term, it would seem that the original intent of the HU–MFA partnership is being well served today.

4.18 Selections from worldwide press coverage following the launch of the Giza 3D website, May–June 2012.

CHAPTER 5

Case Studies: Pyramid, Temple, Tomb, Statue, Human

- -

What constitutes a publication these days? Another volume in this metaLABprojects series asks that important question and considers the future of the library.[1] In this chapter we stretch the concept of traditional publication to include websites fed by online databases and immersive 3D computer models of ancient monuments. Here the question is one of *presentation*—perhaps even inundation—

versus *interpretation* of data. Imagine a printed telephone directory for a major city—aside from the listing in alphabetical order, this is largely undigested data. Compare that with a directory where the names are broken down and sorted by region, by income range, ethnicity, religion, or even by geographic orientation of the dwellings. This is parsed and interpreted data. Knowledge production takes many new forms now, and our task is to evaluate for archaeological heritage and research what our goals are, as well as the means we should choose to reach them. In terms of visualization, we are just beginning to elicit standards in our approach to modeling ancient sites, although there is already a growing body of literature on the subject.[2] Clearly, such digital tools are not for everyone; what is an exciting new window on the past to one researcher may appear to be little more than reveling in technology to another.

A recent publication is provocatively titled *Computer-Generated 3D-Visualisations in Archaeology: Between Added Value and Deception.*[3] Perhaps it is no exaggeration to say that a slightly guilty conscience may accompany the digital archaeologist as she or he attempts to reconstruct the past in 3D. "Even if you follow the rules, the only certain thing about any reconstruction drawing is that it is wrong. The only real question is, how wrong is it?"[4] Jean-Claude Golvin has articulated three elements to every reconstruction image, and our greatest challenge remains how to clearly differentiate them from one another: (1) the archaeological data; (2) a "repositioning" of the site's scattered blocks, fragments, and other items; and (3) the use of ancient documents, testimonies, and other sources. His strategy, relying on the semiotics of Charles Sanders Peirce (1839–1914), involved the creation of still images by hand, but the approach remains valid for digital reconstructions as well.[5]

The previous chapter reviewed some of the 3D models created for the Giza Project; here I will elaborate on the thinking behind the model creation and use Giza to describe some of the challenges inherent in almost any archaeological endeavor in visualization. Foremost among them, of course, is the fact that the ancient dataset is most often fragmentary; how to handle the gaps and, more specifically, in relation to which modern audience, is the critical issue. In the course of the discussion, we would do well to consider whether the much-hyped concepts of "You are there" or "Bringing the past to life" are actually attainable goals or misleading fallacies, as Mark Gillings has argued.[6] But while we strive for archaeological accuracy, we must remember that "visualizations are always interpretations—data [do] not have an inherent visual form that merely gives rise to a graphic expression."[7]

Who Is the Audience?

This is not an easy question to answer when the individual at the other end of the Internet pipeline is unknown. Whereas scholars were once publishing their archaeological results for a relatively small group of peers reading restricted (and expensive) academic journals, today online consumers from any conceivable age group, culture, and level of education, from ignorance to expertise, can access the dataset. Common Western assumptions about terminology, familiarity with reading architectural plans, sections, and perspective renderings, not to mention foreign languages, may not apply to users from distant lands and cultures.[8] Just as we discovered in our experience with the Giza Archives Project that we must weed out (or at least define) specialized Egyptological jargon wherever possible for the benefit of a worldwide audience, so too

must overly westernized approaches to visualization be handled with care. Moreover, gender terminology comes into play
as well, as the computer graphics world has largely been domi-
nated by males for several decades.[9]

In digital archaeology, can one be all things to all people? Certainly one can, with sufficient amounts of money,
time, and personnel. But rarely do the resources suffice, and
so critical compromises must be made. The organization and
presentation of archaeological data, particularly in the case of
visualization, will differ drastically, depending on the intended users. The professional archaeologist who is comfortable
extrapolating from plans and section drawings may wish to
access only what has been firmly attested in the material record. She or he may have no use for or interest in reconstructed wall heights, or theoretical completions of fragmentary or
missing scenes and inscriptions; these may at best distract
and at worst mislead from what archaeologists call "ground
truth". (Fig. 5.1) On the other hand, the armchair archaeologist,
casual historian, interested layman, or grade school student
will need some assistance in understanding the layout and
purpose of a particular structure, ritual, or painting. In this
case, the restoration of color and rooftops or even the addition of animated characters may tip the balance from confusion to comprehension.

What criteria determine whether an ancient monument
is best shown as it originally appeared at the time of construction, millennia ago, or at the time of excavation? What about
its present-day state, or some other point between all these
options? The ultimate use of the model and its intended audience will clarify the nature of the most appropriate workflow.[10]
The other factor that determines what is possible is, of course,
the state of preservation upon discovery and excavation. Good
preservation of ancient structures allows for near complete

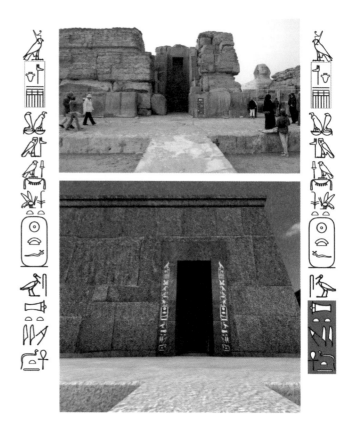

5.1 Khafre Valley Temple, north entrance; restored hieroglyphs are based on scant surviving traces (marked in red) and other contemporary monuments.

virtual restoration, perhaps even with polychromy on the digital walls. (see Fig. 4.9) In other cases, we have little more than foundations, or traces of foundations. For research purposes, whichever point in time one chooses, and however much one attempts to restore, there must be a way to distinguish clearly between ground truth and any digital embellishments. Failure to produce such clear demarcation reduces the visualization to levels unsuitable for serious academic inquiry. This need not be a condemnation; in fact, for educational purposes, embellishment may be exactly what is required, provided that it does not masquerade as ground truth. Other possible goals of virtual reconstruction include conservation and restoration. For purposes of inventory, computer models can serve to document the existing elements of a monument against future changes. How many disputed cases on the art market in recent years would have been rendered moot if proper documentation and virtual inventories had backed up antiquities authorities' claims? Providing guidelines for physical restoration of the ancient monuments represents a further potential benefit of competent examples of visualization.

Digital Archaeology or Artwork and Artistry?

Are we standing at the crossroads, as Steve Jobs used to say, of technology and the humanities? Where does the scholarly documentation end and the artistic embellishment begin? Is experiential learning contributing to knowledge production or are the bells and whistles of these new toys leading us astray? Digital archaeology as a concept comes with certain responsibilities for academic rigor, reconstructive accuracy, and a strict adherence to the archaeological record. How can we stay true to these ideals while still creating a product that enhances teaching and learning and, dare we say, bears some aesthetics in its own right?[11] Are these goals mutually exclusive?

One major advantage of digital over printed content lies in the ability to turn specific elements of a virtual reconstruction on or off. Users can toggle selected features, such as the reconstructed full height of walls, and even roofing over chambers, to "visible" or "hidden" position over the actually excavated remains. The differentiation may also be made through color coding, shading, or tagging of attested versus restored elements. The same illustration then may serve the scholar and the layman alike, its successive layers and levels of detail, real or hypothetical, appropriately tagged so as not to mislead. In the early stages of our construction of the Giza 3D website, we termed these different levels "amateur mode" and "expert mode." In fact, one could design such websites to contain a fork that gives the user the option to choose the amateur path or the expert path, with the ability, of course, to switch from one to the other at will. The same features apply to chronological access to monuments as well, since the successive phasing of a structure can be carefully delineated. (see "Everything Changes," below)

Perhaps a better analogy than Steve Jobs's intersection of technology and humanities is, as noted in our introduction, the American Wild West: at present we seem to lack a comprehensive set of standards for representing ancient structures with our digital tools. Even the definition of "virtual reality" requires some clarification.[12] Factors such as budgets, software sophistication and computer processing power, skill sets of the archaeologists and computer graphics artists involved, and philosophy all play a role. Some believe that deception results from photorealistic reconstructions, and they avoid them intentionally. The more realistic they are, the greater the danger that unsuspecting consumers will fall for their representations as ground truth. Others avoid photorealistic reconstructions because of the dearth of knowledge preserved about the ancient site; wireframe models and untextured, undecorated wall surfaces represent an easier, cheaper, and less time- and labor-intensive procedure that avoids unwarranted speculation and keeps the work progressing. Examples include the Aegaron Project, a joint UCLA–German Archaeological Institute collaboration dedicated to presenting ancient Egyptian architecture online,[13] and the Digital Karnak Project, which to date has not attempted to embellish its pylons, hypostyle halls, or obelisks with photorealistic scenes and inscriptions.[14]

Throughout the process there is always the danger that we are grafting a perceived and imaginary reality onto our reconstructions that is not justified by the data. But does this mean that we should return to simple 2D static line drawings in our attempts to convey the archaeological matrix? Even in this digital age, where new modes of dissemination are constantly springing up, one can still trace a scholarly skepticism for the abundance of illustrations over text, or the use of color invading the traditionally staid realm of academic publication.[15] In time this skepticism may finally disappear, as scholars gain greater comfort not only with color as a bearer of critical information, but even with animation as a legitimate form of scholarly communication.

One solution that might bring some order to our current visualization chaos involves the preparation of downloadable source documents. These supplemental metadata summaries accompany the shading, color coding, and toggle switches inherent in the immersive models themselves, describing precisely what each phase of the digital reconstruction relies on for archaeological documentation. The Aegaron Project includes such source documents with its model files. In fact, the modeling *process* can be every bit as critical as the final result; "how we got there" documents present the user with a layout of the reconstruction workflow, the better to judge its value. Gillings has noted that "archaeologists have to date tended to *apply* VR techniques first and then *think* about them later."[16]

Objectivity

Does objectivity exist in archaeological reconstruction? Despite the proliferation of image-altering tools (*Photoshop* now seems to be a verb as well as the name of an app), we tend to judge reality against photography. But here too someone has composed the reality that we are presented with.[17] If our 3D models are aiming for a photorealistic appearance, are we not caught in a vicious circle, chasing an objective reality that does not exist? Each generation has imbued its documentation with its own perspective and peculiar objectivity. In Egyptological epigraphy, we witness this phenomenon in the scholarly facsimile line drawings of the same ancient wall carving over several generations. In the realm of virtual reality, the immersive environment liberates the user to survey his or her landscape as never before, but it is still a manufactured landscape. Lorraine Daston and Peter Galison traced the evolution of objectivity, from eighteenth-century scientists interested in producing universal, ideal imagery ("truth to nature") to early nineteenth-century scholars determined to display nature in all its asymmetrical, unedited forms ("mechanical objectivity"), to more recent times, when an informed synthesis is the goal ("trained judgment").[18] It is this last approach, trained judgment, that controls Egyptological epigraphy today, the informed decision-making process that presents the data as clearly and realistically as possible, but with an interpretation designed to serve, not mislead, the user.[19] Extrapolating from 2D epigraphy to 3D immersive environments, we find that the same strategy applies. For example, the Sixth Dynasty tomb of Qar (G 7101) contains a series of decorated subterranean chapel rooms, but no superstructure survives. Faced with the options of an open courtyard superstructure, an enclosure wall, or a monolithic, square, mastaba building, our "trained judgment" (the archaeological record combined with our knowledge of Giza mortuary architecture) suggests a small mastaba with enclosure wall that left the sunken courtyard open. (Fig. 5.2) The virtual reality model is therefore not a one-to-one replication of reality, but rather a construct, the more creative aspect of mimesis, beyond its simple definition of mere replication.[20]

Joyce Wittur's volume on computer-generated visualizations concludes with five critical steps for successful digital reconstructions: strict definitions of aims (communication or research, or both); careful planning (including documentation for future reference, and funding for research); collaboration and communication between archaeologists and digital artists; models that are comprehensible (workflow transparency, demarcation of hypothetical areas, multiple versions); and coherent choice of presentation medium (online, museum display, handheld devices, and so on).[21] Debates about all these principles arose during the past several years of creating the Giza 3D Plateau. The rest of this chapter is devoted to describing some of the epistemological dilemmas we encountered along the way, in the hopes that we might assist others in meeting similar challenges.

5.2 Three restoration options for the missing superstructure of the tomb of Qar (G 7101).

Reconstruction: How Much Is Too Much?

We have pointed out the dangers of creating a 3D model so photorealistic that it resembles a photograph and invites blind faith in its accuracy.[22] If photorealism is the goal, then why not just use the photograph and spare oneself much labor? This argument makes sense if the reconstruction desired reflects the monument's current appearance, or at least its appearance at the time the photograph was taken. But virtual reality shows off its greatest advantages in photorealistically re-creating something that is no longer there or has changed substantially. Traveling along the z-axis—time—is where the 3D model best displays its benefits.

Reconstruction is a judgment call, dependent on the aims and goals of the 3D model and the preservation of available archaeological sources. Examples range from the minute and the banal to the wholesale fabrication of entire structures. To illustrate the former, we can revisit the subterranean chapel of Queen Meresankh. On the east wall of the largest room, a window slit allowed rainwater over the millennia to seep in, damaging the painted decoration beneath. The scene shows a papyrus marsh, with the figures of Meresankh and her mother, Hetepheres, farther to the left, in a papyrus skiff. Fig. 5.3 shows two digital renderings of the wall, the one below with the damaged areas restored. For purposes of comparison, the illustration also renders the marsh scene in a modern, Western perspective, drawn by Suzanne E. Chapman.[23] Papyrus stalks are, of course, easier to restore than, say, a lengthy inscription with major lacunae.

The situation is more complex off the edge of the Giza Plateau. Khufu's mortuary complex contained a pyramid temple on the east side attached to a long causeway running eastward off the plateau and ending in a valley temple. These three

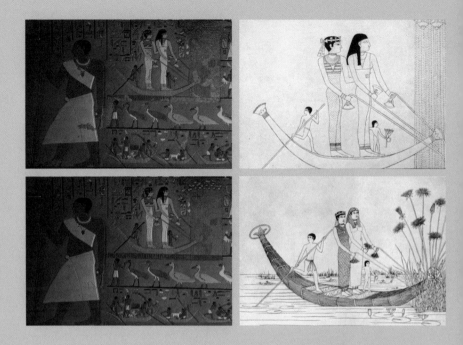

elements are almost completely destroyed today, and the valley temple lies beneath the modern town of Nazlet es-Samman. Its layout and architecture are unknown, save for isolated blocks discovered during sewage project work.[24] (see Chapter 2) Our valley temple model is thus entirely theoretical, based on similar structures from the Old Kingdom. As long as this archaeologically unattested nature of the temple is appropriately flagged, the user should have no trouble distinguishing what the ground truth situation is. Toggling the temple on or off would provide a clean solution as well.

In the case of Khufu's Pyramid Temple, the situation is somewhat clearer, as foundation outlines and floor paving for the structure survive. But here, too, questions remain about the materials used and the nature of the sanctuary (statue niches? false door?). Though the 3D model may rely on the excavation

5.3 *Left*: the chapel of Meresankh (G 7530-sub), east wall damage (above left) and restored (below left). *Right*: a translation of the boating scene into modern perspective by Suzanne E. Chapman.

165

5.4 *Top:* the
Khufu Pyramid
Temple. *Bottom:*
a 3D model of
the temple.

records and architectural plans from the twentieth century,
much is nevertheless left to responsible conjecture. (Fig. 5.4)
Our model omits any decoration or inscriptions, despite the
likelihood that relief sculpture was present, as several blocks
found at Giza and "repurposed" in a Middle Kingdom context
at the site of Lisht attest.[25]

A final example of detailed reconstruction applies to the
unique subterranean shaft of Queen Hetepheres, mother of
Khufu, located just east of the Great Pyramid. In this case the

deterioration of the burial chamber's contents, 89 feet (27 meters) underground, should relegate any reconstruction to the outright fantastical. The HU–MFA Expedition of the 1920s is, however, directly responsible for the 3D model we now refer to for teaching and research in 2016 and, we hope, beyond. Meticulous documentation of the extremely fragmentary contents scattered about the floor allowed us to reconstruct the queen's funeral furniture and other items, in some cases merely on paper, in other cases in physical wood reconstructions (Cairo and Boston). Ground truth and subterranean documentation supported digital archaeology to a degree perhaps previously unattested. (Fig. 5.5) Items restored with a reasonable degree of certainly include the royal bedroom set with canopy, curtain box, and bed, plus the queen's carrying chair, sitting chairs, and even a series of bracelets inlaid with intricate butterfly patterns. (Figs. 5.6–5.7) The tomb provides a classic case for responsible archaeological documentation feeding into new technologies that appeared almost a century after the original excavation. (For an experimental physical reproduction of one of the chairs, see Chapter 6.) Failure to proceed with a digital reconstruction of the tomb for the modern viewer would represent a missed opportunity.

5.5 *Top and middle:* a 1926 photograph and a painting by Joseph Lindon Smith of the discovery condition of the tomb of Hetepheres (G 7000 X). *Bottom:* a 3D model, looking down the shaft into the burial chamber.

5.6 *Top:* the old installation of the reproduction Hetepheres furniture in the Egyptian Museum, Cairo, 1993. *Middle:* the conservator Ahmed Youssef with Hetepheres's reconstructed curtain box and a copy, Harvard Camp, Giza, 1939. *Bottom:* a 3D model of the curtain box.

5.7 *Top:* Hetepheres's bracelets on the floor of G 7000 X, 1926. *Middle left and right:* Hetepheres's bracelets in the Egyptian Museum, Cairo, and Museum of Fine Arts, Boston. *Bottom left and right:* 3D models of the bracelets.

Will It Fit?

Size matters. And it matters even more when the digital reconstruction of ancient buildings casts a number of questions at the archaeologist that he or she may not have considered before embarking on this electronic adventure. As a discussion instigator, then, 3D models often prove their worth before they even come into existence. Such a scenario arose in the reconstruction of the temples associated with the second pyramid at Giza, constructed by Khafre. The edifices in question are the Pyramid Temple, the Valley Temple, and the Sphinx Temple, directly in front (east) of the Sphinx itself. Attribution of the Sphinx has been hotly debated in recent years, and some scholars contend that Khafre's prolific statue program was typical for the Fourth Dynasty, whereas other colleagues, conversely, claim it marked a major break with the more austere tradition of previous reigns. Relocating Khafre's statues virtually to their original locations in these temples, therefore, could not be of greater importance for understanding the development of royal mortuary architecture of the Old Kingdom.

5.8 Aerial view of the Khafre Valley Temple *(left)* and Sphinx Temple, looking west, 2011.

The Khafre Valley Temple and the Sphinx Temple in particular provide tantalizing clues to the original size and number of royal Khafre statues in the form of (now empty) regularly laid-out emplacements in the flooring. (Fig. 5.8) Now restored in modern cement, the Valley Temple emplacements appear to close any debate on the issue, and though most of the Khafre statues today are lost or extremely fragmentary, a number have survived intact enough to help us determine their original heights. What is puzzling, however, is the question of statue bases. In some cases, if the emplacement reflects the size of the statue's actual base, the resulting statue would be colossal. On the other hand, if the emplacements acted as placeholders for stone platforms on which the statues stood (or sat), then the statues take on a more life-size scale. (Fig. 5.9) The most famous Khafre statue, the seated image

of the king in the Egyptian Museum, Cairo, carved from anorthosite gneiss, is by no means colossal. Several scholars have studied the issue, gathering all the fragments and estimating their original locations and poses.[26]

A similar size issue concerns the possibility of four sphinx statues flanking the two entrances of Khafre's Valley Temple. If the statues truly occupied the size suggested in the original excavation report, they would extend partially beyond the edge of the temple facade in an asymmetrical arrangement that the ancient Egyptians would not have found pleasing.[27]

5.9 Digital composite of the Khafre Valley Temple, looking west, showing statue emplacements and various statue sizes.

5.10 *Top:* aerial view of the Khafre Pyramid Temple, looking west, 2011. *Middle and bottom:* two versions of ritual boats, one too large and the other correctly sized for passage through the temple.

A smaller scale fits the spaces better.

The exact functions of these royal mortuary temples are not always clear. Among the uses conjectured are mummification and purification chambers, reanimation ceremonies, funeral processions, provision of offerings, and storage rooms for temple equipment. If sacred barks were part of the funerary equipment, then their storage locations and their size must be carefully calculated. Once borne on the shoulders of priests, these wooden boats had to turn corners between granite or limestone pillars and reach their storage locations safely. Models in 3D allow us to simulate these sizes and determine the possible dimensions of the barks. (Fig. 5.10) Elaine Sullivan has recently described similar experiments for Karnak Temple in the New Kingdom.[28]

Such visualizations enhance our research capabilities. On a more pedestrian front, they allow size comparisons that assist those unfamiliar with the site or with the scale of its individual structures. Such juxtapositions are nothing new; in fact, Dows Dunham, the MFA's former curator, once clothed a plaster cast reproduction of the famous bust of Ankh-haf in modern dress; all that was missing was the ears.[29] Another experiment, conceived by my colleagues Rus Gant and David Hopkins, involved speculation on the proportions of the Sphinx relative to an actual leonine body and human head.[30] They composited a profile view of a lion's skeleton inside the body of the Sphinx, and the resulting proportions seem to be hardly dissimilar, although of course one must replace the lion's skull with a human one to complete the rendering of this fantastical beast. (Fig. 5.11)

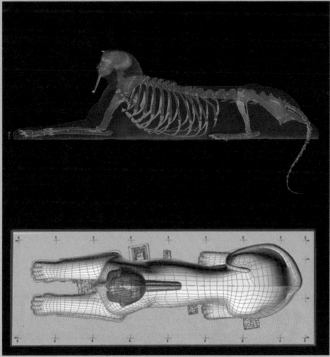

5.11 A panoramic profile of the Sphinx and digital composite with lion skeleton (plus human skull) superimposed on the Sphinx for comparison of proportions.

Everything Changes

Phasing in archaeology refers to the series of occupation levels, construction changes, or successive uses for a specific area, reconstructed from the stratigraphy and other evidence attested in the material record. The most complex example of phasing on the Giza Plateau is probably the Menkaure Valley Temple. In this case 3D visualization becomes indispensable, since Reisner backfilled the structure as he excavated it in 1908 and 1910. In fact, it has never been wholly exposed, and today it lies completely invisible, but for occasional re-excavation of selected areas conducted by Ancient Egypt Research Associates under the direction of Mark Lehner.[31] Despite the absence of a viewable edifice on the ground today, the meticulous documentation by the HU–MFA Expedition has allowed us to experiment with reconstructing the Menkaure Valley Temple's phasing, a complex mixture of mortuary architecture, settlement archaeology, and numerous alterations, in purpose, materials, and form. We began with a vectorized version of Reisner's multilayered plan of the temple from his 1931 excavation report. (Fig. 5.12) A combination of additional plans and sections, augmented with excavation photography by all teams that have worked in the area (George Reisner, Selim Hassan, Vito Maragioglio and Celeste Rinaldi, Mark Lehner),[32] have set us on the path to a better understanding of the building and surrounding area. In particular, Lehner's recent reexamination of the site is updating our knowledge base with state-of-the-art interdisciplinary archaeological techniques absent from Reisner's documentation of more than a century ago.

5.12 A multiphase plan of the Menkaure Valley Temple.

As Chapter 4 notes, Menkaure died before completing his temple in stone; just the outlines of portions of the structure show limestone paving and walls intact. His son Shepseskaf finished major portions of the temple in mud brick. (Fig. 5.13)

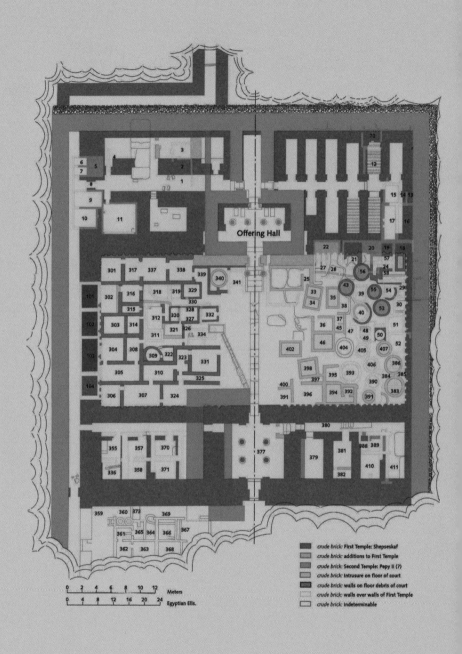

5.13 A 3D
model with
preliminary views
of the phasing
of the Menkaure
Valley Temple,
numbered 1
(earlier) to 5
(later).

Eventually the courtyard, and part of the antetemple east of the complex,[33] filled up during the Fifth Dynasty with storage silos, walls, and apartments or houses. A wadi flood destroyed portions of the temple (and the causeway farther west) and may have led to the abandonment of the "village" nestled within the courtyard. In the Sixth Dynasty the Egyptians renewed the area with the reconstruction of a mud brick "second temple" and additional structures in the courtyard. In all, there were three separate occupation and settlement levels, interspersed with debris layers containing fallen temple walls, statue fragments, and damage from flash floods.[34]

My former Giza Project colleague Diane Flores has contributed more than anyone to deciphering some of Reisner's numbering and other archival documentation discrepancies, and a current Giza Project research associate, Nicholas Picardo, has conducted substantial research into the temple's difficult settlement horizons. The digital visualization of the reburied Menkaure Valley Temple presents an immersive environment that allows for the ability to view changes over time, color coding of different occupation phases, and an enhanced understanding of the chronological sequences. Ideally, such models should always be compared to ground truth wherever possible, and conversely, modern-day excavations might do well to proceed hand in hand with the model-building process, the one process informing the other.[35]

The Sphinx is usually considered a static and timeless figure on the Giza horizon, but it too underwent substantial change over the course of pharaonic history. Among the alterations we may list are the gain and loss of the Sphinx's beard, possible creation of a standing royal figure somewhere below the chin, treatments to the front paws, construction of surrounding shrines, temples, and enclosure walls, and of course erection between its paws of the famous "Dream Stela" of Thutmose IV (Dynasty 18) and subsequent shrine with stelae dedicated by Ramesses II (Dynasty 19). We have yet to model all these diachronic developments, but before tackling this work, a more fundamental question arises: Was the Sphinx painted? Traces of color survive on the striped *nemes* head cloth and the face. Was this the extent of the polychromy, or did a reddish brown (for human males) or even beige-yellow tone (for leonine fur) cover the rest of the monument? How was the beard supported, and was a standing royal statue later added below it? Owing to the fragile state of the geological member formations making up the body beneath the head, and the extensive restorations that have taken place (not all of them for the better), we may never be able to answer this question satisfactorily, but the model can at least provide us with some options to further stimulate a discussion that has rarely taken place in the Egyptological literature. (Fig. 5.14) Moreover, a view of the top of the Sphinx's head reveals an ancient hole; is this simply restoration work, or was some kind of crown or headdress added later to the creature, perhaps in similar fashion to the *nemes* head cloth plus double crown that we see on the sphinxes of Amenhotep III in St. Petersburg, the calcite sphinx of Tutankhamun in the Luxor Museum, or the colossal statues of Ramesses II at Abu Simbel?

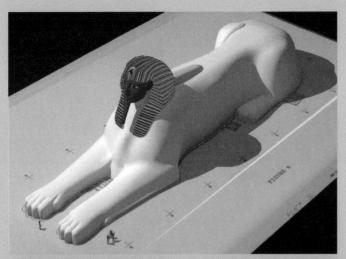

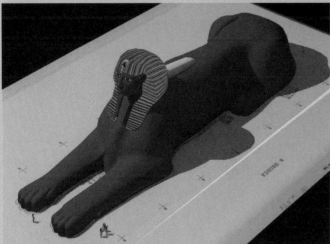

5.14 Two versions of the 3D Sphinx model, showing partial *(top)* and full *(bottom)* polychromy.

Simulation City

Graphics in traditional printed scholarship don't move. Is motion somehow anti-academic? Much may be learned at sites such as Giza by watching processes evolve, buildings change, purposes alter, and the elements attack both the natural and the human landscape. Simulations allows us to witness these changes in action, test some hypotheses, and discard others. They can also position our eye at vantage points that normal mortals cannot attain, such as deep underground or high above the Pyramids. Drag coefficients and the number of individuals needed to haul a block of limestone can be estimated and tested. A recent study has used Dassault Systèmes' software to calculate the date and an explanation for the cracks that emerged in massive granite beams in the roof of the so-called king's chamber in Khufu's Pyramid.[36]

The surrounding geography entered into our research on the tomb of Queen Meresankh (see Chapter 3) in a manner that probably would not have arisen had we not created a 3D model of the subterranean chapel (G 7530-sub). The east wall window referred to earlier appears to take on a significance when studied in the context of a simulation. We have already noted that this window opened to the street outside the subterranean chapel. By re-creating the mastaba, we strove to simulate the effects of morning sunlight streaming in through this window. The beams appear to enter through the large room A, pass through the doorway between two pillars, and illuminate the west wall of room B. This part of the western wall is not flat or undecorated but, rather, contains a recessed "false door," a sacred ritual focus in Egyptian mortuary conceptions at which the living place offerings; the deceased's spirit then magically emerges from the land of the west, through this false door, to partake of the gifts. For this reason false doors always face east, from the western wall of interior spaces, or the eastern facade of exterior spaces. The alignment of the window and the false door would seem to be no accident; (Fig. 5.15) as my digital artist

colleagues Rus Gant and David Hopkins discovered when creating the 3D model, the false door lights up from this direct hit of sunlight. And a cursory look at other windowed tomb chapels at Giza reveals some similar arrangements. Additional research on this topic is needed, but no one doubts the ceremonial significance of false

doors or the realm of the Egyptian sun god in bestowing life-giving benefits on the ancient Egyptians.[37]

Beyond the funerary significance of this noteworthy solar feature, first brought to our attention by the simulation of sunlight entering Meresankh's subterranean chapel, the role played by the window could even assist us in reconstructing the sequential history of the entire cemetery east of the Great Pyramid. Reisner first surmised that the ordered rows of mastabas extended chronologically from west to east, away from Khufu's Pyramid toward the eastern edge of the Giza Plateau.[38] More recently, Peter Jánosi has suggested the reverse development, in part because of the dwindling distance between the rows of altered mastabas as one moves eastward, and the style of the relief carving in certain easternmost mastaba tombs, such as that of Ankh-haf (G 7510).[39] How can Meresankh's window contribute to this debate? The mastaba tombs to the east of her chapel could have blocked the solar illumination of her false door. This in turn

5.15 Exterior and interior 3D models of the chapel of Meresankh, showing the sunlight streaming through the window and illuminating the false door.

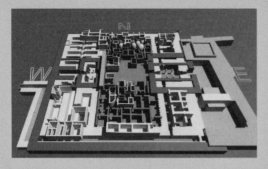

would suggest that Meres-ankh's tomb chapel stood earlier than these later, "intrusive" sepulchers farther to the east. Even more intriguing is the fact that Meresankh's tomb may originally have been constructed for her mother, Hetepheres II, since the inscription on the sarcophagus from the burial chamber states that Hetepheres gave it to her daughter. This has caused speculation that Meresankh predeceased her mother, Hetepheres, whose own burial place remains unknown.[40] Our understanding of parts of Old Kingdom dynastic succession, and the sequential expansion of the Eastern Cemetery, may all be modified by the role played by a window and the sunlight cascading into Meresankh's chapel. More research may clarify the issue, but the discovery is a powerful argument in favor of simulations in archaeological research. Bernard Frischer and John Fillwalk have come to similar conclusions on the significance of solar alignments, solstices, and the uses of simulation and visualization, albeit far from Giza, in the case of Hadrian's villa (Roccabruna).[41]

Moving from private tomb chapels to royal mortuary complexes, we can attest to the benefits of simulations in the case of the Menkaure Valley Temple as well. We have already discussed the complex stratigraphy and multiple occupation levels within the courtyard of this unfinished temple. Color coding is extremely useful in distinguishing the various structures and their chronological sequence. Simulation too can assist us here: an animated model shows the construction, deterioration, and reconstruction of temple walls, and the building and overbuilding of storage bins, chambers, and

5.16 The Menkaure Valley Temple, with different occupation phases color-coded (early to mid to late represented by violet, brown, and yellow).

182

5.17 A 3D model with a subterranean view of burial shafts (G 2100 complex).

houses as well. Such morphing reconstructions may be timed to display the relative length of certain phases; these are tools that assist both research and teaching. (Fig. 5.16)

We could also use a similar approach to inform us about the chronological development of the cemetery west of the Great Pyramid. Here, literally hundreds of burial shafts extend to varying depths beneath the mastabas into the limestone bedrock. To be able to watch the shafts organically "grow" in a real-time sequence would illuminate family relationships, necropolis administration, archival practices (how did they remember where *not* to dig?), and the symbolic significance of geographic proximity between individual burials. (see Chapter 4 and Fig. 5.17) This is urban planning for the dead on a grand scale over hundreds of years, and simulations can help us unlock its secrets.

"The kid stays in the picture"
(Animated Characters and Avatars)

Some of us may fall prey these days to the romantic vision of abandoned ancient landscapes, fallen colossi or temple pylons protruding from the sands, uncolored and pristine stone blocks from long-toppled structures everywhere, and no sound but the swirling desert winds. It's an empty, desolate, if picturesque vision. But how well does it correspond to ancient reality? Vibrantly painted walls covered with polychromed hieroglyphic inscriptions amid bustling hubs of activity, even in ancient Egyptian cemeteries, were probably closer to the mark. We can therefore ask: Should human characters now be added to this landscape? Are they a critical addition to our interpretation of the scene, or do they merely bring needless clutter? Without people in our visualizations, are we turning busy, multiuse spaces into artificially hushed precincts? Which distorts the ancient landscape and purpose of the locality more, the presence or absence of Egyptians? If we place them in the scene, performing a single activity, such as ceramic production, or a religious ritual, are we prejudicing our modern audience in favor of that one activity, when in fact the area had a variety of uses in ancient times? Is our technology (and our screen real estate and computer processing power) sophisticated enough now to show all the functions to which a room, courtyard, house, or temple was put, with all the (gender-appropriate) players present and accounted for?

Teaching experience has shown that students today tend to prefer the presence of ancient human characters. They personalize the scene, add scale, and elucidate how the area functioned. And we can provide the capability to toggle them on and off in a given setting, depending on the needs of the user. (Fig. 5.18) In fact, some scenes, such as a busy limestone quarry, might appear misleading without them, as if the entire crew had knocked off for lunch at the very same time. Even following behind ancient Egyptian characters as they exit the corridor westward between two temples and emerge into the Sphinx courtyard, where the carved colossus towers over them, re-creates an ancient experience and perspective not easily gained through traditional photography, or even a visit to the site itself, for the Sphinx precinct is usually closed to the general public.

Animated figures help us de-fine roles and functions and focus our research processes. For exam-ple, our simulation of Khufu's "opening of the mouth ceremony" (see Chapter 4) forced us to consider numerous questions that rarely surface in common academic discussions. Where did this ceremony actually take place? Is our location correct, inside the king's Pyramid Tem-ple courtyard? Was it in another chamber, or perhaps in a tent in a different location entirely? How many people attended? Should we represent only the immediate royal family members and select priests? Where was the common Egyptian citizen-ry? Clearly, they were not allowed into Egyptian temple sanc-tuaries, but were they prevented from appearing anywhere nearby, even outside the temple walls? Moreover, what time should we set in the model for the ceremony? Did the event take place during the day or at night?

5.18 A 3D model of the Sphinx Temple with and without human figures.

We can also clarify tomb decoration processes at Giza,

from initial quarrying to mastaba construction, to excavation of rock-cut chambers, and finally to outline drafting, carving, and painting of wall decoration. The Egyptians prepared and installed burial equipment, such as furniture, sarcophagi, and canopic jars, with varying degrees of difficulty, usually depending on size. Our admiration for their work increases when we consider our own challenges in removing large items from subterranean burial chambers. We have not yet animated the lowering of a stone sarcophagus down a burial shaft, but the process would doubtless teach us much about the construction sequence of chambers versus shafts, the lowering process, and the cutting and separation of the lid from the body of the box. Protective ancient "bubble wrap" still remains, for example, on a sarcophagus found in the Western Cemetery (G 2150, Kanefer); it clearly prevented denting and scraping of the granite against the sides of the burial shaft as the Egyptians lowered it with ropes.

This discussion has focused on the insertion of ancient Egyptians into our digital reconstructions, to form a more coherent and, with luck, undistracting visualization, for both teaching and research. These figures could open a veritable Pandora's box of potential errors, from misrepresenting the functions of ancient spaces to clothing the Egyptians in garments inappropriate for the space or period—by style, quality, color, or even gender. Nevertheless, we have found a certain value in adding humans to specific virtual reconstructions. And moving beyond the ancient Egyptians, we might briefly mention here the potential value of adding modern human characters at Giza. The digital re-creations of simulated George Reisners, Selim Hassans, Auguste Mariettes, Hermann Junkers, or Georg Steindorffs add more to the pedagogical, rather than academic, research potential for the models. Nevertheless, Giza as an archaeological continuum was altered by these individuals almost as significantly as by Khufu, Hemiunu, Khafre, and Menkaure. Modern human characters, or avatars, could act as lecturers or virtual tour guides at Giza. They could elaborate on some of the documentation processes they used in the field in their day. These range from large-format photography on glass plate negatives (compare Figs. 3.1 and 5.19) to accidental discoveries, such as a reenactment of the slipping tripod leg in a plaster floor fill that led to the burial shaft of Queen Hetepheres (G 7000 X). We have experimented with short educational and interactive video featurettes that make use of such avatars. In one, Queen Hetepheres herself narrates some of the events surrounding the construction of her tomb (in this case a work of informed academic fiction, since she left no autobiographical texts behind). Later, Reisner himself takes over the narrative, elaborating on his reconstruction of the events leading up to the queen's burial.[42] In another educational video, Queen Meresankh leads the visitor on a tour of her subterranean chapel (G 7530-sub), introducing specific family

5.19. *Left*: avatars of George Reisner in the tombs of Kaninisut (G 2155, top) and Hetepheres (G 7000 X, bottom). *Right*: Reisner converses with MFA Director George Edgell at Harvard Camp, looking east, 1938.

members, scenes, and architectural details. In this video, online users may interactively pan and zoom around the scene, interrupting its linearity at any time.[43] In selected cases, they may also click on items represented in the wall paintings, which then pop off the walls and appear in free space as 360-degree rotatable objects.[44] (Fig. 5.20) A desirable, though daunting, project would involve creating the 3D links to every object represented on a complex tomb chapel's walls, as a sort of visual interface to the database of Old Kingdom grave goods and objects of daily use.

Visualization is just one of many tools in the archaeologist's interpretive toolkit. We have seen some case studies of its potential, as well as some of the pitfalls that it presents. Like any maturing technology, it will require further refinement, accepted standards (of both representation and file formats), and a clear path to sustainability and archivability. Moving beyond simple attempts at photographic realism and pretty pictures, we now have the capability to create an exciting new subdiscipline in archaeological research, one that is informed at all stages by traditional ground truth methodology, and that in turn may just modify some of those long-held traditions.

5.20 A 3D model of a chair of Meresankh "released" from the wall decoration (from online interactive, educational video).

CHAPTER 6

Where Can We Go from Here?

Egypt's governing heritage organization has been renamed several times, from the Egyptian Antiquities Organization (EAO) to the Supreme Council of Antiquities (SCA) to the Ministry of State for Antiquities (MSA, or Ministry of Antiquities and Heritage). Perhaps more change will follow. Some archaeological sites and museums have suffered in the recent security vacuum from illicit digging and looting (Dahshur, el-Hibeh, Mallawi), whereas housing construction and modern cemetery expansion have threatened others. Despite these setbacks, however, numerous foreign archaeological missions have been conducting business as usual in recent years up and down the Nile Valley and in the Delta. New technologies are assisting the archeological process, and through social media teams are presenting their discoveries to colleagues and the world community on the very day they occur. It is an odd mix; both the dangers to, and the exciting opportunities for, cultural heritage management and exploration of the human past in Egypt have never been greater.

In the midst of these challenging times in Egypt, preservation (both physical and archival), documentation, and visualization have likewise never been so important. The very survival of some sites relies on assembling recent and not-so-recent inventories and histories, as well as creating a critical mass of public awareness, which in turn leads to resources and support. Archaeologists can no longer work alone or confine their results to a few interested colleagues. Lorna Richardson poignantly asks, "How do we, as a discipline, converse with non-archaeologists through these Internet technologies, with relevance and academic rigour, and in a language that we can all understand?"[1] It is with these challenges and opportunities in mind that we imagine in this final chapter the possible futures of such undertakings as the Giza Project at Harvard University.

Sustainability

A primary goal of the Giza Project, stretching back almost to its inception in 2000, has consisted of serving the international community as the central digital repository for the archaeology of Giza, past, present, and future. This extremely tall order requires a firm data management plan[2] and a path to long-term sustainability. The university, with its educational, nonprofit focus and archival infrastructure (think library science), is a logical storage repository for such an endeavor, better perhaps than even most museums nowadays, whose roles, in the United States at least, have largely shifted—to generalize unfairly—from storehouses of knowledge to entertainment palaces. Step one on the road to digitally collecting and presenting "all things Giza" is the creation of a new Harvard public Giza website that embeds the legacy excavation documentation in the immersive 3D computer model of the entire archaeological site. Moving beyond standard SQL-parsed data systems toward next-generation search engines is also on our to-do list. Between 2014 and 2016 we were fortunate to receive three grants from the National Endowment for the Humanities, for additional data entry and new website preparation.[3] Mockups and layouts of a revised Giza website hosted by Harvard University, enhancing or replacing www.gizapyramids. org, wait in the wings while this important back-end infrastructure is produced.

As noted in Chapter 3, the ancient Egyptians committed much of their legacy to stone. In the early twentieth century archaeologists at sites such as Giza began to convert that legacy from stone to glass plate photo negatives, paper manuscripts, and drawings. Our own era prefers electronic form and digital files. It is perhaps debatable which of these media is best suited to survive for posterity. A Giza hieroglyphic inscription carved in limestone has already proven it can withstand the tests of time, surviving for nearly five thousand years. (Fig. 6.1) A modern twentieth-century glass plate negative, by contrast, can crack or suffer from chemical deterioration; glass plates have notched fewer than two centuries in their life spans so far. The even younger digital files run the risk of binary corruption or failure to keep pace with software and hardware devices re-

quired to access them. We are, alas, resigned to attempting to create a permanent archive using tools that, whether by
unhappy chance or by conscious (capital-
ist) design, march toward obsolescence
with alarming rapidity.

How will these digital environments
be maintained, both archivally and financially? An old line drawing can always be
scanned and converted from bitmap to
vector lines for other uses. But a 3D model might linger in a file format that becomes extinct or reside on a server that
changes its IP address (with no permanent digital object identifier) or becomes
otherwise inaccessible. Until there is in-
teroperability and a set of modeling
standards, this haphazard and risky scenario is bound to continue. The best we
can hope for are well-conceived data
management plans—and the necessary
resources—that allow the conversion of
all our media formats to keep pace with
changing technology.

Future Directions / New Tools

Alongside the ongoing and seemingly endless processing
of traditional excavation records (photos, notes, drawings,
metadata, and so on), a number of new approaches could further enhance access to the Giza Plateau. Many of these technologies are already mature but have yet to be applied to archaeological projects in comprehensive and consistent ways.

6.1 *Top:* slab stela
of Ini (G 1235).
Middle: damaged
glass plate nega-
tive showing the
Menkaure Valley
Temple and Kha-
fre Pyramid, look-
ing northwest,
1910. *Bottom:* CD
and jewel box.

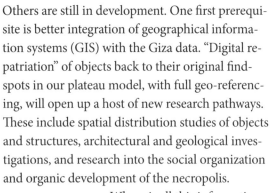

Others are still in development. One first prerequisite is better integration of geographical information systems (GIS) with the Giza data. "Digital repatriation" of objects back to their original findspots in our plateau model, with full geo-referencing, will open up a host of new research pathways. These include spatial distribution studies of objects and structures, architectural and geological investigations, and research into the social organization and organic development of the necropolis.

Where is all this information heading? Perhaps right into your pocket. Mobile technologies should allow for research on-site, including access to a wide range of traditional and visual data. Quick response (QR) codes, radio frequency identification technology (RFID) tags, and augmented reality (AR) can allow visitors

6.2 *Top:* example of smartphone access to museum object information (the Menkaure dyad, MFA 11.1738, with Mansour Boraik in the background). *Bottom:* smartphone access to on-site monuments, such as the Khufu Pyramid Temple, looking northwest.

in Giza galleries in museums to point their devices at an object to reveal its discovery photo and original context, the metadata (in multiple foreign languages), restored colors, or even references to comparable objects found in geographic proximity. (Fig. 6.2, top) A banal example, but one that has disappointed this writer for years is that, for reasons of space, Egyptian statues are often displayed up against museum gallery walls, which tends to obscure the hieroglyphic inscription carved on the back pillar! How convenient it would be to call up images on a smartphone showing the back of the statue, or rotate a 3D model around to reveal the inscription.

Similarly, at the site of Giza itself, portable devices could

194

superimpose the original appearance of a wall onto what is today merely a deteriorated foundation, or demarcate the findspots of specific types of objects as one pans the device across the landscape. The lower image in fig. 6.2 shows our hypothetical reconstruction of the Khufu Pyramid Temple superimposed over the present-day image of its remains. The entire Giza Plateau should be laid out virtually as a grid, and using portable smart devices and satellite connections, both excavator and casual tourist could access the entire corpus of Giza material from any position on the plateau. This is "edu-tourism" and a researcher's portable, virtual Giza encyclope-dia, all rolled into one. For those not physically at Giza, the successor to my own 1,300 QTVR rotating standpoints virtu-ally planted all over the site would naturally resemble Google Street View, a walk up and down all the streets of Giza masta-ba tombs with a 360-degree camera rig, just as web users to-day browse streets of cities and towns online.[4] Such compre-hensive documentation will no doubt happen soon. Google Earth satellite images contain a chronology or history slider, morphing from one image or year to the next; so, too, could a "Google Ancient Earth" approach make use of our 3D models to slide along the time-axis to view the site at different points in time. These changes extend from predynastic times to the present day.

Back in the classroom, these new research technologies will continue to alter teaching methods. At present, Giza ar-chaeology at Harvard is taught in the university's small Visual-ization Center. (Fig. 6.3) This expensive classroom uses two high-resolution digital projectors in active stereo mode dis-playing on a cylindrical screen 23 × 8 feet (7 × 2.4 meters). The resolution of the combined image is 1,200 × 3,600 pixels, and the curved screen covers 120 degrees. Students don 3D glasses to view the Giza content in an immersive environment.

Tomorrow's trends, however, may lead us away from such expensive setups to rear-projection portable 3D stations, where any classroom can be instantly transformed into a 3D theater or, even further, to smaller, personal devices. If the answer is not of the ilk of Google Glass, perhaps the Oculus Rift, Samsung GearVR, Google Cardboard, or other devices will transform visualization in archaeology. These 3D stereo headsets seem to have finally solved most of the latency problems between head motion and computer processing that cause the queasy discomfort that many people experience in 3D environments. There are of course some unwanted implications worth watching out for—if students today can waste valuable class time browsing on Facebook, in future they could virtually wander off to other locations of a site in 360-degree space rather than focusing on the instructor's content. Nevertheless, the technology shows great potential for distance learning, where entire classrooms of hundreds or perhaps even thousands of people around the world "meet" simultaneously at the Giza Necropolis for lectures and walking tours. This is public archaeology at its virtual finest. Students, edutourists, or whatever we wish to call them could view one another or stand at the site alone with the instructor in a digital one-on-one private class. This may tie in well with the strategies of massive

6.3 Students study Giza in the Harvard University Visualization Center.

open online courses (MOOCs). In a consortium with MIT and other universities, Harvard has recently invested heavily in these technologies (https://www.edx.org), which go far beyond merely filming a professor's lecture and should enhance on-campus instruction as well.[5] With the development of these new immersive systems, one wonders: Could custom contact lenses or visual implants be far behind? "Embedded files triggered by environmental sensors or ambient experience provoked by our presence will situate us in a hybrid sensorium. Utopian or dystopian, this future is upon us."[6]

The ability to move around digital objects, view them from different vantage points, or light them from various angles, is a critically useful tool for scholarly research. Reflectance Transformation Imaging (RTI) is particularly helpful for reading wall carvings and inscriptions or viewing sculpture in the round under diverse lighting conditions. Imagine a carved hieroglyphic inscription in a difficult state of preservation, where lighting from the upper left might reveal certain details, and lighting from the lower right elucidates others. (Fig. 6.4) Funding and page length limitations prevent most print publications from reproducing multiple images of the same object lit from eight or twelve different angles. Online publishing is less limited, of course, but even better are RTI images, where all the separately lit images are combined in a single file, and the viewer has the ability to control the light source him- or herself.

6.4 The slab stela of Wepemnefret, lit for Reflectance Transformation Imaging (RTI).

Let us move beyond 2D RTI imaging, however, to 3D printing in archaeology. In this case, we may learn much about ancient artifacts in the course of producing 3D models that can be printed or carved in the round, either with dedicated printing machines in wax, plastic, resin, metal, or other materials, or with computer-driven, multiaxis milling machines. The most instructive piece we have worked on at the Giza Project thus far is one of the chairs of Queen Hetepheres from her subterranean burial shaft, excavated between 1925 and 1927 by the HU–MFA Expedition. Unlike the queen's other furniture, whose modern wood reproductions are on view in Cairo (a second set is in Boston), this chair was never replicated, for its tiny fragments and complex patterning present a restorer's nightmare (none of the wood from Hetepheres's tomb has survived). (Fig. 6.5) Our attempts at restoration have taught us about the chair's construction methods and its gilding layers and inlays, and the project has even served to correct many of the drawings and suggestions of the original excavators from the 1920s and 1930s.[7] (Fig. 6.6) Using computer-driven milling machines provided by Shopbot Tools, and with the assistance of Neil Gershenfeld, director of the Center for Bits and Atoms at MIT, we carved theriomorphic (animal-legged) furniture. With the collaboration of Kathryn King, director of Education at the Ceramics Program, Office for the Arts at Harvard University, we have re-created ancient faience in molds for the inlays. Beyond the academic exercise of producing 3D models of artifacts for recontextualization in our Giza Plateau rendering, such 3D-printed products have a display value for museum visitors—they can be handled and can supplement collections not as rich in actual artifacts as those of major metropolitan museums. These new 3D-milled and 3D-printed replicas continue a virtual reality tradition that was all the fashion in museums in the Victorian era,

when plaster casts served as teaching tools all over the world. The practice is even making a comeback of sorts.[8] Should we aim for an educational "library" of 3D models for reproduction, sort of a digital *Gipsformerei* (plaster form factory)? This would not only enhance the study potential for any given object, but would also allow for the flexibility of reproduction at different scales from the original, useful for a wide variety of pedagogical purposes. After all, who could bring a full-scale physical model of the Sphinx into the classroom?

Throughout the creation and display of all these technologies, it is the underlying search engine that remains paramount to archaeological knowledge production. Should we be able to move beyond our Giza SQL databases, there waits for us such programs as Watson, IBM's cognitive computer sys-

6.5 Fragments of Hetepheres's chair B and other items in situ on the floor in G 7000 X, 1926.

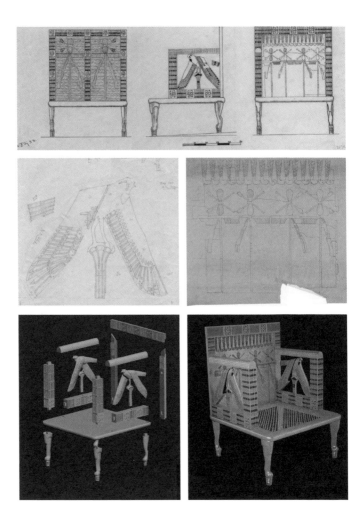

6.6 Chair B of Hetepheres, from fragments in G 7000 X. *Top and middle:* HU–MFA Expedition drawings. *Bottom:* 3D models.

tem. This artificial intelligence–based interface can handle search queries in natural spoken language.[9] How convenient it would be to rid the user of the frustrating semantics that can currently ruin well-intentioned search queries, such as simply mistyping tomb prefix numbers or being forced to guess if a drawing lies in the "published" or "unpublished" documentation module, to cite some banal examples of a systemwide problem. No user knows a database structure as well as its creators do, and too often ambiguities in organization leave users unsure of where to look next. The possibilities for streamlining and naturalizing search queries are extremely attractive and would level the playing field for experts and lay public alike.

Challenges and Economies of Scale

Content builders must have the necessary resources to create, maintain, and improve the virtual Giza environment and its links to traditional archaeological data. To avoid inaccurate models and a general descent into inauthentic, popular-media type ("infotainment") simulations, the digital environment is wholly dependent on the ground truth of responsible documentation from past and present excavations and publications. Long-term strategies are critical to building such a massive interface that can serve all parties, from K–12 children through postdoctoral researchers, each at his or her desired level of expertise.

In some cases, recent work has been frustrated by bandwidth and processor power limitations that will, we hope, disappear in the near future. The most prominent example lies in the discrepancy between high-resolution, locally stored models, where the digital objects are based on thousands if not millions of underlying polygons, and their counterpart low-polygon ("dumbed-down") versions that are necessary for rapid builds and display over the Internet within the interactive model. It is already time-consuming and labor-intensive enough to create these 3D models; having to "freeze" them and then spend yet more time eliminating polygons— and which ones to eliminate is always a judgment call—for

the Internet seems like a counterintuitive workflow. (Fig. 6.7) In the case of Giza statuary, for example, laser-scanning or other 3D-capture technologies today can produce extremely accurate and faithful renderings of fine ancient craftsmanship. Yet these 3D models, which are based on point clouds, often bear *too much* information to be used in some virtual environments. As a solution, manual labor must step in with artistic approximations of the statuary instead. The results are usually less than satisfactory, particularly in the case of recognizable masterpieces. We cite here the famous pair statue of Menkaure and possibly his queen (MFA 11.1738), where it is clear that no amount of digital tweaking of an artist's model can match the proportions and features that a laser scan would produce (and in fact has produced) of the same statue. (Fig. 6.8) Map streaming data, as currently served by Google, may provide one future solution. High-resolution point clouds could be broken up into individual cubes, each with several levels of detail. Then only the cubes around the user's current position need be loaded, as higher levels of detail would stream during navigation to other locations. We hope that future versions of virtual environments and increasing Internet bandwidth will allow us to serve more accurate, high-polygon 3D models even

6.7 *Left:* wireframe polygon editing of engaged statuary in the chapel of Meresankh. *Right:* a 3D model superimposed over a Joseph Lindon Smith painting.

to lowest-common-denom-inator PCs and other devic-es. This would eliminate the time-consuming creation of low-polygon versions of 3D landscapes and objects.[10]

The costs of 3D scan-ning decrease each year, and the methodology choices increase, from pro-fessional equipment to on-board smartphone cameras. Though one may dream of

creating accurate 3D models of all the objects ever excavated at Giza, the political hurdles involved outweigh the advances in technology. Gaining access to ancient artifacts in museum dis-play cases, behind glass or Plexiglas, or hidden away in storage basements, represents a significant pull on understaffed muse-um curators, not to mention issues of security and supervi-sion, while depriving the museum-visiting public of its right to view objects that are temporarily removed from exhibition. Colossal objects, too, present special scanning challenges, re-quiring scaffolding or other heavy equipment, or nighttime photography, depending on the room-darkening capabilities of a given gallery. Imagine the various intellectual property issues that Google encountered in its worldwide book-scan-ning endeavors, and then consider if each of the millions of books were a priceless antiquity requiring special access and handling by trained professionals. Simple photograph-based 3D model creation will help alleviate this problem, but curato-rial permissions, reflective vitrines, intellectual property con-siderations, and inaccessible storage depots will continue to slow our progress on this front for some time.

6.8 *Left:* the Menkaure dyad. *Right:* an unsatisfactory 3D model created by hand editing.

Openness / Share and Share Alike?

In 2014 Chinese entrepreneurs built a replica of the Sphinx in Shijiazhuang, Hebei Province, at a cost of about $1.3 million, ostensibly for use in a theme park, and for offering TV and movie filming opportunities as well. (Fig. 6.9) Once word broke out, the Egyptian reaction was harsh and swift. The Egyptians felt that this fake Sphinx harmed and insulted their cultural heritage, which in turn prompted apologies and assurances from the Chinese that the structure was only temporary and would be removed in due course. As a consequence, Egyptian antiquities authorities became suspicious of all sorts of laser-scanning projects and other similar types of photorealistic image-capturing technology in their country.

Can one actually argue in such cases that one's cultural heritage "brand," represented in this case by the Sphinx, is being "diluted"? Did Egypt stand to suffer financially? Would Chinese citizens actually cancel a trip to the land of the pharaohs, depriving the Egyptian economy of needed support, all because of a full-scale Sphinx replica in China's own backyard? One could argue that no such cancellations or revenue losses are likely, and perhaps even the opposite perspective is true. Chinese citizens, intrigued by this colossal temporary "ambassador," might find the motivation to go visit the real thing. In short, the replica Sphinx could be said to have created positive "buzz." This trend, namely, the release, rather than the hoarding, of cultural assets, is gaining traction now. Major museums such as the Metropolitan Museum of Art and the British Museum have begun to release high-resolution images of their collections free of charge for academic and other fair-use purposes. They have rightly reasoned that in many cases the old traditional licensing fees charged fail to support the rights and licensing staff salaries at their own institutions.

Moreover, the business model was punishing scholars and students, the very sector endeavoring to study and publicize—at no cost to the museum—the works of art in their collections.

Institutions such as the Metropolitan Museum, the Oriental Institute Museum, the Giza Project, and eventually the Harvard Semitic Museum are similarly placing PDF document versions of their publications backlists online for universal access and free downloading. An out-of-print volume that once enjoyed a meager run of five hundred copies is now available to millions around the world 24/7. At a Harvard symposium on linking libraries, ar-

chives, and museums (LAM) held in April 2012, Holly Witchey, interim director of the Marcus Institute for Digital Education in the Arts, at Johns Hopkins University, said, "'Our job as curators is LAM integration, but we all do it so idiosyncratically'. . . Witchey described a split among museum curators dividing those who prefer the old, idiosyncratic systems of organization and those who recognize the value added by integration . . . 'Our audiences simply expect integration,' and there's no escaping it."[11] Perhaps we should be arguing for *more* full-scale replica Sphinxes around the world.

There are of course some legal implications beyond basic fair-use policies for intellectual property. It is one thing to share Giza documentation among Egyptological institutions in a purely research and pedagogical endeavor. But publishers need to make a living, too. And what happens when new derivative digital content is created that is based, or partly based,

6.9 *Top:* replica Sphinx built in Hebei Province, China. *Bottom:* actual Sphinx at Giza.

on the archaeological holdings of multiple copyright owners? An example might be the mapping of a museum's photographs onto a 3D model of the tomb chapel in question, and then colorizing it to restore its original polychromy. At what point should the original copyright holder of the photographs be informed of the new creation? Only if revenue is generated in some fashion? Might some revenue-generating schemes be developed to support the academic research, while simultaneously fulfilling some of our educational goals? Imagine "Giza: The Archaeology Simulation," in which users take on the avatar identities of the great excavators and reenact the historical development of the excavation of the Giza Plateau, punctuated by two world wars and a host of other challenges. My Egyptological colleagues might roll their eyes at such a suggestion, and yet such accurate role-playing simulations could represent a critical example of the "digital public archaeology" conversation that Lorna Richardson alluded to in the quote at the start of this chapter. Digital immersion in a building environment is one thing; immersion in an excavator's environment and decision-making process is quite another. In addition to learning about the ancient monuments themselves and Old Kingdom history, students might benefit from experiencing the challenges of working in an expatriate mission amid competing cultural heritage agendas. Archaeology under such circumstances hardly exists in a vacuum, as excavators confronted issues of nationalism, colonialism, repatriation, and the rush to be the first into print. We have already re-created digital Harvard Camp and plan to simulate George Reisner's archaeological workflow, from discoveries in the ground to registration and study in the lab, to documentation in the photo studio, and finally to the formal division, packing, and shipping to either Cairo or Boston. (Fig. 6.10) Should an institution that develops such educational content share revenue

among other institutions that contributed material, even if the derivative results are almost completely removed from the original intellectual property?

Until such a "serious" gaming landscape appears, perhaps one of the best ways to share the Giza repository, beyond the Internet of course, will be in the forthcoming Grand Egyptian Museum, currently under construction about one mile north of the Giza Plateau.[12] Sited with a view of the Pyramids, the new museum is set to become one of the world's largest, and the treasures of Tutankhamun, not to mention the Khufu boats excavated south of the Great Pyramid, are on the list at present to move there. (Fig. 6.11) It would seem appropriate then, that some of the educational technology galleries in the new museum might provide access to the richest assemblage of Giza data ever collected.

6.10 A 3D model of Harvard Camp, Giza.

Picking Up the Pace

The amount of realism in digital archaeology reconstructions depends directly on the resources available, a fact that in turn forces us to consider the scope and scale of our projects. At the Giza Necropolis, the numbers reach into the hundreds (complex architecture, often with decoration), the thousands (individual burials), the tens of thousands (finds), and the hundreds of thousands (modern images and illustrations). This sobering realization tempers our ideal objective, which is the faithful digital reconstruction of all the monuments on the plateau, in all their construction phases, their ornamentation intact, finds recontextualized, and all relevant archaeological documentation linked. Despite the contributions of more than five hundred people to the Giza Project, (see Chapter 3) both at the Museum of Fine Arts, Boston, and at

6.11 Top: a 3D model of the first Khufu boat. *Bottom:* a view of the Giza Plateau from the boat, sailing on the Nile.

Harvard University, only a small portion of the Giza Necropolis exists today in our Giza 3D model in granular detail.

The Pyramids are indeed stationary, but modeling the entire site is a moving target; we must deal with constant changes to the landscape, the incorporation of new discoveries, and revisions to old ones. Two strategies exist that might accelerate the workflow—and preserve the sanity of our overworked project staff. One is to increase personnel, the other to schematize and simplify a series of templates for representing the monuments. Without major financial contributions from foundations or individuals—and I shamelessly confess that we are always on the lookout for these—the project staff numbers are unlikely to increase dramatically. But for 3D model creation, some form of crowdsourcing might bring us closer to our goals. Following the lead of 3D structures currently being added to Google Earth by individuals all over the world, we could write and distribute a system or "kit" for mastaba construction. Interested individuals could, for example, "adopt a mastaba," submit their model file for vetting, and eventually see their edifice take its place on our virtual Giza Plateau. One wonders if a similar "adopt-a-mastaba" program for the actual mastabas at Giza might improve site management and conservation, in exchange for some sort of acknowledgment or special status for the donor (e.g., "The restoration of Mastaba G 2370 was made possible through contributions by John Smith"). A sort of Kickstarter campaign for virtual Giza, with or without a financial component for the archaeological site as well, is worth exploring.

The second strategy for increasing coverage of the vast Giza Plateau is to rethink a slavish concern for block-by-block fidelity to individual monuments. For example, Reisner determined a useful typology for the exterior casing types of the many Giza mastabas. Adopting and adapting this system,

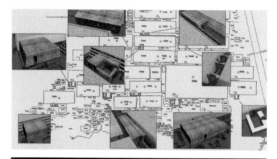

one could quickly "case" the structures with a pattern of blocks (large, small, vertical, sloping, and so on) appropriate to the tomb in question. As fig. 6.12 shows, we have experimented with this strategy for portions of the Giza cemeteries. The Eastern Cemetery gains somewhat in photorealism, as the varied casing types differentiate the mastabas' appearance, but it should be clarified that these structures are not faithful block-by-block reconstructions.

In Chapter 5 we considered whether a 3D computer model of a Giza tomb should present its appearance in 2500 BCE, on the day of the deceased tomb owner's interment; or whether it should illustrate the tomb's condition upon discovery, millennia later, such as in 1912 CE? Finally, should the model display the tomb's condition now, in the present day? All these choices are valid, and all have something to teach us, so the Giza Project has experimented with each of these phases. We have restored painted wall decoration to its original luster in the Fourth Dynasty. (Figs. 4.11, 5.5, 5.17; chapel of Meresankh, G 7530-sub) We have restored and placed objects back in their funerary contexts at the time of burial. (Figs. 4.13–4.14, 5.7–5.9; Queen Hetepheres, G 7000 X) We have shown the condition upon discovery in 1906 (Figs. 4.7–4.8; Sedit, G 2100 shaft A) and presented the current condition of other monuments. In many cases the

6.12 Casing types, following Reisner's typology for Eastern Cemetery mastabas.

nature of the surviving data will make the choice for us. We plan to develop additional user-controlled, online toggle switches for displaying such different phases, as well as standards for rendering restorations more distinctly from the preserved archaeological record.

The digital renderings in this volume may soon start to resemble dated period pieces, primitive attempts at reproducing the complexities of ancient Egyptian material culture. Indeed, we hope for this outcome, for it will signify technological progress, not just in the aesthetics of the landscapes, buildings, and animated characters in our Giza models, but in the digital archaeology workflow itself. As our renderings have built on the work of our predecessors, so too might we hope that our contribution proves to be of some value to the next generation of archaeological visualizations. May our renderings present a useful stop, but not an end station, toward picturing the past.

Free Lunches?

As large-scale projects struggle with ever-shrinking funds, the challenge remains to create an archive for posterity and ensure that all interested parties continue to enjoy free access. In the absence of federal grants, individual donations, or endowments, such initiatives as the Giza Project may be forced to move to some sort of subscription-based model. The brunt of the expenses would then be borne either by subscribing libraries and institutions or by broad-based, crowdfunded support. Punishing individual researchers—or worse, students—with registration and fee-based access runs counter to the overriding premise and mission of this centralized repository. Perhaps this small publication may serve in part as a call for support not only to develop the next "killer Giza app," but also to solve the sustainability challenge that our efforts at Giza, like so many worthy documentation projects, currently face.

Let us assume for a moment that the long-term financing issues are solved. How then to solve the problem of each archaeological site's dataset (in Egypt and elsewhere) forming its own "digital silo"? In other words, tomb numbers, feature numbers, architecture—or the lack thereof—are all elements with specific designations assigned on a site-by-site, culture-by-culture basis to fit the material record at hand. Can we eventually reach a federated search ideal standard—from one expedition to another at Giza; then from one Egyptian site to another; then from one ancient Near Eastern excavation to another; and finally across all of world archaeology? That solution must probably await the creation of much better artificial intelligence–based search algorithms to replace today's SQL databases, or the creation of federated searches that can delve into all types of proprietary content-management systems to aggregate the results in an intelligible manner. These and other new technologies will continue to sort and display Giza records online in new and exciting ways.[13] For now, we can already pose research questions that previously could not be formulated, and the next frontier will incorporate additional archaeological sciences. We look forward to online delivery of more precise structure and object geo-referencing, augmented reality, perhaps with new technologies such as defocused point-light sources for 3D augmented reality glasses, satellite and low aerial drone photography, "street view" type access, remote sensing techniques, and enhanced, interactive 3D modeling of the tombs, temples, and settlements covering the Giza Plateau. The next generation of Giza documentation, using infrared thermography and cosmic particle detectors, was already under way as this book went to press. The Giza Project is part of a new initiative, cofounded by Mehdi Tayoubi and colleagues, to scan the entire archaeological site.[14] By the time we reach the age when all these approaches work together seamlessly, then beyond Khufu's Fourth Dynasty, past George Reisner's twentieth-century era of great excavations, and after our current digital conversions, Giza may be ready for its fourth "golden age." (Fig 6.13)

6.13 A 3D model
of the Giza Plateau,
looking west

Endnotes

2. Archaeological Explorations at Giza from 1800 to the Present

1   For a summary of the rediscovery of ancient Egypt by both Europeans and Egyptians, see **D. M. Reid**, *Whose Pharaohs? Archaeology, Museums, and Egyptian National Identity from Napoleon to World War I* (Berkeley: University of California Press, 2002), 21–63; **O. El-Daly**, *Egyptology: The Missing Millennium. Ancient Egypt in Medieval Arabic Writings* (London: University College London, 2005); and **M. Lehner**, *The Complete Pyramids: Solving the Ancient Mysteries* (New York: Thames & Hudson, 1997), 38–45.

2   **B. M. Fagan**, *The Rape of the Nile: Tomb Robbers, Tourists, and Archaeologists in Egypt*, 3rd ed. (Boulder: Westview Press, 2004).

3   **D. Manley** and **P. Rée**, *Henry Salt: Artist, Traveller, Diplomat, Egyptologist* (London: Libri, 2001); **R. T. Ridley**, *Napoleon's Proconsul in Egypt: The Life and Times of Bernardino Drovetti* (London: Rubicon Press, 1998).

4   **E. Vassilika**, *Art Treasures from the Museo Egizio* (New York: Umberto Allemandi, 2006), and **Vassilika**, *Masterpieces of the Museo Egizio in Turin* (Turin: Fondazione Museo delle Antichità Egizie di Torino, 2009).

5   **P. Usick** and **D. Manley**, *The Sphinx Revealed: A Forgotten Record of Pioneering Excavations* (London: British Museum, 2007), including Salt's overview sketch plan on pl. 1, which shows one of the earliest attempts to number many of the monuments.

6   **G. Belzoni**, *Narrative of the Operations and Recent Discoveries within the Pyramids, Temples, Tombs, and Excavations in Egypt and Nubia . . .* (Brussels: H. Remy, 1835), 255; **Stanley Mayes**, *The Great Belzoni: The Circus Strongman Who Discovered Egypt's Ancient Treasure* (London: Tauris Parke, 2003), 202–203.

7   **Lehner**, *The Complete Pyramids*, 52; **Fagan**, *The Rape of the Nile*, 117.

8   **J.-F. Champollion**, *Lettres écrites d'Egypte et de la Nubia en 1828 et 1829* (Paris: Didier, 1868); **I. Rosellini**, *I monumenti dell'Egitto e della Nubia, disegnati dalla spedizione scientifico-letteraria toscana in Egitto; distribuiti in ordine di materie, interpretati ed illustrati dal dottore Ippolito Rosellini*, 9 vols. (Pisa: Presso N. Capurro, 1832–1844).

9   **J. S. Perring**, *The Pyramids of Gizeh*, 3 vols. (London: J. Fraser, 1839–1842); **R. W. H. Vyse**, *Operations Carried on at the Pyramids of Gizeh in 1837*, 3 vols. (London: J. Fraser, 1840–1842). The British Egyptologist Samuel Birch (1813–1885) assisted in transcribing some of the inscriptions unearthed by Vyse and Perring.

10 **Perring**, *The Pyramids of Gizeh*, 2: pl. v; **Vyse**, *Operations Carried on at the Pyramids of Gizeh in 1837*, 2: pl. facing p. 84; **A. M. Donadoni Roveri**, *I sarcofagi egizi dalle origini alla fine dell'antico regno* (Rome: Istituto di Studi del Vicino Oriente, Università, 1969), 105 [A 6], fig. 14 [b].

11 British Museum EA6647; **Vyse**, *Operations Carried on at the Pyramids of Gizeh in 1837*, 1:86, 87, 93–96, 2: pl. opp. p. 94; **C. M. Zivie-Coche**, *Giza au premier millénaire: Autour du temple d'Isis dame des pyramides* (Boston: Museum of Fine Arts, 1991), 97–101; **J. Taylor**, "Coffin of

king Menkaure," in N. Strudwick, *Masterpieces of Ancient Egypt* (Austin: University of Texas Press, 2006), 264–265; **Lehner**, *The Complete Pyramids*, 52.

12 **J.-J. Fiechter**, *Mikerinos: Le dieu englouti* (Paris: Maisonneuve et Larose, 2001), 221–231.

13 There is some confusion about whether Colonel Coutelle had already cleared one of these pyramids; see **Vyse**, *Operations Carried on at the Pyramids of Gizeh in 1837*, 1:36n2. For detailed descriptions of these pyramids and their possible owners, see **P. Jánosi**, *Die Pyramidenanlagen der Königinnen: Untersuchungen zu einem Grabtyp des Alten und Mittleren Reiches* (Vienna: Österreichische Akademie der Wissenschaften, 1996), 21–28.

14 **K. R. Lepsius**, *Briefe aus Ägypten, Äthiopien und der Halbinsel des Sinai* (Berlin: Verlag von Wilhelm Hertz, 1852); **G. Ebers**, *Richard Lepsius, Ein Lebensbild* (Berlin: W. Engelmann, 1885); **H. Mehlitz**, *Richard Lepsius: Ägypten und die Ordnung der Wissenschaft* (Berlin: Kulturverlag Kadmos, 2011).

15 **A. von Specht**, ed., *Lepsius: Die deutsche Expedition an den Nil* (Berlin: Staatliche Museen zu Berlin, Stiftung Preussischer Kulturbesitz, 2006), 12–15; **H. G. Fischer**, "The Mark of a Second Hand on Ancient Egyptian Antiquities," *Metropolitan Museum Journal* 9 (1974): 8, fig. 5.

16 For the fascinating history of this panorama, see **B. Lepsius**, *Das Haus Lepsius: Vom geistigen Aufstieg Berlins zur Reichshauptstadt* (Berlin: Klinkhardt & Biermann, 1933), 178; **Horst Beinlich**, *Mit Richard Lepsius auf die Cheops-Pyramide* (Dettelbach: J. H. Röll, 2012), 1–22, 24–27, foldout plate, and esp. 9–10. The panorama returned briefly to Egypt as part of a

special Lepsius exhibition at the Egyptian Museum, Cairo: **von Specht**, *Lepsius, Die deutsche Expedition an den Nil*, 156–157, cat. no. 48 (Berlin Inv. Nr. 2548).

17 **R. Lepsius**, *Denkmaeler aus Aegypten und Aethiopien nach den zeichnungen der von Seiner Majestät dem koenige von Preussen Friedrich Wilhelm IV*, 12 vols. (Berlin: Nicolai, 1849–1856), 3: pl. 68.

18 In fact, some 15,000 objects and plaster casts were eventually sent to Berlin.

19 As noted by **G. A. Reisner**, *A History of the Giza Necropolis*, vol. 1 (Cambridge: Harvard University Press, 1942), 22, these included Champollion (1790–1832), Ippolito Rosellini (1800–1843), John Gardner Wilkinson (1797–1875), Robert Hay (1799–1863), James Burton (1788–1862), Théodule Devéria (1831–1871), Giuseppe Passalacqua (1797–1865), Nestor L'Hôte (1804–1842), Freiherr von Minutoli (1772–1846), Emile Prisse d'Avennes (1807–1879), Emmanuel de Rougé (1811–1872) and Jacques de Rougé (1842–1928), and Heinrich Brugsch Pasha (1827–1894).

20 **E. David**, *Mariette Pacha, 1821–1881* (Paris: Pygmalion/G. Watelet, 1994).

21 **Zivie-Coche**, *Giza au premier millénaire*, 218–246, pls. 39–40.

22 Egyptian Museum JE 10062 = CG 14; **M. Saleh and H. Sourouzian**, *The Egyptian Museum Cairo: Official Guide* (Mainz: Philipp von Zabern, 1987), cat. 31.

23 **A. Mariette**, *Les mastabas de l'ancien empire* (Paris: F. Vieweg, 1889), 488–571, with pl. 1.

24 Commission des Sciences et Arts d'Egypte, *Description de l'Egypte, ou, Recueil des observations et des recherches qui ont été faites en Egypte pendant l'éxpédition de l'armée français* (Paris: Imprimerie Impériale, 1822–1823), pl. 6; **Perring**, *The*

Pyramids of Gizeh; Lepsius, *Denkmaeler,* 1: pl. 14; **C. Piazzi Smyth**, *Our Inheritance in the Great Pyramid* (London: A. Strahan, 1864), 228, pl. III. See also the plan in **Sir J. G. Wilkinson**, *Modern Egypt and Thebes* (London: J. Murray, 1843), 363. Survey work at Giza had come quite some way since the somewhat fanciful plan by **R. Pococke**, *A Description of the East, and Some Other Countries,* vol. 1, *Observations on Egypt* (London: W. Bowyer, 1743), pl. 16.

25 **E. Prisse d'Avennes**, *Atlas de l'histoire de l'art égyptien d'après les monuments depuis les temps les plus reculés jusqu'à la domination romaine* (Paris: Arthur Bertrand, 1878–1879), pls. 3, 5, 6, and 50. A modern reprint of this volume is available by **Prisse d'Avennes**, *Atlas of Egyptian Art,* introduction by M. J. Raven, captions by O. Kaper (Cairo: American University in Cairo Press, 1997). For a more recent work, see **Sylvie Aubenas** et al., *Visions d'Égypt: Émile Prisse d'Avennes (1807–1879)* (Paris: Bibliothèque Nationale de France), 2011.

26 **W. de Famars Testas**, *Reisschetsen uit Egypte, 1858–1860* (Maarssen: SDU, 1988).

27 **H. W. C.**, "Recent Discoveries in the Great Pyramid of Egypt—Ancient Egyptian Weight," *Nature* 7, no. 165, (1872): 146–149; an anonymously authored article in *The Graphic* 158 (December 7, 1872): 544–545; **R. G. Bauval** and **J. Sierra**, "Carbon-14 Dating the Giza Pyramids? The Small Relics Found inside the Pyramids," *Discussions in Egyptology* 49 (2001): 6–21.

28 The Dixons also sent a casing stone fragment from the Khufu Pyramid back to London; *The Graphic* 158 (December 7, 1872): 530.

29 **A. Wiedemann** and **B. Pörtner**, *Aegyptische Grabreliefs aus der Grossherzoglichen Altertümer-Sammlung zu Karlsruhe* (Strassburg: Schlesier & Schweikhard, 1906); **S. Albersmeier**, *Ägyptische Kunst: Bestandskatalog Badisches Landesmuseum Karlsruhe* (Munich: Edition Minerva, 2007), 14–26; **W. Schürmann**, *Die Reliefs aus dem Grab des Pyramidenvorstehers Ii-nefret: Eine Bilddokumentation des Badischen Landesmuseums Karlsruhe* (Karlsruhe: C. F. Müller, 1983); **A. Bolshakov**, "Some Notes on the Reliefs of *Ij-nfr.t* (Karlsruhe)," *Göttinger Miszellen* 115 (1990): 15–27; **I. Gamer-Wallert** and **R. Grieshammer**, *Ägyptische Kunst: Badisches Landesmuseum Karlsruhe* (Karlsruhe: Badisches Landesmuseum, 1992), 28–31 (4).

30 On Maspero, see **E. David**, *Gaston Maspero, 1846–1916: Le gentleman égyptologue* (Paris: Pygmalion/G. Watelet, 1999; and **David**, *Lettres d'Egypte: Correspondance avec Louise Maspero, 1883–1914* (Paris: Seuil, 2003).

31 **W. M. F. Petrie**, *Seventy Years in Archaeology* (New York: H. Holt, 1932), esp. 21–38; **M. S. Drower**, *Flinders Petrie: A Life in Archaeology* (Madison: University of Wisconsin Press, 1985); **Drower**, *Letters from the Desert: The Correspondence of Flinders and Hilda Petrie* (Oxford: Aris and Phillips, 2004).

32 **S. Quirke**, *Hidden Hands: Egyptian Workforces in Petrie Excavation Archives, 1880–1924* (London: Duckworth, 2010); **M. Golia**, *Photography and Egypt* (London: Reaktion, 2010), 33–37; **W. Doyon**, "On Archaeological Labor in Modern Egypt," in *Histories of Egyptology: Interdisciplinary Measures,* ed. W. Carruthers (London: Routledge, 2014), 141–156.

33 W. M. F. **Petrie**, *The Pyramids and Temples of Gizeh* (London: Field and Tuer, 1883). A second, shorter edition was published in 1885. In 1990 Zahi Hawass added a Giza update as an appendix to this volume.

34 J. H. **Breasted**, *Egypt through the Stereoscope* (New York: Underwood and Underwood, 1905), esp. images 16–27. The stereography firm Underwood and Underwood produced the box set, and several reprints have since appeared, including online versions. See also J. **Abt**, *American Egyptologist: The Life of James Henry Breasted and the Creation of His Oriental Institute* (Chicago: University of Chicago Press, 2011), 84–91.

35 C. **Ziegler**, *Catalogue des steles, peintures et reliefs égyptiens de l'Ancien Empire* (Paris: Musée du Louvre, Département des Antiquités Égyptiennes, 1990), 187–189, cat. 29; P. D. **Manuelian**, *Slab Stelae of the Giza Necropolis* (New Haven: Peabody Museum of Natural History, Yale University, 2003), 58–62, pls. 11–12. We know that Ballard cleared mastaba G 2091 of Kapi in a "search for serdabs" in 1901–1902; **Reisner**, "A History of the Giza Necropolis," vol. 2 (unpublished), app. L, 142 (http://www.gizapyramids.org; search for UM3650) and 148 (http://www.gizapyramids.org; search for UM3656).

36 D. **Covington**, "Mastaba Mount Excavations," *Annale du Service des Antiquités de l'Egypte* 6 (1905): 193–218. For the inventory list allegedly from Covington's tomb, see E. **Brovarski**, "An Inventory List from 'Covington's Tomb' and Nomenclature for Furniture in the Old Kingdom," in *Studies in Honor of William Kelly Simpson*, ed. P. D. Manuelian, 2 vols. (Boston: Museum of Fine Arts, 1996), 1:117–155 (where it

is ascribed as more likely belonging to the stone mastaba nearby, dated to the Fourth Dynasty).

37 K. **Kromer**, *Nezlet Batran: Eine Mastaba aus dem Alten Reich bei Giseh (Ägypten). Österreichische Ausgrabungen 1981–1983* (Vienna: Österreichische Akademie der Wissenschaften, 1991).

38 For a plan of the excavations drawn by Covington and recently rediscovered, see G. **Martin**, "'Covington's Tomb' and Related Early Monuments at Giza," in *Etudes sur l'Ancien Empire et la nécropole des Saqqâra dédiées à Jean-Philippe Lauer*, ed. C. Berger and B. Mathieu (Montpellier: Université Paul Valéry), 279–288.

39 Ibid., 34–38.

40 **Reisner**, unpublished autobiographical statement, Harvard–MFA Expedition archives.

41 See **Reisner**, *A History of the Giza Necropolis* 1:23.

42 G. A. **Reisner**, "The Work of the Hearst Egyptian Expedition of the University of California in 1903–04," *Records of the Past* 4, pt. 5 (May 1905): 133–134.

43 P. D. **Manuelian**, "On the Early History of Giza: The 'Lost' Wadi Cemetery (Giza Archives Gleanings: III)," *Journal of Egyptian Archaeology* 95 (2009): 105–140.

44 A. **Spiekermann** and F. **Kampp-Seyfried**, *Ausgrabungen im Friedhof der Cheopspyramide von Georg Steindorff* (Leipzig: Ägyptisches Museum, 2003); G. **Steindorff** and U. **Hölscher**, *Die Mastabas westlich der Cheopspyramide*, ed. A. Grimm (Frankfurt am Main: Peter Lang, 1991).

45 H. **Kayser**, *Die Mastaba des Uhemka: Ein Grab in der Wüste* (Hannover: Fackelträger-Verlag, Schmidt-Küster GmbH, 1964). This was one of a total of five Giza

chapels sent to Europe by German and Austrian excavators.

46 For a summary of Steindorff's field seasons, see **Spiekermann** and **Kampp-Seyfried**, *Ausgrabungen im Friedhof der Cheopspyramide von Georg Steindorff*, 24–26.

47 **Mariette**, *Les mastabas de l'ancien empire*, 566–567, and **A. Mariette**, *Notice des principaux monuments exposés dans les galeries provisoires du Musée d'antiquités égyptiennes à Boulaq* (Paris: A. Franck, 1869), 286 (8); **I. Gamer-Wallert**, *Von Giza bis Tübingen: Die bewegte Geschichte der Mastaba G 5170* (Tübingen: Klöpfer & Meyer, 1998), 17, 18.

48 **I. Gamer-Wallert**, *Die Tübinger Mastaba: Eine altägyptische Opferkammer aus Giza* (Tübingen: Museum der Universität Tübingen, 2014); **E. Brunner-Traut**, *Die altägyptische Grabkammer Seschemnofers III. aus Gîsa*, 2nd ed. (Mainz am Rhein: Philipp von Zabern, 1995), 13–26.

49 **U. Hölscher**, *Das Grabdenkmal des Königs Chephren* (Leipzig: J. C. Hinrichs, 1912).

50 **S. Curto**, *Gli Scavi Italiani a el-Ghiza (1903)* (Rome: Centro per le Antichita e la Storia dell'Arte del Vicino Oriente, 1963); figs. 2–3 highlight plans of the Eastern and Western Cemeteries, including tombs excavated by the Italian mission.

51 For the history of German Egyptology during this era, both in Berlin and in Cairo, see **T. L. Gertzen**, *École de Berlin und "Goldenes Zeitalter" (1882–1914) der Ägyptologie als Wissenschaft: Das Lehrer-Schüler-Verhältnis von Ebers, Erman und Sethe* (Berlin: De Gruyter, 2013); **Gertzen**, *Jean Pierre Adolphe Erman und die Begründung der Ägyptologie als Wissenschaft* (Berlin: Hentrich & Hentrich, 2015); **S. Voss**, *Die Geschichte der Abteilung Kairo des DAI im Spannungsfeld deutscher politischer Interessen*, +, *Die Jahre 1881 bis 1929* (Rahden: Marie Leidorf, 2013), and **S. Bickel, H.-W. Fischer-Eifert, Antonio Loprieno**, and **S. Richter**, eds., *Ägyptologen und Ägyptologien zwischen Kaiserreich und Gründung der beiden deutschen Staaten . . .* (Berlin: Akademie Verlag, 2013).

52 **G. A. Reisner** and **William Stevenson Smith**, *A History of the Giza Necropolis*, vol. 2, *The Tomb of Hetep-Heres, the Mother of Cheops: A Study of Egyptian Civilization in the Old Kingdom* (Cambridge: Harvard University Press, 1955); **M. Lehner**, *The Pyramid Tomb of Hetep-heres and the Satellite Pyramid of Khufu* (Mainz: Philipp von Zabern, 1985); **M. Eaton-Krauss**, "Embalming Caches," *Journal of Egyptian Archaeology* 94 (2008): 292–293; **H.-H. Münch**, "Categorizing Archaeological Finds: The Funerary Material of Queen Hetepheres I at Giza," *Antiquity* 74 (2000): 898–908.

53 **C. S. Fisher**, *The Minor Cemetery at Giza* (Philadelphia: University Museum, 1924). Fisher's expedition worked from January 28 to March 9, 1915.

54 **D. Dunham** and **W. K. Simpson**, *The Mastaba of Queen Mersyankh III (G 7530–7540)* (Boston: Museum of Fine Arts, 1976); **A. Bolshakov**, "What Did the Bust of Ankh-haf Originally Look Like?" *Journal of the Museum of Fine Arts, Boston* 3 (1991): 4–14.

55 **H. Junker**, *Gîza*, vol. 1, *Die Mastabas der IV. Dynastie auf dem Westfriedhof* (Vienna: Hölder-Pichler-Tempsky, 1929), 153–157, pls. 18–23; **K. Lembke** and **B. Schmitz**, eds., *Giza: Am Fuß der großen Pyramiden*, exhibition catalogue (Hildesheim: Roemer- und Pelizaeus-Museum, 2011), 98, fig. 2, 108, fig. 5; **M. von**

Falck and **B. Schmitz**, *Das Alte Reich: Ägypten von den Anfängen zur Hochkultur* (Mainz: Philipp von Zabern, 2009), 56–57, cat. no. 5.

56 See **P. Jánosi**, *Österreich vor den Pyramiden: Die Grabungungen Hermann Junkers im Auftrag der Österreichischen Akademie der Wissenschafte in Wien bei der Grossen Pyramide in Giza* (Vienna: Österreichische Akademie der Wissenschaften, 1997), 62.

57 Seneb's chapel niche: Cairo JE 51297; family statue group: JE 51280; see **H. Junker**, *Gîza*, vol. 5, *Die Mastaba des Snb (Seneb) und die umliegenden Gräber* (Vienna: Hölder-Pichler-Tempsky, 1941), 3–128; **Saleh** and **Sourouzian**, *Cairo Museum Official Catalogue*, cat. no. 39.

58 **Selim Hassan**, *Excavations at Gîza*, vol. 1, *1929–1930* (Oxford: Oxford University Press, 1932), 1–61, esp. 18, fig. 13, pl. 18; **J. P. Allen**, "Reᶜ-wer's Accident," in *Studies in Pharaonic Religion and Society in Honour of J. G. Griffiths*, ed. Alan B. Lloyd (London: Egypt Exploration Society, 1992), 14–20; **N. Strudwick**, *Texts from the Pyramid Age* (Atlanta: Society of Biblical Literature, 2005), 305–306 (text 227).

59 **S. Hassan**, *Excavations at Gîza*, vol. 2, *1930–1931* (Cairo: Government Press, Bulâq, 1936), 190, fig. 219, pls. 74–75.

60 On Queen Khentkaus see **S. Hassan**, *Excavations at Gîza*, vol. 4, *1932–1933* (Cairo: Government Press, Bulâq, 1943), 1–62; on Debehen see ibid., 159–184; on the controversial "Galarza" mastaba of Queen Khamerernebty II, see **Hassan**, *Excavations at Gîza*, 1:8, 10; **Hassan**, *Excavations at Gîza*, vol. 3, *1931–1932* (Cairo: Government Press, Bulâq, 1941), 31; **Hassan**, *Excavations at Gîza*, 4:5, 10; **S. Hassan**, *Excavations at Gîza*, vol. 7,

1935–1936 (Cairo: Government Press, 1953), 13, 17; **S. Hassan**, *Excavations at Gîza*, vol. 9, *1936–37–38* (Cairo: Government Organisation for Government Printing Offices, 1960), 64; **B. S. Lesko**, "Queen Khamerernebty II and Her Sculpture," in *Ancient Egyptian and Mediterranean Studies in Memory of William A. Ward*, ed. L. H. Lesko (Providence: Department of Egyptology, Brown University, 1998), 149–162; **V. G. Callender** and **P. Jánosi**, "The Tomb of Queen Khamerernebty II at Giza: A Reassessment," *Mitteilungen des deutschen archäologischen Instituts, Abteilung Kairo* 53 (1997): 1–22; **Jánosi**, *Giza in der 4. Dynastie: Die Baugeschichte und Belegung einer Nekropole des Alten Reiches*, vol. 1, *Die Mastabas der Kernfriedhöfe und die Felsgräber* (Vienna: Österreichische Akademie der Wissenschaften, 2005), 306; on the Khufu Pyramid Temple see **Hassan**, *Excavations at Gîza*, vol. 9; on the Sphinx and associated later temples see **Hassan**, *Excavations at Gîza*, vol. 8, *1936–1937* (Cairo: Government Press, 1953); on the Sphinx Temple of Amenhotep II see **Hassan**, "The Great Limestone Stela of Amenhotep II," *Annales du Service des Antiquités de l'Egypte* 37 (1937): 129–134; **P. D. Manuelian**, *Studies in the Reign of Amenophis II* (Hildesheim: Gerstenberg Verlag, 1987), 181–188.

61 See "Bernard Bruyère's Archives (1879–1971)," http://www.ifao.egnet.net/bases/archives/bruyere/ (search term "Gizeh"). From a diary entry in the Harvard–MFA Expedition diaries (vol. 21, 774, dated October 16, 1927), it seems that Baraize was also working in the Central Field, for his small finds from the tomb of Rawer (G 8988) are listed.

62 **A. Fakhry**, *Sept tombeaux à l'est de la Grande Pyramide de Guizeh* (Cairo: Institut Français d'Archéologie Orientale, 1935).

63 **G. A. Reisner**, *Mycerinus: The Temples of the Third Pyramid at Giza* (Cambridge: Harvard University Press, 1931).

64 See **Reisner**, *A History of the Giza Necropolis,* vol. 1, loose-leaf maps at back of the volume; **H. Junker**, *Gîza,* vol. 12, *Schlußband mit Zusammenfassungen und Gesamt-Verzeichnissen von Band 1–12* (Vienna: Rudolf M. Rohrer, 1955), plans; **Hassan**, *Excavations at Gîza,* vol. 9, frontispiece foldout plan of the Central Field.

65 **Z. Hawass**, "The Discovery of the Osiris Shaft at Giza," in *The Archaeology and Art of Ancient Egypt: Essays in Honor of David B. O'Connor,* ed. Z. Hawass and J. Richards, vol. 1 (Cairo: Supreme Council of Antiquities, 2007), 379–397.

66 Originally found by Petrie in 1907, then reburied by Maspero, this tomb was later the subject of a Vienna doctoral dissertation by an Egyptian Egyptologist: **W. el-Sadeek**, *Twenty-sixth Dynasty Necropolis at Gizeh: An Analysis of the Tomb of Thery and Its Place in the Development of Saite Funerary Art and Architecture* (Universität Wien, 1984).

67 **U. Schweitzer**, "Archäologischer Bericht aus Ägypten," *Orientalia* 19 (1950): 118–119.

68 **A. M. Abu-Bakr**, *Excavations at Giza, 1949–1950* (Cairo: Government Press, 1953).

69 **G. Goyon**, "Les ports des pyramides et le Grand Canal de Memphis," *Revue d'Egyptologie* 23 (1971): 137–153.

70 **A. H. Abd el-'Al** and **A. Youssef**, "An Enigmatic Wooden Object Discovered beside the Southern Side of the Giza Second Pyramid," *Annales du Service des Antiquités de l'Egypte* 62 (1977): 103–120, pls. i–xv. See also **M. Lehner** and **P. Lacovara**, "An Enigmatic Object Explained," *Journal of Egyptian Archaeology* 71 (1985): 169–174.

71 **A. A. Saleh**, "Excavations around Mycerinus Pyramid Complex," *Mitteilungen des deutschen archäologischen Instituts Abteilung Kairo* 30 (1974): 137–154.

72 **K. Kromer**, *Siedlungsfunde aus dem frühen Alten Reich in Giseh: Österreichische Ausgrabungen, 1971–75* (Vienna: Österreichische Akademie der Wissenschaften, 1978). In 1981 Kromer returned to explore Tomb 3, south of Giza; see **K. Kromer**, *Nezlet Batran.*

73 **Dunham** and **Simpson**, *The Mastaba of Queen Mersyankh III.*

74 **W. K. Simpson**, *The Mastabas of Qar and Idu* (*G 7101 and G 7102*) (Boston: Museum of Fine Arts, 1976); **Simpson**, *The Mastabas of Kawab, Khafkhufu I and II: G 7110–20, 7130–40, and 7150, and Subsidiary Mastabas of Street G 7100* (Boston: Museum of Fine Arts, 1978); **Simpson**, *Mastabas of the Western Cemetery, Part I* (Boston: Museum of Fine Arts, 1980).

75 **A. Badawy**, *The Tombs of Iteti, Sekhem-ankh-Ptah and Kaemnofret at Giza* (Berkeley: University of California Press, 1976); **Badawy**, *The Tomb of Nyhetep-Ptah at Giza and the Tomb of 'Ankhm'ahor at Saqqara* (Berkeley: University of California Press, 1978).

76 **M. Lehner**, "Archaeology of an Image: The Great Sphinx of Giza" (PhD diss., Yale University, 1991). In 1987 a conference on Sphinx conservation took place in Cairo: **F. A. Esmael**, ed., *Proceedings of the First International Symposium on the Application of Modern Technology to Archaeological Explorations at the Giza*

Necropolis, Cairo, December 14–17, 1987 (Cairo: Egyptian Antiquities Organization Press, 1992). See also **K. Lal Gauri**, "Geologic Study of the Sphinx," *Newsletter of the American Research Center in Egypt* 127 (1984): 24–43; **Lal Gauri**, "Deterioration of the Stone of the Great Sphinx," *Newsletter of the American Research Center in Egypt* 114 (1981): 35–47.

77 See **M. Lehner** and **W. Wetterstrom**, *Giza Reports*, vol. 1, *The Giza Plateau Mapping Project: Project History, Survey, Ceramics, and the Main Street and Gallery Operations* (Boston: AERA, 2007), 53–94. For more on updates to the original Giza mapping work, see **Lehner**, "GPMP Full Circle," *Aeragram* 13, no. 1 (2012): 16–18.

78 **H. Messiha**, "The Valley Temple of Khufu (Cheops)," *Annales du Service des Antiquités de l'Egypte* 55 (1983): 9–18; **Z. Hawass**, "Recent Discoveries at Giza Plateau," in *Sesto Congresso Internazionale di Egittologia, Atti*, ed. **G. M. Zaccone** and **T. R. di Netro**, vol. 1 (Turin: International Association of Egyptologists, 1993), 241–242; **Hawass**, "The Discovery of the Harbors of Khufu and Khafre at Giza," in Berger and Mathieu, *Etudes sur l'Ancien Empire et la nécropole des Saqqâra*, 245–256; **Z. Hawass** and **A. Senussi**, *Old Kingdom Pottery from Giza* (Cairo: Supreme Council of Antiquities, 2008), 127–128; **Petrie**, *The Pyramids and Temples of Gizeh* (with appendix by Zahi Hawass); **A. M. Roth**, *A Cemetery of Palace Attendants* (Boston: Museum of Fine Arts, 2001); **Z. Hawass**, "The Excavation at Kafr el Gebel Season 1987–1988," in *The World of Ancient Egypt: Essays in Honor of Ahmed Abd el-Qader el-Sawi*, ed. K. Daoud and S. Abd el-Fatah (Cairo: Supreme Council of Antiquities, 2006), 121–145; **N. J. Conard** and **M. Lehner**,

"The 1988/1989 Excavation of Petrie's 'Workmen's Barracks' at Giza," *Journal of the American Research Center in Egypt* 38 (2001): 21–60 ("Lehner's Area C").

79 **Esmael**, *Proceedings of the First International Symposium on the Application of Modern Technology to Archaeological Explorations at the Giza Necropolis;* **T. Aigner**, *Geology and Geoarchaeology of the Egyptian Pyramids Plateau in Giza* (diploma thesis, University of Tübingen, 1982); **Aigner**, "A Pliocene Cliff-line around the Giza Pyramids Plateau, Egypt," *Palaeogeography, Palaeoclimatology, Palaeoecology* 42 (1983): 313–322; **Aigner**, "Zur Geologie und Geoarchäologie des Pyramidenplateaus von Giza, Ägypten," *Natur und Museum* 112 (1982): 377–388.

80 **M. Lehner**, "The Heit el-Ghurab Site Reveals a New Face: The Lost Port City of the Pyramids," *Aeragram* 14, no. 1 (Spring 2013): 2–7.

81 See **Lehner** and **Wetterstrom**, *Giza Reports*, vol. 1; **Lehner** et al., Giza Occasional Papers Series, and AERAgram newsletters. The AERA website is at www.aeraweb.org.

82 Hawass received his PhD in Egyptology from the University of Pennsylvania in 1987 and was appointed secretary general of the Egyptian Supreme Council of Antiquities in 2002.

83 Some sample publications include **Z. Hawass**, "The Tombs of the Pyramids Builders—The Tomb of the Artisan Petety and His Curse," in *Egypt, Israel, and the Ancient Mediterranean World: Studies in Honor of Donald B. Redford*, ed. G. N. Knoppers and A. Hirsch (Leiden: Brill, 2004), 21–39; **Hawass**, "The Workmen's Community at Giza," in *Haus und Palast im alten Ägypten: Internationales Symposium 8. bis 11. April 1992 in Kairo*, ed. M.

Bietak (Vienna: Österreichische Akademie der Wissenschaften 1996), 54–67; **Hawass**, *Mountains of the Pharaohs: The Untold Story of the Pyramid Builders* (New York: American University in Cairo Press, 2006), 157–176; **Hawass**, *Secrets from the Sand: My Search for Egypt's Past* (London: Thames & Hudson, 2003), 96–131.

84 **Z. Hawass**, "The Statue of the Dwarf *Prn(j)anx(w)* Discovered at Giza," *Mitteilungen des deutschen archäologischen Instituts Abteilung Kairo* 47 (1991): 157–162; **Hawass**, "Unique Statues at Giza V: The Exceptional Statue of the Priest Kai and His Family," in *Studies in Honor of Ali Radwan*, ed. K. Daoud, S. Bedier, and S. Abd el-Fatah (Cairo: Supreme Council of Antiquities, 2005), 25–38; **Hawass**, "The Discovery of the Satellite Pyramid of Khufu (GI-d)," in Manuelian, *Studies in Honor of William Kelly Simpson*, 1:379–398; **Hawass**, "The Discovery of the Pyramidion of the Satellite Pyramid of Khufu [GID], with an Appendix by Josef Dorner," in *Iubilate Conlegae: Studies in Memory of Abdel Aziz Sadek*, pt. 1, *Varia Aegyptiaca*, ed. C. C. Van Siclen III, 10, nos. 2–3 (1995): 105–124; **Hawass**, "The Discovery of a Pair-Statue Near the Pyramid of Menkaure at Giza," *Mitteilungen des deutschen archäologischen Instituts Abteilung Kairo* 53 (1997): 289–293; **Hawass**, "The Discovery of the Osiris Shaft at Giza," in Hawass and Richards, *The Archaeology and Art of Ancient Egypt*, 1:379–397; **Hawass**, *Secrets from the Sand*, 69–73.

85 **Z. Hawass** et al., "First Report: Video Survey of the Southern Shaft of the Queen's Chamber in the Great Pyramid," *Annales du Service des Antiquités de l'Egypte* 84 (2010): 203–216.

86 **G. Steindorff** and **U. Hölscher**, *Die Mastabas westlich der Cheopspyramide*, ed. Alfred Grimm (Frankfurt am Main: P. Lang, 1991); reviewed by **P. Jánosi**, *Wiener Zeitschrift für die Kunde des Morgenlands* 83 (1993): 255–259.

87 **N. Kanawati**, *Tombs at Giza*, vol. 1, *Kaiemankh (G 4561) and Seshemnefer I (G 4940)* (Warminster, UK: Aris and Phillips, 2001); **Kanawati**, *Tombs at Giza*, vol. 2. *Seshathetep/Heti (G 5150), Nesutnefer (G 4970) and Seshemnefer II (G 5080)* (Warminster, UK: Aris and Phillips, 2002).

88 **G. Dreyer**, "Im Schatten der Pyramiden: Beamtengräber im Chephren 'Quarry-Cemetery' (Giza)," in *Begegnung mit der Vergangenheit—100 Jahre in Ägypten: Deutsches Archäologishes Institut Kairo, 1907–2007*, ed. G. Dreyer and D. Polz (Mainz: Philipp von Zabern, 2007), 114–119.

89 **S. Phillips**, "Two Enigmatic Circular Mud Brick Structures in the Western Field at Giza: A Preliminary Report," in *The Old Kingdom Art and Archaeology: Proceedings of the Conference Held in Prague, May 31–June 4, 2004*, ed. Miroslav Bárta (Prague: Publishing House of the Academy of Sciences of the Czech Republic, 2006), 239–258. See also **E. Brovarski** et al., "Preliminary Report on the Fifth Field Season of the Cairo University–Brown University Expedition at Giza, 2005," *Annales du Service des Antiquités de l'Egypte* 80 (2006): 221–227.

90 **E. Kormysheva**, **S. Malykh**, and **S. Vetokhov**, *Giza Eastern Necropolis*, vol. 1, *The Tomb of Khafraankh*; vol. 2, *The Minor Cemetery to the East from the Tomb G7948*; vol. 3 (with M. Lebedev), *Tombs of Tjenty II, Khufuhotep, and Anonymous Tombs GE 17, GE 18, GE 47, GE 48, and GE 49* (Moscow: Institute of Oriental

Studies, Russian Academy of Sciences, 2010, 2012, 2015).

91 A. M. **Roth**, "In Reisner's Footsteps: Three Seasons' Work in the Western Cemetery at Giza," *Annales du Service des Antiquités de l'Egypte,* forthcoming; D. M. **Mulhern**, "A Probable Case of Gigantism in a Fifth Dynasty Skeleton from the Western Cemetery at Giza, Egypt," *International Journal of Osteoarchaeology* 15, no. 4 (2005): 261–275. Additional Egyptian Supreme Council of Antiquities excavations by Wahiba Saleh in the 1990s revealed mastabas off the northwest corner of the Khentkaus pyramid.

92 Some examples of recent exhibition catalogues include Metropolitan Museum of Art, *Egyptian Art in the Age of the Pyramids,* exhibition catalogue (New York: Metropolitan Museum of Art, 1999); **Y. Markowitz, J. L. Haynes,** and **R. E. Freed,** *Egypt in the Age of the Pyramids: Highlights from the Harvard University Museum of Fine Arts, Boston, Expedition* (Boston: Museum of Fine Arts, 2002); **K. Lembke** and **B. Schmitz,** *Giza: Am Fuß der großen Pyramiden. Katalog zur Sonderausstellung* (Hildesheim: Hirmer Verlag, 2011); and **S. Haag, R. Hölzl,** and **P. Jánosi,** eds., *Im Schatten der Pyramiden. Die österreichischen Grabungen in Giza (1912–1929)* (Vienna: Kunsthistorisches Museum, 2013).

93 For some recent attempts at synthesis, expanding beyond Giza to other Old Kingdom sites, see **S. Verma,** *Cultural Expression in the Old Kingdom Elite Tomb* (Oxford: Archaeopress, 2014); **J. Swinton,** *Dating the Tombs of the Egyptian Old Kingdom* (Oxford: Archaeopress, 2014).

94 Candidates for identification with the Sphinx include Khafre: **M. Lehner,** "The Sphinx," in *The Treasures of the Pyramids,* ed. Z. Hawass (Vercelli: White Star, 2003), 176–177; **Lehner,** "Unfinished Business: The Great Sphinx. Why It Is Most Probable That Khafre Created the Sphinx," *Aeragram* 5, no. 2 (2002): 10–14; Khufu: R. **Stadelmann,** "The Great Sphinx—A Puzzle Is Solved," in *Egypt: The World of the Pharaohs,* ed. R. Schulz and M. Seidel (Cologne: Könemann, 1998), 73–75; Djedefre: V. Dobrev, cited in **M. Verner,** *The Pyramids: The Mystery, Culture, and Science of Egypt's Great Monuments* (New York: Grove Press, 2001), 236; and even individuals predating the rise of the Egyptian state altogether. For some controversial discussions of Giza individuals, see **R. Stadelmann,** "Khaefkhufu = Chephren: Beiträge zur Geschichte der 4. Dynastie," *Studien zur altägyptischen Kultur* 11 (1984), 165–172; **Stadelmann,** "The Prince Kawab, Oldest Son of Khufu," in *Offerings to the Discerning Eye: An Egyptological Medley in Honor of Jack A. Josephson,* ed. S. D'Auria (Leiden: Brill, 2010), 295–299.

Window 2.1
Napoleon in Egypt

1 For recent investigations into the Napoleonic expedition, see **N. Burleigh**, *Mirage: Napoleon's Scientists and the Unveiling of Egypt* (New York: Harper, 2007), and **P. Strathern**, *Napoleon in Egypt* (New York: Bantam Books, 2007).

2 **R. B. Parkinson**, *Cracking Codes: The Rosetta Stone and Decipherment* (Berkeley: University of California Press, 1999); **L. Adkins** and **R. Adkins**, *The Keys to Egypt: The Race to Read the Hieroglyphs* (London: HarperCollins, 2000).

3 Commission des Sciences et Arts d'Égypte, France, *Description de l'Égypte, ou, Recueil des observations et des recherches qui ont été faites en Egypte pendant l'éxpédition de l'armée française, publié par les ordres de Sa Majesté l'empereur Napoléon le Grand*, vol. 5 (Paris: Imprimerie Impériale, 1822–1823), pls. 6–18, http://descegy.bibalex.org/index1.html.

Window 2.2
Thutmose IV

1 Louvre B 18, B 19. For Salt's drawings of these monuments, along with the Dream Stela, see **P. Usick** and **D. Manley**, *The Sphinx Revealed: A Forgotten Record of Pioneering Excavations* (London: British Museum, 2007), 40 (sketch 36), 41 (sketches 36a, 37), 49 (sketch 53), 50 (sketch 54). See also **A. Piankoff**, "Two Reliefs in the Louvre Representing the Giza Sphinx," *Journal of Egyptian Archaeology* 18 (1932): 155–158.

Window 2.3
Karl Richard Lepsius

1 Merib's tomb received the number L 24 (later G 2100-I); **P. D. Manuelian**, *Mastabas of Nucleus Cemetery G 2100* (Boston: Museum of Fine Arts, 2009), 69–115; **O. Zorn** and **D. Bisping-Isermann**, *Die Opferkammern im Neuen Museum Berlin* (Berlin: Verlag Michael Haase, 2011).

2 Based on these illustrations, later published as plates 19–22 of the second volume of **Lepsius**'s *Denkmaeler aus Aegypten und Aethiopien nach den Zeichnungen der von Seiner Majestät dem Koenige von Preussen Friedrich Wilhelm IV . . .* , 12 vols. (Berlin: Nicolai, 1849–1856), a full-scale, painted plaster reproduction of the four chapel walls was produced in Berlin between 1982 and 1984 and exhibited in the Bode Museum for many years; see **K.-H. Priese**, *Die Opferkammer des Merib* (Berlin: Ägyptisches Museum, 1984).

3 **G. A. Reisner**, *A History of the Giza Necropolis*, vol. 1 (Cambridge: Harvard University Press, 1942), 419–421; **H. Junker**, *Gîza*, vol. 2, *Die Mastabas der beginnenden V. Dynastie auf dem Westfriedhof* (Vienna & Leipzig: Hölder-Pichler-Tempsky, 1934), 121–135; **Zorn** and **Bisping-Isermann**, *Die Opferkammern im Neuen Museum Berlin*; Manuelian, *Mastabas of Nucleus Cemetery G 2100*, 69–115.

4 **K. R. Weeks**, *Mastabas of Cemetery G 6000* (Boston: Museum of Fine Arts, 1994), pls. 3–5 (G 6010, chamber 2; Berlin, Inv. Nr. 1114). This tomb lies southwest of that of Merib, likewise in the Western Cemetery.

Window 2.4
George Reisner

1. **Manuelian**, *Mastabas of Nucleus Cemetery G 2100*, 429–433.

2. **G. A. Reisner**, "The Dog Which Was Honored by the King of Upper and Lower Egypt," *Bulletin of the Museum of Fine Arts, Boston* 34, no. 206 (1936): 96–99; **O. Goldwasser**, *Prophets, Lovers and Giraffes: Wor(l)d Classification in Ancient Egypt* (Wiesbaden: Otto Harrassowitz, 2002), 93–94.

3. **M. Lehner**, "Shareholders: The Menkaure Valley Temple Occupation in Context," in *Towards a New History for the Egyptian Old Kingdom: Perspectives on the Pyramid Age. Papers from a Symposium at Harvard University, April 26, 2012*, ed. P. D. Manuelian and T. Schneider, Harvard Egyptological Studies 1 (Leiden: Brill, 2015), 227–314.

4. **G. A. Reisner**, *Mycerinus: The Temples of the Third Pyramid at Giza* (Cambridge: Harvard University Press, 1931), 108–129. Reconstructions of the Menkaure statue program continue: **F. Friedman**, "The Menkaure Dyad(s)," in *Egypt and Beyond: Essays Presented to Leonard H. Lesko upon His Retirement from the Wilbour Chair of Egyptology at Brown University, June 2005*, ed. S. E. Thompson and P. D. Manuelian, eds. (Providence, RI: Department of Egyptology and Ancient Western Asian Studies, Brown University, 2008), 109–144; **Friedman**, "Reading the Menkaure Triads, Part I," in *Palace and Temple, 5. Symposium zur ägyptischen Königsideologie I, Cambridge, July, 16th–17th, 2007*, ed. Rolf Gundlach and K. Spence (Wiesbaden: Harrassowitz Verlag, 2011), 23–55; **Friedman**, "Reading

the Menkaure Triads, Part II (Multi-directionality)," in *Old Kingdom, New Perspectives: Egyptian Art and Archaeology, 2750–2160 BC*, ed. N. Strudwick and H. Strudwick (Oxford: Oxbow Books, 2011), 93–114; **Friedman**, "Economic Implications of the Menkaure Triads," in Manuelian and Schneider, *Towards a New History for the Egyptian Old Kingdom*, 18–59.

Window 2.5
Hermann Junker

1. **R. Hölzl**, *Die Kultkammer des Ka-ni-nisut im Kunsthistorischen Museum Wien* (Vienna: Brandstätter, 2005).

Window 2.6
The Boats of Khufu

1. **M. Z. Nour, Z. Iskander, M. S. Osman, and A. Y. Moustafa**, *The Cheops Boats*, pt. 1 (Cairo: General Organization for Govt. Printing Offices, 1960); **A. M. Abu-Bakr and A. Y. Mustafa**, "The Funerary Boat of Khufu," in *Aufsätze zum 70. Geburtstag von Herbert Ricke* (Wiesbaden: F. Steiner Verlag, 1971), 1–16; **Z. Hawass**, "The Royal Boats at Giza," in *The Treasures of the Pyramids*, ed. Zahi Hawass (Vercelli: White Star, 2003), 164–171.

3. From Stone to Silicon: Translating the Medium

1 The author is preparing a biography of Reisner's life. See http://gizapyramids.org/static/html/reisnerbio.jsp; **P. D. Manuelian**, "George Andrew Reisner (1867–1942)—Ein Leben für die Archäologie," in *Giza: Am Fuß der großen Pyramiden. Katalog zur Sonderausstellung*, ed. K. Lembke and B. Schmitz, exhibition catalogue (Hildesheim: Roemer- und Pelizaeus-Museum, 2011), 28–35; **Manuelian**, "March 1912: A Month in the Life of American Egyptologist George A. Reisner," *KMT* 7, no. 2 (1996): 60–75.

2 Nevertheless, Harvard Camp formed the seeds of the fledgling American Research Center in Egypt, founded on May 14, 1948; see http://www.arce.org/main/about/historyandmission.

3 Timothy Kendall, formerly MFA Egyptian Department associate curator, had overseen the microfilm conversion project for the expedition volumes, a resource that remains invaluable to this day.

4 I would like to thank here the many MFA museum associates for their tireless devotion to the Giza Archives Project over an entire decade: Jennie Lou Brockelman, Joan Cook, Anne Harper, Elaine Marquis, Nancy Riegel, and Evelyn Umlas. Additional MFA volunteers who devoted years to the work include Ruth Bigio, Steven Klitgord, Myron Seiden, Soisic Brill, Jessie Ring, Judy Donovan, Nancy Methelis, Elizabeth Rowe, and Louis Kamentsky.

5 **G. A. Reisner**, "Note on Objects Assigned to the Museum by the Egyptian Government," *Bulletin of the Museum of Fine Arts, Boston* 36, no. 214 (1938): 26–27, illustrated on p. 29, fig. 5.

6 **P. D. Manuelian**, "Digital Epigraphy: An Approach to Streamlining Egyptological Epigraphic Method," *Journal of the American Research Center in Egypt* 35 (1998): 97–113; **Manuelian**, "Digital Epigraphy at Giza," *Egyptian Archaeology* 17 (Autumn 2000): 25–27. For the Chicago House method, see **W. R. Johnson**, "The Epigraphic Survey and the 'Chicago Method,'" in *Picturing the Past: Imaging and Imagining the Ancient Middle East*, ed. J. Green, E. Teeter, and J. A. Larson (Chicago: Oriental Institute, University of Chicago, 2012), 31–38; and on epigraphy in general see **P. F. Dorman**, "Epigraphy and Recording," in *Egyptology Today*, ed. R. H. Wilkinson (Cambridge: Cambridge University Press, 2008), 77–97. For a recent manual detailing the digital conversion of the Chicago House method, see **K. Vértes**, *Digital Epigraphy* (Chicago: Epigraphic Survey, Oriental Institute, University of Chicago, 2014), http://oi.uchicago.edu/research/publications/misc/digital-epigraphy.

7 The following institutions in Europe joined the international Giza collaboration in 2006 and have since renewed their partnership with Harvard University: in Berlin, the Ägyptisches Museum and the Berlin-Brandenburgische Akademie der Wissenschaften; in Hildesheim, the Pelizaeus-Museum and the Stadtarchiv; in Leipzig, the Ägyptisches Museum, Universität; in Turin, the Ministero per i Beni e le Attività Culturali and the Museo Egizio; in Vienna, the Ägyptologisches Institut der Universität Wien, and the Kunsthistorisches Museum. Here in the United States, our partners included, in Berkeley, the Hearst Museum of Anthropology; and, in Philadelphia, the University of Penn-

sylvania Museum of Archaeology and Anthropology.

8   I thank my colleagues in Europe, the US, and Egypt for their kind assistance: Joan Knudsen (Berkeley), Stephan Seidlmayer (Berlin), Dietrich Wildung (Berlin), Wafaa el-Saddik (Cairo), Zahi Hawass (Cairo), Mansour Boraik (Giza), Mohamed Shiha (Giza), Katja Lembke (Hildesheim), Bettina Schmitz (Hildesheim), Regine Schulz (Hildesheim), Antje Spiekermann (Hildesheim), Hans-Werner Fischer-Elfert (Leipzig), Friederike Kampp-Seyfried (Leipzig and Berlin), David Silverman and Stephen Phillips (Philadelphia) Eleni Vassilika (Turin), Regina Hölzl (Vienna), and Peter Jánosi (Vienna).

9   The ABC-CLIO Online History Awards are offered biennially to developers of freely available and sustainable online history resources that are useful and innovative. The award is administered by the History Section of the Reference and User Services Association (RUSA) of the American Library Association (ALA). It is the first ALA award of its kind to acknowledge the importance of Internet-based historical resources.

10 The Society of American Archivists selected the Giza Archives as the winner of the 2010 Philip M. Hamer and Elizabeth Hamer Kegan Award (established in 1973) in recognition of its outstanding efforts in promoting the knowledge and use of collections. Erin Lawrimore, chair of the award committee and associate head and curator of the Special Collections Research Center, North Carolina State University Libraries, wrote: "The award committee expresses its high regard for your team's efforts to increase public awareness of your vast holdings of 20th century archaeological expedition records. Additionally, the website's creative display, visual search, and high resolution zoom features effectively use today's technology to provide insight into ancient Egyptian civilization during the Pyramid Age."

11 This award "honors visionary applications in computer technology promoting positive social, economic, and educational change."

12 **Juan Carlos Meno García**, "A New Old Kingdom Inscription from Giza (CGC 57163), and the Problem of sn-$\underline{d}t$ in Pharaonic Third Millennium Society," *Journal of Egyptian Archaeology* 93 (2007), http://www.gizapyramids.org/pdf_library/garcia_jea_93_2007.pdf.

13 **Stéphane Pasquali**, "Les fouilles de S. Hassan à Gîza en 1938 et le temple d'Osiris de Ro-Sétaou au Nouvel Empire," *Göttinger Miszellen* 216 (2008), http://www.gizapyramids.org/pdf_library/pasquali_gm_216_2008.pdf.

14 **May Farouk Mahmoud**, "GIS-based Study of Cemetery en Echelon" (PhD thesis, Freie Universität, Berlin, 2010), http://www.gizapyramids.org/pdf_library/farouk_cem_en_eschelon_diss.pdf.

15 **F. D. Friedman**, "The Menkaure Dyad(s)," in *Egypt and Beyond: Essays Presented to Leonard H. Lesko*, ed. S. E. Thompson and P. D. Manuelian (Providence, RI: Department of Egyptology and Ancient Western Asian Studies, Brown University, 2008), 109–144, http://www.gizapyramids.org/pdf_library/friedman_fs_lesko.pdf.

16 **Antje Spiekermann**, "Steindorff und Mastaba G 2005," in *Zur Zierde gereicht . . . : Festschrift Bettina Schmitz* (Hildesheim: Verlag Gebrüder Gerstenberg, 2008), 241–250, http://www.gizapyramids.org/pdf_library/spiekermann_fs_schmitz.pdf.

17 Available at Projekt Giza, http://www. giza-projekt.org.

18 **B. Stangl**, "Simulation of Interactive Virtual Spaces: Creating a Virtual Archaeological Model of the Queen Meresankh III Mastaba" (MA thesis, Technische Universität, Vienna, 2010), http://www.ub. tuwien.ac.at/dipl/2010/AC07808887.pdf.

19 **E. M. Pastore**, "Access to the Archives? Art Museum Websites and Online Archives in the Public Domain" (MA thesis, State University of New York, 2008).

20 **I. Kulitz** and **P. Ferschin**, "Archaeological Information Systems: Creating a Visual Index to Aid Architectural Reconstruction," in *Scientific Computing and Cultural Heritage: Contributions in Computational Humanities,* ed. H. G. Bock et al. (Berlin: Springer, 2012), 147–155. See also **Kulitz** and **Ferschin**, "Von der Grabung zur virtuellen Präsentation: Digitale visuelle Dokumentationsmethoden in der Archäologie," in *Im Schatten der Pyramiden: Die österreichischen Grabungen in Giza (1912–1929),* exhibition catalogue, ed. S. Haag, R. Hölzl, and P. Jánosi (Vienna: Kunsthistorisches Museum, 2013), 154–171.

21 "UCLA Encyclopedia of Egyptology," http://escholarship.org/uc/nelc_uee.

22 I am grateful to Dr. Zahi Hawass, at that time secretary general of the Supreme Council of Antiquities, for his assistance with this project, and to Mr. Hassan Diraz and his family for preserving the books for over sixty-five years. Mr. Mohamed Shiha and Mr. Mansour Boreik, then inspectors at the Giza Antiquities Inspectorate, were instrumental in locating Mr. Diraz on my behalf. I also thank Lauren Thomas, Ramadan Hussein, Catherine Pate, Christine End, David Pendlebury, and Sara Wald-heim for their contributions (logistical, translational, and financial).

23 **P. D. Manuelian**, "Giza 3D: Digital Archaeology and Scholarly Access to the Giza Pyramids. The Giza Project at Harvard University," *Digital Heritage 2013,* papers from the Digital Heritage International Conference, Marseille (October 28–November 1, 2013), 727–734, https://www.academia.edu/7572994/_Giza_3D_Digital_Archaeology_and_Scholarly_Access_to_the_Giza_Pyramids._The_Giza_Project_at_Harvard_University_; **Manuelian**, "Eight Years at the Giza Archives Project: Past Experiences and Future Plans for the Giza Digital Archive," *Egyptian and Egyptological Archives and Libraries* 1 (2009): 139–148.

24 **S. D. Gillespie** and **M. Volk**, "A 3d Model of Complex A, La Venta, Mexico," *Digital Applications in Archaeology and Cultural Heritage* 1, nos. 3–4 (2014): 72–81.

25 I wish to thank in particular Jeff Steward, who, in his role as MFA database programmer–analyst, solved countless problems for us with plug-ins, customization, and other adjustments tailored to the needs of our data. He is currently director of Digital Infrastructure and Emerging Technology at the Harvard Art Museums. I am also indebted to Linda Pulliam (now retired) and Kenneth Leibe of the MFA's Conservation and Collections Management Department.

4. Giza 3D:
The Real-Time Immersive Experience

1 **Dassault Systèmes**, http://www.3ds.com.

2 **J. Drucker**, *Graphesis: Visual Forms of Knowledge Production* (Cambridge: meta-LABprojects, Harvard University Press, 2014), 65; emphasis in original.

3 For Schlumberger see http://slb.com; for the Schlumberger-Doll Research Center see http://www.slb.com/about/rd/research/sdr.aspx.

4 Among them were Richard Coates, Michael Oristaglio, Douglas Miller, Jakob Haldorsen, David Nichols, and James Martin, whom I thank for their interest in and support of our Giza work.

5 **M. Oristaglio, J. Haldorsen**, and **P. Englund**, "Ground-Penetrating Radar Surveys on the Giza Plateau," *Technical Program and Expanded Abstracts, Society of Exploration Geophysicists 75th Annual Meeting* (Houston: Society of Exploration Geophysicists, 2005), 1101–1104; see also **M. Oristaglio, J. Haldorsen**, and **P. Englund**, "Ground-Penetrating Imaging Radar on the Giza Plateau: Area Near Khafre's Causeway," report to Schor Foundation, October 2001.

6 Data sources for these images include ASTER DEM: NASA Land Processes Distributed Active Archive Center (LP DAAC); ASTER L1B; USGS/Earth Resources Observation and Science (EROS) Center, Sioux Falls, SD, 2001. Landsat satellite imagery: these data are distributed by the Land Processes Distributed Active Archive Center (LP DAAC), located at USGS/EROS, Sioux Falls, SD, http://lpdaac.usgs.gov. QuickBird imagery was by produced by DigitalGlobe's QuickBird satellite.

7 I am especially grateful to Mark Lehner for sharing his views during many visits to Harvard on the geomorphology of the Giza Plateau, the layout of the ancient harbors, and course of the Nile during the Old Kingdom. See **K. Lutley** and **J. Bunbury**, "The Nile on the Move," *Egyptian Archaeology* 32 (2008): 3–5, and **David Jeffreys**, "Archaeological Implications of the moving Nile," ibid., 6–7.

8 See **P. D. Manuelian**, *Mastabas of Nucleus Cemetery G 2100* (Boston: Museum of Fine Arts, 2009), 69–116, 367–414.

9 A poster for the exhibition can be found on the museum's website, http://www.rpmuseum.de/index.php?id=83.

10 The exhibition is described at http://oi.uchicago.edu/museum/special/picturing/.

11 **K.-H. Priese**, *Die Opferkammer des Merib* (Berlin: Ägyptisches Museum, 1984), and **O. Zorn** and **D. Bisping-Isermann**, *Die Opferkammern im Neuen Museum Berlin* (Berlin: Verlag Michael Haase, 2011).

12 **R. Hölzl**, *Die Kultkammer des Ka-ni-nisut im Kunsthistorischen Museum Wien* (Vienna: Kunsthistorisches Museum, 2005).

13 The sarcophagus, HU–MFA Expedition field number 27-6-20, is in the Egyptian Museum, Cairo, JE 54935. The four canopic jars are in the MFA, 27.1551.1–4.

14 **M. Lehner**, "Unfinished Business: The Great Sphinx. Why It Is Most Probable That Khafre Created the Sphinx," *Aeragram* 5, no. 4 (2002): 10–14.

15 **G. A. Reisner**, *Mycerinus: The Temples of the Third Pyramid at Giza* (Cambridge: Harvard University Press, 1931).

16 **M. Lehner**, "Shareholders: The Menkaure Valley Temple Occupation in Context," in *Towards a New History for the Egyptian Old Kingdom: Perspectives on the Pyramid*

Age. Papers from a Symposium at Harvard University, April 26, 2012, ed. P. D. Manuelian and T. Schneider (Leiden: Brill, 2015), 227–314.

17 I am grateful to my colleague Florence Friedman for generously sharing preliminary results from her ongoing study of the Menkaure statuary program with our Giza Project. See **F. Friedman**, "The Menkaure Dyad(s)," in *Egypt and Beyond: Essays Presented to Leonard H. Lesko*, ed. S. E. Thompson and P. D. Manuelian (Providence, RI: Department of Egyptology and Ancient Western Asian Studies, Brown University, 2008), 109–144, http://www.gizapyramids.org/pdf_library/friedman_fs_lesko.pdf; **Friedman**, "Reading the Menkaure Triads, Part I," in *Palace and Temple: 5. Symposium zur ägyptischen Königsideologie I, Cambridge, July 16th–17th, 2007*, ed. R. Gundlach and K. Spence (Wiesbaden: Harrassowitz Verlag, 2011), 23–55; **Friedman**, "Reading the Menkaure Triads, Part II (Multi-directionality)," in *Old Kingdom, New Perspectives: Egyptian Art and Archaeology, 2750–2160 BC*, ed. N. Strudwick and H. Strudwick (Oxford: Oxbow Books, 2011), 93–114.

18 "Giza 3D Experience," http://www.youtube.com/watch?v=r46ADKia6l0. See also "Dassault Systèmes & MFA Boston: Giza 3D Preview," http://www.youtube.com/watch?v=0QY_Cxo9d88.

19 A website for this conference is at http://www.digitalheritage2013.org. See **P. D. Manuelian**, "Giza 3D: Digital Archaeology and Scholarly Access to the Giza Pyramids. The Giza Project at Harvard University," *Digital Heritage 2013*, papers from the Digital Heritage International Conference, Marseille (October 28–November 1, 2013), https://www.academia.edu/7572994/_Giza_3D_Digital_Archaeology_and_Scholarly_Access_to_the_Giza_Pyramids._The_Giza_Project_at_Harvard_University_.

20 A selection of presentations includes the annual meetings of the American Research Center in Egypt, Providence, RI, April 27–29, 2012 (R. Aronin, R. Gant, P. D. Manuelian, N. Picardo), http://www.arce.org/files/user/page157/2012_AM_booklet.pdf, and Portland, OR, April 4–6, 2013 (R. Aronin), http://www.arce.org/files/user/page157/2014_Abstract_Booklet.pdf; at South by Southwest Interactive, Austin, TX, March 8–17, 2013 (R. Gant), https://storify.com/Dassault3DS/live-from-sxswi.html; and at a National Museum Publishing Seminar, Boston, June 12–14, 2014 (P. D. Manuelian).

21 For their dedication to forging the 2013 HU–MFA collaboration agreement, I am grateful to Thomas Lentz, Peter Katz, Lori Gross, Laura Fisher, and Diana Sorensen on the Harvard side, and to Malcolm Rogers, Katie Getchell, Debra Lakind, and Rita E. Freed, Larry Berman, and Denise Doxey on the MFA side.

5. Case Studies:
Pyramid, Temple, Tomb, Statue, Human

1 **J. T. Schnapp** and **M. Battles**, *The Library beyond the Book* (Cambridge: Harvard University Press, 2014).

2 For just a few examples, see **L. Meskell**, "Electronic Egypt: The Shape of Archaeological Knowledge on the Net," *Antiquity* 71 (1997): 1073–1076; **P. S. Murgatroyd**, "Appropriate Levels of Detail in 3-D Visualisation: The House of the Surgeon,

Pompeii," *Internet Archaeology* 23, no. 3 (2008), http://intarch.ac.uk/journal/issue23/3/toc.html; **R. M. Van Dyke**, "Seeing the Past: Visual Media in Archaeology," *Visual Anthropologist* 108, no. 2 (2006): 370–384; **F. Remondino** and **S. Campana**, eds., *3D Recording and Modelling in Archaeology and Cultural Heritage Theory and Best Practices* (Oxford: BAR International, 2014); **S. Eve**, *Dead Men's Eyes: Embodied GIS, Mixed Reality and Landscape Archaeology* (Oxford: Archaeopress, 2014); **W. Wendrich**, "Visual Archaeology," in *Beyond the Horizon: Studies in Egyptian Art, Archaeology and History in Honour of Barry J. Kemp,* ed. S. Ikram and A. Dodson, vol. 2 (Cairo: Supreme Council of Antiquities, 2009), 583–603; **M. Llobera**, "Archaeological Visualization: Towards an Archaeological Information Science (AISc)," *Journal of Archaeological Method and Theory* 18, no. 3 (2011): 193–223; Llobera, "Life on a Pixel: Challenges in the Development of Digital Methods within an 'Interpretive' Landscape Archaeology Framework," *Journal of Archaeological Method and Theory* 19, no. 4 (2012): 495–509; **Llobera**, "Reconstructing Visual Landscapes," *World Archaeology* 39, no. 1 (2007): 51–69. See also the online journal *Digital Applications in Archaeology and Cultural Heritage,* edited by B. Frischer (http://www.journals.elsevier.com/digital-applications-in-archaeology-and-cultural-heritage/), and the series of international conferences called Cultural Heritage and New Technologies (http://www.chnt.at/program-2014/).

3 **J. Wittur**, *Computer-Generated 3D-Visualisations in Archaeology: Between Added Value and Deception* (Oxford: BAR International, 2013).

4 **S. James**, "Drawing Inferences: Visual Reconstructions in Theory and Practice," in *The Cultural Life of Images: Visual Representation in Archaeology,* ed. B. L. Molyneaux (London: Routledge, 1997), 25.

5 **J.-C. Golvin**, "Drawing Reconstruction Images of Ancient Sites," in *Picturing the Past: Imaging and Imagining the Ancient Middle East,* ed. J. Green, E. Teeter, and J. A. Larson (Chicago: Oriental Institute, University of Chicago, 2012), 80.

6 **M. Gillings**, "The Real, the Virtually Real, and the Hyperreal: The Role of VR in Archaeology," in *Envisioning the Past: Archaeology and the Image,* ed. Sam Smiles and Stephanie Moser (Malden, MA: Blackwell, 2005), 223–239. For a blatant attempt to demonstrate the "you are there" concept, see the time-lapse sequence of the Vesuvius eruption on August 24, 79 CE, from a single, fixed vantage point, created by Museum Victoria in Melbourne, at http://museumvictoria.com.au/education/learning-lab/ancient-roman-empire/recreation-of-vesuvius-erupting/.

7 **J. Drucker**, *Graphesis: Visual Forms of Knowledge Production* (Cambridge: meta-LABprojects, Harvard University Press, 2014), 7.

8 **James**, "Drawing Inferences," 34.

9 **S. Chattoo**, "Representing a Past: A Historical Analysis of How Gender Biases Influence the Interpretation of Archaeological Remains," *Constellations* 1, no. 1 (2009): 34–58.

10 Unintended or extended uses, beyond what the originators conceived, will also play a role in the evolution of virtual reconstructions.

11 **James**, "Drawing Inferences," esp. 23.

12 **D. H. Sanders**, "A Brief History of Virtual Heritage," in *Picturing the Past: Imaging*

and Imagining the Ancient Middle East,
ed. J. Green, E. Teeter, and J. A. Larson
(Chicago: Oriental Institute, University of
Chicago, 2012), 95.

13 Ancient Egyptian Architecture Online,
http://dai.aegaron.ucla.edu.

14 Digital Karnak, http://dlib.etc.ucla.edu/
projects/Karnak/.

15 **James**, "Drawing Inferences," 24–25.

16 **Gillings**, "The Real, the Virtually Real,
and the Hyperreal," 224; emphasis in original.

17 Ibid., 228–230.

18 **L. Daston** and **P. Galison**, *Objectivity*
(New York: Zone Books, 2007).

19 **W. R. Johnson**, "The Epigraphic Survey
and the 'Chicago Method,'" in Green et al.,
Picturing the Past, 31–38; **P. D. Manue-
lian**, "Digital Epigraphy: An Approach to
Streamlining Egyptological Epigraphic
Method," *Journal of the American Research
Center in Egypt* 35 (1998): 97–113.

20 **Gillings**, "The Real, the Virtually Real,
and the Hyperreal," 234–236.

21 **Wittur**, *Computer-Generated 3D-Visuali-
sations in Archaeology*, 253–257.

22 For a spectacular example of photorealistic
modeling that "estimates spatially-varying
surface reflectance of a complex scene
observed under natural illumination conditions," see "Unlighting the Parthenon," a
2004 Siggraph presentation by **C. Tchou**,
J. Stumpfel, **P. Einarsson**, **M. Fajardo**,
and **P. Debevec**, available at http://gl.ict.
usc.edu/Research/reflectance/.

23 After **D. Dunham**, *The Egyptian Department and Its Excavations* (Boston: Museum of Fine Arts, 1958), 49, figs. 31–32.

24 **H. Messiha**, "The Valley Temple of Khufu
(Cheops)," *Annales du Service des An-
tiquités de l'Egypte* 55 (1983): 9–18; **Z.
Hawass**, "The Discovery of the Harbors of

Khufu and Khafre at Giza," in *Etudes sur
l'Ancien Empire et la nécropole de Saqqâra
dédiées à Jean-Philippe Lauer*, ed. C. Berger and B. Mathieu (Montpellier: Université Paul Valéry, 1997), 245–256; **Z. Hawass** and **A. Senussi**, *Old Kingdom Pottery
from Giza* (Cairo: SCA Press, 2008),
127–128, pls. 40–55.

25 **H. Goedicke**, *Re-used Blocks from the
Pyramid of Amenemhet I at Lisht* (New
York: Metropolitan Museum of Art, 1971).

26 See, for example, **M. Seidel**, *Die könig-
lichen Statuengruppen*, vol. 1, *Die Denk-
mäler vom Alten Reich bis zum Ende der
18. Dynastie* (Hildesheim: Gerstenberg
Verlag, 1996).

27 **U. Hölscher**, *Das Grabdenkmal des Königs
Chephren* (Leipzig: J. C. Hinrichs, 1912),
15, fig. 5, 16–17, pls. III, VIII, XVII.

28 **E. A. Sullivan**, "Visualizing the Size and
Movement of the Portable Festival Barks
at Karnak Temple," *British Museum Studies in Ancient Egypt and Sudan* 19 (2012):
1–37, http://www.britishmuseum.org/
research/publications/online_journals/
bmsaes/issue_19/sullivan.aspx.

29 **D. Dunham**, "An Experiment with an
Egyptian Portrait: Ankh-haf in Modern
Dress," *Bulletin of the Museum of Fine Arts
Boston* 41, no. 243 (1943): 10, http://www.
gizapyramids.org/static/pdf%20library/
bmfa_pdfs/bmfa41_1943_10.pdf.

30 **M. Lehner**, *The Complete Pyramids* (New
York: Thames and Hudson, 1997), 127,
believed the lion's body was too elongated
to be realistic.

31 Many AERA publications are available at
http://www.aeraweb.org/publications/.

32 **Hassan**, *Excavations at Giza*, vol. 4, *1932–
1933* (Cairo: Government Press, 1943); **V.
Maragioglio** and **C. Rinaldi**, *L'Architettu-
ra delle Piramidi Menfite*, vol. 6, *La Grande*

Fosse di Zauiet el-Aryan, la Piramidi di Micerino, il Mastabat Faraun, la Tomba di Khenkaus (Rapallo: Officine Grafiche Canessa, 1967); M. **Lehner**, "Shareholders: The Menkaure Valley Temple Occupation in Context," in *Towards a New History for the Egyptian Old Kingdom: Perspectives on the Pyramid Age. Papers from a Symposium at Harvard University, April 26, 2012,* ed. P. D. Manuelian and T. Schneider, Harvard Egyptological Studies 1 (Leiden: Brill, 2015), 227–314.

33 **Selim Hassan**, who excavated this area, called it the valley temple of Queen Khentkaus; see his *Excavations at Giza,* 4:51–62.

34 See **G. A. Reisner**, *Mycerinus: The Temples of the Third Pyramid at Giza* (Cambridge: Harvard University Press, 1931), 34–54, and **Lehner**, "Shareholders: The Menkaure Valley Temple Occupation in Context"; M. **Lehner**, M. **Kamel**, and A. **Tavares**, "The Khentkawes Town (KKT)," in *Giza Plateau Mapping Project Season 2008 Preliminary Report,* ed. M. Lehner, M. Kamel, and A. Tavares (Boston: Ancient Egypt Research Associates, 2009), 9–44; and M. **Lehner**, "KKT-AI: Between Khentkawes Town and the Menkaure Valley Temple," in *Giza Plateau Mapping Project Season 2009 Preliminary Report,* ed. M. Lehner (Boston: Ancient Egypt Research Associates, 2011), 53–92.

35 **Wittur**, *Computer-Generated 3D-Visualisations in Archaeology,* 255 (under 11.3).

36 **R. Breitner, J.-P. Houdin**, and **B. Brier**, "A Computer Simulation to Determine When the Beams in the King's Chamber of the Great Pyramid Cracked," *Journal of the American Research Center in Egypt* 48 (2012): 23–33.

37 My Giza Project colleague Rachel Aronin is currently preparing a study of Meresankh's window arrangement.

38 **G. A. Reisner**, *A History of the Giza Necropolis,* vol. 1 (Cambridge: Harvard University Press, 1942), 70–74.

39 **P. Jánosi**, *Giza in der 4. Dynastie: Die Baugeschichte und Belegung einer Nekropole des Alten Reiches,* vol. 1, *Die Mastabas der Kernfriedhöfe und die Felsgräber* (Vienna: Österreichische Akademie der Wissenschaften, 2005), esp. 92–93.

40 For a recent summary of Meresankh's chapel and its historical implications, see **V. G. Callender**, *In Hathor's Image,* vol. 1, *The Wives and Mothers of Egyptian Kings from Dynasties I–VI* (Prague: Charles University in Prague, 2011), 119–129.

41 **B. Frischer** and **J. Fillwalk**, "The Digital Hadrian's Villa Project: Using Virtual Worlds to Control Suspected Solar Alignments," *Proceedings of the Annual Conference of the International Society for Virtual Systems and Multimedia, 2–5 Sept. 2012* (Milan: IEEE, 2013), 49–55.

42 Giza 3D, http://giza3d.3ds.com/en-bonus.html?L=en; also available on YouTube: "Hetepheres Giza3D Full," http://www.youtube.com/watch?v=-yAibZvP6pY.

43 Giza 3D, http://giza3d.3ds.com/en-bonus2.html?L=en.

44 For a similar project concept, see Jeffrey Shaw's 3D display of the caves of Dunhuang, a joint project by the City University of Hong Kong's Applied Laboratory for Interactive Visualization and Embodiment (ALiVE) and the Dunhuang Academy and the Friends of Dunhuang Hong Kong; https://www.youtube.com/watch?v=BbU7LvPhLSE.

6. Where Can We Go from Here?

1 **L. Richardson**, "A Digital Public Archaeology?" *Papers from the Institute of Archaeology, University College, London* 23, no. 1 (2013): 8.

2 For one innovative online system, see Open Context, edited by S. Whitcher Kansa and E. Kansa (http://opencontext.org), which "reviews, edits, and publishes archaeological research data and archives data with university-backed repositories, including the California Digital Library." The National Science Foundation and the National Endowment for the Humanities refer to Open Context for archaeological data management.

3 We are extremely grateful to Mary Downs and Marc Ruppel, senior program officers of the Divisions of Preservation and Access and of Public Programs, respectively, at the National Endowment for the Humanities. My thanks also go to my colleagues at Harvard's Office of Sponsored Research: Susan Gomes, Samantha Schwartz, and Erin Cromack.

4 Google has recently released Street View images for a general walk around Giza, but they do not provide comprehensive access to the major cemeteries: http://www.google.com/maps/about/behind-the-scenes/streetview/treks/pyramids-of-giza.

5 EdX, https://www.edx.org; HarvardX, http://harvardx.harvard.edu; "Harvard University MOOCs," https://www.edx.org/school/harvardx.

6 **J. Drucker**, *Graphesis: Visual Forms of Knowledge Production* (Cambridge: meta-LABprojects, Harvard University Press, 2014), 194.

7 **G. A. Reisner** and **W. S. Smith**, *A History of the Giza Necropolis,* vol. 2, *The Tomb of Hetep-Heres, the Mother of Cheops: A Study of Egyptian Civilization in the Old Kingdom* (Cambridge: Harvard University Press, 1955), 28–32.

8 **W. H. Peck**, "Preserving the Past in Plaster," in *Picturing the Past: Imaging and Imagining the Ancient Middle East,* ed. J. Green, E. Teeter, and J. A. Larson (Chicago: Oriental Institute, University of Chicago, 2012), 71–75; **R. Frederiksen** and **E. Marchand**, eds., *Plaster Casts: Making, Collecting and Displaying from Classical Antiquity to the Present* (New York: De Gruyter, 2010); **H. G. H. von Gaertringen**, *Masterpieces of the Gipsformerei: Art Manufactory of the Staatliche Museen zu Berlin since 1819* (Berlin: Gipsformerei of the Staatliche Museen zu Berlin, 2012).

9 "Meet Watson: The Platform for Cognitive Business," http://www.ibm.com/smarterplanet/us/en/ibmwatson/.

10 I am grateful to Pierre Gable, Dassault Systèmes' Passion for Innovation Institute, for discussing these issues with me.

11 **Chuck Leddy**, "Linking Libraries, Museum, Archives," *Harvard Gazette,* April 10, 2012, http://news.harvard.edu/gazette/story/2012/04/linking-libraries-museums-archives/

12 The Grand Egyptian Museum is at http://www.gem.gov.eg.

13 **S. Eve**, *Dead Men's Eyes: Embodied GIS, Mixed Reality and Landscape Archaeology* (Oxford: Archaeopress, 2014).

14 Heritage, Innovation, Preservation Institute, www.hip.institute.

Linkography and Further Reading

Digital Projects

Giza Archives Project
http://www.gizapyramids.org.
At this writing, hundreds of Giza-related publications, including the Giza Mastabas Series and works by George Reisner, Hermann Junker, and Selim Hassan, are available for downloading at http://www.gizapyramids.org/static/html/authors_list.jsp. At this writing a new Giza website is in preparation at Harvard University.

Ancient Egypt Research Associates (AERA)
Publications are available at http://www.aeraweb.org/publications/.

Cultural Heritage and New Technologies
http://www.chnt.at/program-2014/.

The Gordion Archaeological Project, University of Pennsylvania
http://sites.museum.upenn.edu/gordion/.

Meketre: an online repository for Middle Kingdom Scenes
Institute of Egyptology and the research group Multimedia Information Systems at the University of Vienna,
http://www.meketre.org.

Open Access Antiquarianism
http://openaccessantiquarianism.wordpress.com.

Oxford Expedition to Egypt: Scene-details Database, Linacre College
http://archaeologydataservice.ac.uk/archives/view/oee_ahrc_2006/.

The Ur Digitization Project, the British Museum, and the University of Pennsylvania
http://www.britishmuseum.org/research/research_projects/all_current_projects/ur_project.aspx.

The Cuneiform Digital Library Initiative
A joint project of UCLA, Oxford University, and the Max Planck Institute for the History of Science, Berlin,
http://cdli.ucla.edu.

OsirisNet.net
This is a project to photograph tombs and mastabas,
http://osirisnet.net/e_centra.htm.

Giza 3D
A collaboration between Dassault Systèmes and the Giza Project, Harvard University (at present PC users only),
http://giza3d.3ds.com.

Projekt-Giza Pelizaeus-Museum, Hildesheim (Georg Steindorff excavations)
http://www.giza-projekt.org.

Museum of Fine Arts, Boston
Collections database,
http://www.mfa.org/collections.

Center for Documentation of Cultural and National Heritage
http://www.cultnat.org/General/Cultnat.aspx.

Eternal Egypt: The Giza Plateau
A collaboration between the Center for Documentation of Cultural and Natural Heritage (CULTNAT) and IBM,
http://www.eternalegypt.org.

NOVA's Egyptian website
The emphasis is on Giza,
http://www.pbs.org/wgbh/nova/egypt/.

Visualizing Giza
A digital collection of Giza's inspiration to
artists, explorers, engravers, and photographers,
1400–1923,
http://egypt.musicfilmbroth.com/
minishowcase/index.php.

Museums with Giza Collections

**Museum of Fine Arts, Boston:
Art of the Ancient World Collection**
http://www.mfa.org/node/9457.

The Egyptian Museum, Cairo
The largest and most important collection of
Egyptian antiquities in the world. The official
website is currently unavailable, but see
http://en.wikipedia.org/wiki/Egyptian_
Museum.

Kunsthistorisches Museum, Vienna
http://www.khm.at/en/visit/collections/
egyptian-and-near-eastern-collection/.

Pelizaeus-Museum, Hildesheim
http://www.rpmuseum.de/english/egypt.html.

**Phoebe A. Hearst Museum of Anthropology,
Berkeley, California**
http://hearstmuseum.berkeley.edu/collections/
ancient-egypt.

Ägyptisches Museum, Berlin
http://www.egyptian-museum-berlin.com/a01.
php?fs=0.5.

**Ägyptisches Museum—Gerog Steindorff—
der Universität Leipzig**
http://www.gko.uni-leipzig.de/aegyptisches-
museum/.

Museo Egizio, Turin
http://www.museoegizio.org.

**University of Pennsylvania Museum of
Archaeology and Anthropology**
http://www.penn.museum/about-our-
collections/egyptian-section.html.

Further Reading

**Bock, Hans Georg, Willi Jäger, and
Otmar Venjakob**, eds. *Scientific Computing
and Cultural Heritage: Contributions in
Mathematical and Computational Sciences,* vol.
3. Berlin: Springer-Verlag, 2013.

**Breitner, Richard, Jean-Pierre Houdin,
and Bob Brier**. "A Computer Simulation to
Determine When the Beams in the King's
Chamber of the Great Pyramid Cracked."
*Journal of the American Research Center in
Egypt* 48 (2012): 23–33.

Callender, Vivienne Gae. *In Hathor's Image,*
vol. 1, *The Wives and Mothers of Egyptian Kings
from Dynasties I–VI.* Prague: Charles University
in Prague, 2011.

Chattoo, Saliha. "Representing a Past: A
Historical Analysis of How Gender Biases
Influence the Interpretation of Archaeological
Remains." *Constellations* 1, no. 1 (2009): 34–58.

Corteggiani, Jean-Pierre. *The Great Pyramids.*
New York: Abrams, 2007.

Daston, Lorraine, and **Peter Galison.** *Objectivity.* New York: Zone Books, 2007.

Drucker, Johanna. *Graphesis: Visual Forms of Knowledge Production.* Cambridge: metaLABprojects, Harvard University Press, 2014.

Evans, Thomas, and **Patrick Daly,** eds. *Digital Archaeology: Bridging Method and Theory.* London: Routledge, 2006.

Eve, Stuart. *Dead Men's Eyes: Embodied GIS, Mixed Reality and Landscape Archaeology.* Oxford: Archaeopress, 2014.

Faniel, Ixchel, Eric Kansa, Sarah Whitcher Kansa, Julianna Barrera-Gomez, and Elizabeth Yakel. "The Challenges of Digging Data: A Study of Context in Archaeological Data Reuse." *2013 Proceedings of the 13th ACM/IEEE-CS Joint Conference on Digital Libraries,* 295–304. New York: Association for Computing Machinery, 2013.

Forte, Maurizio. "3D Archaeology: New Perspectives and Challenges—The Example of Çatalhöyük." *Journal of Eastern Mediterranean Archaeology and Heritage Studies* 2, no. 1 (2014): 1–29.

Frischer, Bernard, and **John Fillwalk.** "The Digital Hadrian's Villa Project: Using Virtual Worlds to Control Suspected Solar Alignments." In *Proceedings of the Annual Conference of the International Society for Virtual Systems and Multimedia, 2–5 Sept. 2012* (Milan: IEEE, 2013), 49–55.

Gillings, Mark. "The Real, the Virtually Real, and the Hyperreal: The Role of VR in Archaeology." In *Envisioning the Past: Archaeology and the Image,* 223–239. Edited by Sam Smiles and Stephanie Moser. Oxford: Blackwell, 2005.

Golvin, Jean-Claude. "Drawing Reconstruction Images of Ancient Sites." In *Picturing the Past: Imaging and Imagining the Ancient Middle East,* 77–82. Edited by Jack Green, Emily Teeter, and John A. Larson. Chicago: Oriental Institute, University of Chicago, 2012.

Green, Jack, Emily Teeter, and **John A. Larson,** eds. *Picturing the Past: Imaging and Imagining the Ancient Middle East.* Chicago: Oriental Institute, University of Chicago, 2012. Available at http://oi.uchicago.edu/research/publications/oimp/oimp-34-picturing-past-imaging-and-imagining-ancient-middle-east.

Grosman, Leore, Avshalom Karasik, Ortal Harush, and **Uzy Smilanksy.** "Archaeology in Three Dimensions: Computer-Based Methods in Archaeological Research." *Journal of Eastern Mediterranean Archaeology and Heritage Studies* 2, no. 1 (2014): 48–64.

Haag, Sabine, Regina Hölzl, and **Peter Jánosi,** eds. *Im Schatten der Pyramiden: Die Österreichischen Grabungen in Giza (1912–1929).* Exhibition catalogue. Vienna: Kunsthistorisches Museum, 2013.

Hawass, Zahi, ed. *The Treasures of the Pyramids.* Cairo: American University in Cairo Press, 2003.

Houston, Stephen D. "Telling It Slant: Imaginative Reconstructions of Classic Maya Life." In *Past Presented: Archaeological*

Illustration and the Ancient Americas, 387–411. Edited by Joanne Pillsbury. Washington, DC: Dumbarton Oaks Research Library and Collection, 2012.

Hu, Di. "Advancing Theory? Landscape Archaeology and Geographical Information Systems." *Papers from the Institute of Archaeology, University College, London* 21 (2011): 80–90.

James, Simon. "Drawing Inferences: Visual Reconstructions in Theory and Practice." In *The Cultural Life of Images: Visual Representation in Archaeology*, 22–48. Edited by B. L. Molyneaux. London: Routledge, 1997.

Jánosi, Peter. *Giza in der 4. Dynastie: Die Baugeschichte und Belegung einer Nekropole des Alten Reiches*, vol. 1, *Die Mastabas der Kernfriedhöfe und die Felsgräber*. Vienna: Österreichische Akademie der Wissenschaften, 2005.

Johnson, W. Raymond. "The Epigraphic Survey and the 'Chicago Method.'" In *Picturing the Past: Imaging and Imagining the Ancient Middle East*, 31–38. Edited by Jack Green, Emily Teeter, and John A. Larson. Chicago: Oriental Institute, University of Chicago, 2012.

Kansa, Eric. "Openness and Archaeology's Information Ecosystem." *World Archaeology* 44, no. 4 (2012): 498–520.

Kansa, Eric, Sarah Whitcher Kansa, and Benjamin Arbuckle. "Publishing and Pushing: Mixing Models for Communicating Research Data in Archaeology." *International Journal for Digital Curation* 9, no. 1 (2014). Available at http://alexandriaarchive.org/wp-content/uploads/2012/11/idcc14-Kansa-Kansa-Arbuckle-researchpaper-final.pdf.

Kulitz, Iman, and Peter Ferschin. "Archaeological Information Systems: Creating a Visual Index to Aid Architectural Reconstruction." In *Scientific Computing and Cultural Heritage: Contributions in Mathematical and Computational Sciences*, 3:147–155. Edited by Hans Georg Bock, Willi Jäger, and Otmar Venjakob. Berlin: Springer-Verlag, 2013.

Lehner, Mark. *The Complete Pyramids: Solving the Ancient Mysteries.* New York: Thames & Hudson, 1997.

Lembke, Katja, and Bettina Schmitz, eds. *Giza: Am Fuß der großen Pyramiden.* Exhibition catalogue. Hildesheim: Roemer- und Pelizaeus-Museum, 2011.

Llobera, Marcos. "Archaeological Visualization: Towards an Archaeological Information Science (AISc)." *Journal of Archaeological Method and Theory* 18, no. 3 (2011): 193–223.

———. "Life on a Pixel: Challenges in the Development of Digital Methods within an 'Interpretive' Landscape Archaeology Framework." *Journal of Archaeological Method and Theory* 19, no. 4 (December 2012): 495–509.

———. "Reconstructing Visual Landscapes." *World Archaeology* 39, no. 1 (2007): 51–69.

Loring, Edward. "Educational Images on the Web." In *Information Technology and Egyptology in 2008: Proceedings of the Meeting of the Computer Working Group of the International Association of Egyptologists (Informatique et Egyptologie), Vienna, 8–11 July 2008*, 45–48. Edited by Nigel Strudwick. Piscataway, NJ: Gorgias Press, 2008.

Manuelian, Peter Der. "Digital Epigraphy: An Approach to Streamlining Egyptological Epigraphic Method." *Journal of the American Research Center in Egypt* 35 (1998): 97–113.

——. "Digital Epigraphy at Giza." *Egyptian Archaeology* 17 (Autumn 2000): 25–27.

——. "Eight Years at the Giza Archives Project: Past Experiences and Future Plans for the Giza Digital Archive." *Egyptian and Egyptological Archives and Libraries* 1 (2009): 139–148.

——. "Giza 3D: Digital Archaeology and Scholarly Access to the Giza Pyramids. The Giza Project at Harvard University." *Digital Heritage 2013,* papers from the Digital Heritage International Conference, Marseille (Oct. 28–Nov. 1, 2013). Available at https://www.academia.edu/7572994/_Giza_3D_Digital_Archaeology_and_Scholarly_Access_to_the_Giza_Pyramids._The_Giza_Project_at_Harvard_University_.

——. "Harvard University–Boston Museum of Fine Arts Expedition Contributions to Old Kingdom History at Giza: Some Rights and Wrongs." In *Towards a New History for the Egyptian Old Kingdom: Perspectives on the Pyramid Age. Papers from a Symposium at Harvard University, April 26, 2012,* 315–336. Edited by Peter Der Manuelian and Thomas Schneider. Leiden: Brill, 2015.

——. "Virtual Pyramids—Real Research: The Giza Archives Project Goes Live Online." *KMT* 16, no. 3 (Fall 2005): 68–80.

Markowitz, Yvonne J., Joyce L. Haynes, and Rita E. Freed. *Egypt in the Age of the Pyramids: Highlights from the Harvard University Museum of Fine Arts, Boston, Expedition.* Boston: Museum of Fine Arts, 2002.

Matei, Sorin Adam, Eric Kansa, and Nicholas Rauh. "The Visible Past/Open Context Loosely Coupled Model for Digital Humanities Ubiquitous Collaboration and Publishing: Collaborating across Print, Mobile, and Online Media." *Spaces and Flows: An International Journal of Urban and ExtraUrban Studies* 1, no. 3 (2011): 33–48.

Meskell, Lynn. "Electronic Egypt: The Shape of Archaeological Knowledge on the Net." *Antiquity* 71 (1997): 1073–1076.

Metropolitan Museum of Art. *Egyptian Art in the Age of the Pyramids*. Exhibition catalogue. New York: Metropolitan Museum of Art, 1999.

Moser, Stephanie. "Archaeological Representation: The Visual Conventions for Constructing Knowledge about the Past." In *Archaeological Theory Today,* 262–283. Edited by Ian Hodder. Cambridge: Polity Press, 2001.

Murgatroyd, P. S. "Appropriate Levels of Detail in 3-D Visualisation: The House of the Surgeon, Pompeii." *Internet Archaeology* 23, no. 3 (2008). Available at http://intarch.ac.uk/journal/issue23/3/toc.html.

Reisner, George A. *A History of the Giza Necropolis,* vol. 1. Cambridge: Harvard University Press, 1942.

——. *Mycerinus: The Temples of the Third Pyramid at Giza*. Cambridge: Harvard University Press, 1931.

Reisner, George A., and William Stevenson Smith. *A History of the Giza Necropolis,* vol. 2, *The Tomb of Hetep-Heres, the Mother of Cheops: A Study of Egyptian Civilization in the Old Kingdom.* Cambridge: Harvard University Press, 1955.

Remondino, Fabio, and Stefano Campana, eds. *3D Recording and Modelling in Archaeology and Cultural Heritage Theory and Best Practices.* Oxford: BAR International, 2014.

Richardson, Lorna. "A Digital Public Archaeology?" *Papers from the Institute of Archaeology, University College, London* 23, no. 1 (2013): 1–12.

Rick, John. "Realizing the Illustration Potential of Digital Models and Images: Beyond Visualization." In *Past Presented: Archaeological Illustration and the Ancient Americas,* 413–446. Edited by Joanne Pillsbury. Washington, DC: Dumbarton Oaks Research Library and Collection, 2012.

Sanders, Donald H. "A Brief History of Virtual Heritage." In *Picturing the Past: Imaging and Imagining the Ancient Middle East,* 95–103. Edited by Jack Green, Emily Teeter, and John A. Larson. Chicago: Oriental Institute, University of Chicago, 2012.

———. "Virtual Heritage: Researching and Visualizing the Past in 3D." *Journal of Eastern Mediterranean Archaeology and Heritage Studies* 2, no. 1 (2014): 30–47.

Schnapp, Jeffrey T., and Matthew Battles. *The Library beyond the Book.* Cambridge: Harvard University Press, 2014.

Smiles, Sam, and Stephanie Moser, eds. *Envisioning the Past: Archaeology and the Image.* Malden, MA: Blackwell, 2005.

Sullivan, Elaine A. "Visualizing the Size and Movement of the Portable Festival Barks at Karnak Temple." *British Museum Studies in Ancient Egypt and Sudan* 19 (2012): 1–37. Available at http://www.britishmuseum.org/research/publications/online_journals/bmsaes/issue_19/sullivan.aspx.

Sullivan, Elaine, and Willeke Wendrich. "An Offering to Amun-Ra: Building a Virtual Reality Model of Karnak." In *Information Technology and Egyptology in 2008: Proceedings of the Meeting of the Computer Working Group of the International Association of Egyptologists (Informatique et Egyptologie), Vienna, 8–11 July 2008,* 109–128. Edited by Nigel Strudwick. Piscataway, NJ: Gorgias Press. 2008.

Van Dyke, Ruth M. "Seeing the Past: Visual Media in Archaeology." *Visual Anthropologist* 108, no. 2 (2006): 370–384.

Wendrich, Willeke. "Visual Archaeology." In *Beyond the Horizon: Studies in Egyptian Art, Archaeology and History in Honour of Barry J. Kemp,* 2:583–603. Edited by Salima Ikram and Aidan Dodson. Cairo: Supreme Council of Antiquities, 2009.

Wittur, Joyce. *Computer-Generated 3D-Visualisations in Archaeology: Between Added Value and Deception.* Oxford: BAR International, 2013.

Acknowledgments

As the long list below attests, a site as large as the Giza Pyramids, and an initiative as ambitious as the Giza Project, depends on the expertise, collaboration, and support of a wide variety of colleagues with an impressive array of skills. These individuals have my gratitude for making possible whatever success we have achieved. Unfortunately omitted from the list are the many hundreds of undergraduate and graduate students who have also contributed to the work since the year 2000.

I am grateful to Jeffrey Schnapp for his invitation to contribute to the metaLABprojects series, and to the staff at Harvard University Press for their expertise and patience. My Egyptological colleague Bob Brier kindly read through the manuscript and caught many an inelegant and unclear phrase, for which I thank him. For publishing collaboration over many years that resulted in thirty Egyptological monographs, I wish to acknowledge my friend and colleague Jonathan Sawyer, formerly of Henry N. Sawyer Printers, Charlestown. My Egyptological colleagues at the Museum of Fine Arts, Boston, over more than thirty years have also contributed, directly and indirectly, to the genesis and evolution of the Giza Project: William Kelly Simpson, Rita E. Freed, Edward Brovarski, Timothy Kendall, Peter Lacovara, Sue D'Auria, Yvonne J. Markowitz, Joyce L. Haynes, Catharine Roehrig, Lawrence Berman, and Denise Doxey. Institutions and individuals are acknowledged below, and I hope I might be forgiven for any inadvertent omissions.

Institutions
Harvard University
Andrew W. Mellon Foundation
Museum of Fine Arts, Boston

The Giza Project, Harvard University
Nicholas Picardo
Rachel Aronin
Jeremy Kisala
Rus Gant
David Hopkins

Harvard University Deans, Administrators, and Colleagues
Michael D. Smith
Diana Sorensen
Laura Fisher
Peter Katz
Thomas Lentz
Lori Gross
Mathilda van Es
Judson Harward
John Shaw
Andreas Plesch
Alexandre Tokovinine
Barbara Fash
William Fash
Linda Mishkin
Lawrence Stager
Peter Machinist

Giza Archives Project, Museum of Fine Arts, Boston

Egyptologists
Diane Flores
Heidi Saleh
Heather Evans
Christine End
Nicholas Picardo
Rachel Aronin
Jeremy Kisala
Ramadan Hussein

Project Archivist
Catherine Pate

Museum Associates
Judy Donovan
Jennie Lou Brockelman
Joan Cook
Kate Diamond
Elaine Marquis
Dorothy Robbins
Anne Harper
Evelyn Umlas
Nancy Riegel

Other Volunteers
Steven Klitgord
Myron Seiden
Ruth Bigio
Louis Kamentsky
Hayley Monroe
Joel Hoff
Soisic Brill
Harriet Heyman
Nancy Methelis
Jessie Ring
Elizabeth Rowe
Lisa Jobe Carmack
Doug Hall
Tarek M. Hussain

Colin Newton
Meghan Place
Barbara Tobey
Barbara Wilhelm
Anat Yakobi
Sara Zaia

Giza Interns
Amanda Pavlick
Jennifer Adler
Heather Roughton
Anne Austin
Marisa Coutts
Noémie Bonnet
Virginia Hunt
Rachael Robinson
Mina Gumrukcuoglu
Rebecca Mountain
Ariana Dunning
Meredith Fraser
Samantha Grantham
Francesca Tronchin
Brittany Perham
Elizabeth Stewart
Dalia Linssen
Kate Grossman
Rachel Mittelman
Laurel Darcy Hackley
Marisa Privitera
Francisco Robledo
Elise Ramsey
Rashmi Singhal
Loren Sparling
Pauline Stanton
Natalie Susmann
Kristen Vagliardo

Department of Art of the Ancient World, Museum of Fine Arts, Boston
Rita E. Freed
Lawrence Berman
Denise Doxey
Laura Gadbery

Project Administrators, Museum of Fine Arts, Boston
Malcolm Rogers
Katie Getchell
Nancy Allen (later Andrew W. Mellon Foundation)
Maureen Melton
Arthur Beale
Matthew Siegal
Linda Pulliam

Staff Assistance, Museum of Fine Arts, Boston
Jeff Steward
Kenneth Leibe
Kay Satomi
Emily Dean
Nicole Linderman
Debra Lakind
Jennifer Riley
Jonathan DelGaizo
Bob Wilson

Andrew W. Mellon Foundation
Angelica Zander Rudenstine
Donald Waters
Helen Cullyer

**Dassault Systèmes, Passion
for Innovation Institute
(and Partners)**
Mehdi Tayoubi
Karine Guilbert
Isabelle Estebe
Reichard Breitner
Nicolas Serikoff
Emmanuel Guerriero
Fabien Barati
Pierre Gable
Jean-Pierre Houdin

Gallery Systems, New York
Jay Hoffman
Kevin Arista (eMuseum)

**Ancient Egypt Research
Associates (AERA)**
Mark Lehner
Wilma Wetterstrom
John Nolan
Glen Dash (Dash
Foundation)
Joan Dash
Peggy Sanders
Ana Tavares
Rebekah Miracle
Camilla Mazzucato
David Goodman
Alexandra Witsell
Mohsen Kamel

Credits

1. The Giza Necropolis in Time and Space

1.1 Menkaure Pyramid Temple, room 29, looking northeast to the sunlit Khafre Pyramid. Jan. 7, 2004. Photo by author (PDM_00311).

1.2 Map of Egypt. Drawing by author.

1.3 Comparison views of the Western Cemetery, looking southeast toward the Great Pyramid. *Top:* 1905–1906. Photo by Albert M. Lythgoe (B772 = B7243). *Middle:* Apr. 4, 1936. Photo by Mohhamedani Ibrahim (A7558), both images courtesy of Museum of Fine Arts, Boston. *Bottom:* Jan. 19, 2011. Photo by author (PDM_DSC01287).

1.4 Aerial view of Giza, indicating direction of hypothetical walking tour. July 11, 2013. Image copyright Google Earth.

1.5 The Great Pyramid "restored." Courtesy of Giza Project, Harvard University, with contributions by Dassault Systèmes and Ancient Egypt Research Associates.

1.6 Aerial view of the Eastern Cemetery, looking southeast. Oct. 7, 2011. Courtesy of AirPano.com.

1.7 The Sphinx and associated temples, looking southwest. Oct. 7, 2011. Courtesy of AirPano.com.

1.8 Central Field quarry, looking west; some of the tops of the limestone bedrock surfaces are indicated in red. Oct. 7, 2011. Courtesy of AirPano.com, with author's additions.

1.9 Nighttime view of the Khafre Pyramid and Western Cemetery, looking southwest. Mar. 27, 2013. Photo courtesy of Vadim Makharov.

1.10 Aerial view of the Western Cemetery, looking northwest. Oct. 7, 2011. Courtesy of Air.Pano.com.

1.11 The Menkaure Pyramid complex, looking southwest. Oct. 7, 2011. Courtesy of Air-Pano.com.

2. Archaeological Explorations at Giza from 1800 to the Present

2.1 The buried Sphinx, looking east, 1886. Photo by Emil Brugsch. Courtesy of Ägyptisches Museum Berlin (Ph.P. 01098).

2.2 Aerial comparison views of the Central Field and beyond, looking southeast. *Top:* Sept. 13, 1913. Photo by Mohamed Shadduf (A1076P). *Middle:* May 28, 1938. Photo by Dahi Ahmed (A8030); both images HU–MFA Expedition, courtesy of Museum of Fine Arts, Boston. *Bottom:* Oct. 7, 2011. Courtesy of AirPano.com.

2.3 Cutaway section view of the Great Pyramid, showing the king's chamber and five relieving chambers above it. Courtesy of Dassault Systèmes.

2.4 Twenty-sixth Dynasty coffin from the Menkaure Pyramid. British Museum EA6647. *Left:* Courtesy of The Trustees of the British Museum. *Right:* from R. W. H. Vyse, *Operations Carried on at the Pyramids of Gizeh in 1837,* vol. 2 (London: J. Fraser, 1842), after p. 94.

2.5 Seated statue of Khafre (Egyptian Museum Cairo, Cairo JE 10062 = CD 14), in a painting by Joseph Lindon Smith; MFA 24.12. Photo by author.

2.6 Plan of the Giza Necropolis, from Prisse d'Avennes, *Histoire de l'art égyptien* (Paris, 1878).

2.7 *Left:* George Reisner at Giza, Apr. 11, 1927. Photo by Mustapha Abu el-Hamd (B6205, detail). HU–MFA Expedition, courtesy of Museum of Fine Arts, Boston. *Center, seated from left to right:* Selim Hassan,

Hermann Junker, and Georg Steindorff. Courtesy of CULTNAT, Cairo. *Right:* bust of Ernesto Schiaparelli, Egyptian Museum Turin. June 25, 2006. Photo by author (PDM_CIMG2265).

2.8 Giza concession divisions and modifications. Illustration by the author, with contributions by Dassault Systèmes, Ancient Egypt Research Associates, and the Giza Project, Harvard University.

2.9 *Top:* Hermann Junker's expedition at work on tomb G 5340, looking northwest (Junker stands on the tomb of Khufudinef-ankh in front), 1913–1914. Courtesy of Kunsthistorisches Museum Vienna (AE-OS_I_5785). *Bottom:* Cemetery G 5000, mastaba of Ptahshepses [I], serdab 1 (S 1), statues in situ, looking east (including, Hildesheim 2140, 2141, 2144, Cairo JE 43961, 43963, 43964, 43966, KHM Vienna ÄS 7499, 7500, 7508). 1913–1914. Courtesy Kunsthistorisches Museum Vienna (AEOS_I_5468).

2.10 Noel F. Wheeler excavating in the tomb of Hetepheres, G 7000 X, looking north. July 22, 1926. Photo by Mustapha Abu el-Hamd (A3992). HU–MFA Expedition, courtesy of Museum of Fine Arts, Boston.

2.11 Modern reconstructions of Hetepheres's furniture in the Museum of Fine Arts, Boston: canopy (38.873), headrest (29.1859), chair (38.957), curtain box (39.746), and bed (29.1858) (SC63207). Courtesy of Museum of Fine Arts, Boston.

2.12 The will of Wepemnefret, from G 8882. Painting by Joseph Lindon Smith, MFA 36.261. Photo by author.

2.13 Ancient Egypt Research Associates (AERA) 2012 excavations of the Silo Building Complex and the Fourth Dynasty Khentkaus I basin, with the pyramids of Menkaure, the tomb of Khentkawes I, and

the pyramid of Khafre in the background, looking northwest. Feb. 25, 2012. Photograph by Mark Lehner.

3. From Stone to Silicon: Translating the Medium

3.1 Large-format camera setup in the burial chamber of Hetepheres, G 7000 X. Dec. 5, 1926. Photo by Mustapha Abu el-Hamd (A4500). HU–MFA Expedition, courtesy of Museum of Fine Arts, Boston.

3.2 Then-and-now comparison of the north wall engaged statuary in room C of the chapel of Meresankh (G 7530-sub). *Top:* June 25, 1930. Photo by Mohammedani Ibrahim (A5640). HU–MFA Expedition, courtesy of Museum of Fine Arts, Boston. *Bottom:* Apr. 20, 1999. Photo by author (PDM_1999.019.24).

3.3 Then-and-now comparison of the sarcophagus of Akhethetep (G 7650), showing the disappearance of painted decoration. *Top:* Mar. 22, 1929. Photo by Mustapha Abu el-Hamd (A5084). HU–MFA Expedition, courtesy of Museum of Fine Arts, Boston. *Bottom:* Brooklyn Museum 48.110; Charles Edwin Wilbour Fund. Oct. 24, 2008. Courtesy of Brooklyn Museum of Art (CUR.48.110_erg2).

3.4 HU–MFA Expedition Object Register, vol. 25, p. 1190, handwritten by Hansmartin Handrick. Courtesy Museum of Fine Arts, Boston.

3.5 Jousting in the papyrus marsh, from the east wall of the chapel of Sekhemka (G 1029); painting by Norman de Garis Davies. Courtesy of Museum of Fine Arts, Boston.

3.6 Schematic diagram of data relationships used in the current Giza database structure. Concept by Jeff Steward with additions by Nicholas Picardo.

3.7 Statue of Khui-en-khufu (MFA 37.638) lying in G 2407, shaft D. Apr. 19, 1936. Photo by Mohammedani Ibrahim (B8651). HU–MFA Expedition, courtesy of Museum of Fine Arts, Boston.

3.8 HU–MFA Expedition Object Register, vol. 28, p. 1354. Courtesy of Museum of Fine Arts, Boston.

3.9 Harvard Camp studio photographs of the statue of Khui-en-khufu (MFA 37.638). Apr. 24, 1936. Photos by Mohammedani Ibrahim. HU–MFA Expedition, courtesy of Museum of Fine Arts, Boston (A7566 and A7567).

3.10 MFA studio photograph of the statue of Khui-en-khufu, MFA 37.638. Courtesy of Museum of Fine Arts, Boston (E7219CR-d1).

3.11 The Giza website amalgamated tomb record for G 2407.

3.12 The Giza website Visual Search page.

3.13 *Left:* QTVR camera rig in the chapel of Meresankh (G 7530-sub). Jan. 13, 2004. *Right:* the resulting panoramic image, before unwrapping by means of software. June 7, 2005. Photos by author (PDM_DSCN00060 and PDM_00772).

3.14 Digital epigraphy, showing the on-screen tracing process, from top to bottom; this example is from the chapel of Nefer (G 2110). Drawings by the author.

3.15 HU–MFA Expedition Arabic Diary, book 29, written by Duwy Mahmoud, p. 2341, with the description of tomb G 2407 (Khui-en-khufu). Courtesy of Museum of Fine Arts, Boston.

3.16 *Top:* some of the MFA museum associates and staff who contributed years of work to the Giza Archives Project. *Bottom:* MFA Deputy Director Katie Getchell addresses Giza Project staff, volunteers, and Art of the Ancient World curators at the project's final party, June 28, 2011. Photos by author.

4. Giza 3D:
The Real-Time Immersive Experience

4.1 A screenshot of the Giza website records totals as of February 1, 2016 (www.giza pyramids.org).

4.2 Topographic map of the Giza Plateau overlaid with the archaeological map produced by Ancient Egypt Research Associates showing potential flooding extent during the Fourth Dynasty. Courtesy of A. Laake, WesternGeco.

4.3 Aerial view render from the Giza Plateau model, with contributions by Ancient Egypt Research Associates, Rus Gant, and David Hopkins. Courtesy of Giza Project, Harvard University.

4.4 Sample casing stone types at Giza: G 4550, Jan.16, 2004. PDM_01249. G 2150, Aug. 1989. AAW253. G 2155, Mar. 11, 1993. PDM_1993002.09. G 2100-I, G 2100, Mar. 12, 1993. PDM_1993.029.10. G 7440, Jan. 11, 2004. PDM_00634. G 4000, Nov. 19, 1993. PDM_1993.099.16. Photos by author.

4.5 *Top:* Wireframe computer images for reconstructing the G 2100 family complex, looking northwest, based on original HU–MFA and German-Austrian Expedition plans and survey data. Courtesy of Dassault Systèmes, 2009. *Bottom:* the rendered computer model. Courtesy of Dassault Systèmes, 2009.

4.6 Sequence showing the computer modeling process, from an excavation photograph of

250

the burial chamber of G 2100 A to a wire-frame build, to the final, rendered image. *Top:* Jan. 5, 1936. Photo by Mohammedani Ibrahim. HU–MFA Expedition photograph, courtesy of Museum of Fine Arts, Boston (A7363). *Middle and bottom images:* courtesy of Dassault Systèmes.

4.7 A 3D reconstruction of G 2100 A, looking southeast, showing the portcullis stone in the shaft, corridor blocking, and burial chamber. Courtesy Dassault Systèmes.

4.8 A 3D reconstruction of the burial shaft arrangement for the G 2100 family complex, looking east toward the Khufu Pyramid. Courtesy of Dassault Systèmes.

4.9 The north wall of Meresankh's, chapel room A (G 7530-sub). *Top:* May 8, 1927. Photo by Mustapha Abu el-Hamd (A4676). HU–MFA Expedition, courtesy of Museum of Fine Arts, Boston. *Middle:* Apr. 20, 1999. Photo by Brian Snyder (AAW1223). *Bottom:* 3D model by David Hopkins and Rus Gant. Courtesy of Giza Project, Harvard University.

4.10 A 3D model of the chapel of Meresankh (G 7530-sub) with original excavators' plans and sections superimposed. Image by David Hopkins and Rus Gant. Courtesy of Giza Project, Harvard University.

4.11 *Top:* Harvard students study the 1925 appearance of the burial chamber of Hetepheres (G 7000 X). Apr. 1, 2013. Photo by author. *Bottom:* a 3D model of the same burial chamber. Courtesy of Giza Project, Harvard University, and Dassault Systèmes.

4.12 A 3D model of Hetepheres's furniture. Courtesy of Giza Project, Harvard University.

4.13 "Time-lapse" sequence of the excavation of the Menkaure Pyramid Temple, 1906–1907, taken from one-third of the

distance up the east face of the Menkaure Pyramid. HU–MFA Expedition, courtesy of Museum of Fine Arts, Boston.
1. Nov. 1906. Photo by George Reisner (A11P).
2. Jan. 5, 1907. Photo by Said Ahmed (A63).
3. Jan. 27, 1907. Photo by Said Ahmed (A87).
4. Mar. 8, 1907. Photo by Said Ahmed (A128).
5. Mar. 17, 1907. Photo by Said Ahmed (137).
6. May 18, 1907. Photo by Said Ahmed (A221).

4.14 Excavation of the Menkaure Valley Temple. *Top:* looking southeast. Feb. 9, 1910. Photo by Badawi Ahmed (A329). *Middle:* looking west. Feb. 15, 1910. Photo by Badawi Ahmed (A334). *Bottom:* looking north. Mar. 10, 1910. Photo by Bishari Mahfud (A354P). HU–MFA Expedition, courtesy of Museum of Fine Arts, Boston.

4.15 The Giza 3D website homepage. Courtesy of Dassault Systèmes.

4.16 Two screenshots from http://giza.3ds.com, one in 2D, one in 3D.

4.17 Giza 3D launch event at the Museum of Fine Arts, Boston, May 8, 2012. Photos by Dassault Systèmes and the author.

4.18 Selections from worldwide press coverage following the launch of the Giza 3D website, May–June 2012.

5. Case Studies: Pyramid, Temple, Tomb, Statue, Human

5.1 Khafre Valley Temple, north entrance; restored hieroglyphs are based on scant surviving traces (marked in red) and other contemporary monuments. *Top:* Jan. 17,

2011. Photo by author (PDM_DSC00189). *Bottom:* 3D model by David Hopkins and Rus Gant. Courtesy of Giza Project, Harvard University.

5.2   Three restoration options for the missing superstructure of the tomb of Qar (G 7101). Image by David Hopkins and Rus Gant. Courtesy of Giza Project, Harvard University.

5.3   *Left:* the chapel of Meresankh (G 7530-sub), east wall damage (top left) and restored (bottom left). Courtesy of Giza Project, Harvard University. *Right:* a translation of the boating scene into modern perspective by Suzanne E. Chapman.

5.4   Khufu Pyramid Temple. *Top:* Oct. 7, 2011. Courtesy of AirPano.com. *Bottom:* 3D model of the temple. Courtesy of Giza Project, Harvard University, and Dassault Systèmes.

5.5   *Top:* Discovery condition of the tomb of Hetepheres (G 7000 X). Feb. 5, 1926. Photo by Mohammedani Ibrahim (A3685). HU–MFA Expedition, courtesy of Museum of Fine Arts, Boston. *Middle:* painting by Joseph Lindon Smith. MFA 27.388. Photo by author. *Bottom:* 3D model, looking down the shaft into the burial chamber. Image by Rus Gant and David Hopkins, courtesy of Giza Project, Harvard University, and Dassault Systèmes.

5.6   *Top:* the old installation of the reproduction Hetepheres furniture in the Egyptian Museum, Cairo. Nov. 10, 1993. Photo by author (PDM_1993.067.35). *Middle:* the conservator Ahmed Youssef with Hetepheres's reconstructed curtain box and a copy, Harvard Camp, Giza. May 12, 1939. Photo by Mohammedani Ibrahim (A8233). HU–MFA Expedition, courtesy of Museum of Fine Arts, Boston. *Bottom:* a 3D model of the curtain box. Image by Rus Gant and

David Hopkins. Courtesy of Giza Project, Harvard University, and Dassault Systèmes.

5.7   *Top:* Hetepheres's bracelets on the floor of G 7000 X. July 29, 1926. Photo by Mustapha Abu el-Hamd (A4019). HU–MFA Expedition, courtesy of Museum of Fine Arts, Boston. *Middle left:* Hetepheres's bracelets in the Egyptian Museum, Cairo. Nov. 10, 1993. Photo by author (PDM_1993.067.37). *Middle right:* Hetepheres's bracelet at the Museum of Fine Arts, Boston (47.1700). Courtesy of Museum of Fine Arts, Boston (SC209057). *Bottom left and right:* 3D models of the bracelets. Courtesy of Giza Project, Harvard University, and Dassault Systèmes.

5.8   Aerial view of the Khafre Valley Temple *(left)* and Sphinx Temple, looking west. Oct. 7, 2011. Courtesy of AirPano.com.

5.9   Digital composite of the Khafre Valley Temple, looking west, showing statue emplacements and various statue sizes. Jan. 17, 2011. Photo by author (PDM_DSC00206). Digital composite by Rus Gant and David Hopkins, courtesy of Giza Project, Harvard University.

5.10 *Top:* aerial view of the Khafre Pyramid Temple, looking west. Oct. 7, 2011. Courtesy of AirPano.com. *Middle and bottom:* two versions of ritual boats, one too large and the other correctly sized for passage through the temple. 3D model by Rus Gant and David Hopkins, courtesy of Giza Project, Harvard University.

5.11 *Top:* a panoramic profile of the Sphinx. Jan. 17, 2011. Photo by author (PDM_DSC00239). *Bottom:* a digital composite with a lion skeleton (plus human skull) superimposed on the Sphinx for comparison of proportions. 3D model by Rus Gant and David Hopkins, courtesy of Giza Project, Harvard University.

5.12 A multiphase plan of the Menkaure Valley Temple, after Reisner, *Mycerinus* (Cambridge: Harvard University Press, 1931), plan VIII.

5.13 Preliminary views of the phasing of the Menkaure Valley Temple, numbered 1 (earlier) to 5 (later). 3D model by Rus Gant and David Hopkins, and Dassault Systèmes. Courtesy of Giza Project, Harvard University.

5.14 Two versions of the 3D Sphinx model, showing partial *(top)* and full *(bottom)* polychromy. Images by Rus Gant, David Hopkins, and Dassault Systèmes. Courtesy of Giza Project, Harvard University.

5.15 Exterior and interior 3D models of the chapel of Meresankh (G 7530-sub), showing the sunlight streaming through the window and illuminating the false door. 3D model by Rus Gant and David Hopkins. Courtesy of Giza Project, Harvard University.

5.16 The Menkaure Valley Temple, with different occupation phases color-coded (early to mid to late represented by violet, brown, and yellow). 3D model by Rus Gant, David Hopkins, and Nicholas Picardo. Courtesy of Giza Project, Harvard University.

5.17 A 3D model with a subterranean view of burial shafts (G 2100 complex). Image by Dassault Systèmes. Courtesy of Giza Project, Harvard University.

5.18 The Sphinx Temple with and without human figures. 3D model by Rus Gant and David Hopkins. Courtesy of Giza Project, Harvard University.

5.19 *Left:* avatars of George Reisner in the tombs of Kaninisut (G 2155, top) and Hetepheres (G 7000 X, bottom). 3D models by Dassault Systèmes, Rus Gant, and David Hopkins. Courtesy of Giza Project, Harvard University. *Right:* Reisner con-

verses with MFA director George Edgell at Harvard Camp, looking east. Feb. 26, 1938. Photo by Mohammedani Ibrahim (A7911), courtesy of Museum of Fine Arts, Boston.

5.20 A 3D model of a chair of Meresankh "released" from the wall decoration (from an online interactive educational video). 3D model by Rus Gant, David Hopkins, and Dassault Systèmes. Courtesy of Giza Project, Harvard University.

6. Where Can We Go from Here?

6.1 *Top:* slab stela of Ini (G 1235), Port Said Museum P4083 (JE37727). Apr. 15, 1999. Photo by Brian Snyder (AAW2072). *Middle:* Damaged glass plate negative showing the Menkaure Valley Temple and Khafre Pyramid, looking northwest. Feb. 28, 1910. Photo by Bishari Mahfud (A344). HU–MFA Expedition, courtesy of Museum of Fine Arts, Boston. *Bottom:* CD and jewel box.

6.2 *Top:* example of smartphone access to museum object information (the Menkaure dyad, MFA 11.1738, with Mansour Boraik in the background). Sept. 13, 2005. Photo by author. *Bottom:* smartphone access to on-site monuments, such as the Khufu Pyramid Temple, looking northwest. Apr. 20, 1999. Photo by author (PDM_1999.018.25).

6.3 Students study Giza in the Harvard University Visualization Center. Mar. 25 and Apr. 17, 2014. Photos by author.

6.4 The slab stela of Wepemnefret, from G 1201, Hearst Museum Berkeley 6-19825, lit for Reflectance Transformation Imaging (RTI). Aug. 22, 2012. Photos by Elizabeth Minor. Copyright Phoebe A. Hearst Museum of Anthropology and the Regents of the University of California (*top:* 6-19825_2012-08-22_14-07-09; *bottom:* 6-19825_2012-08-22_14-09-29).

6.5 Fragments of Hetepheres's chair in situ on the floor in G 7000 X. Mar. 10, 1926. Photo by Mustapha Abu el-Hamd (A3718). HU–MFA Expedition, courtesy of Museum of Fine Arts, Boston.

6.6. Chair B of Hetepheres, from fragments in G 7000 X. *Top:* three chair views (EG022087); *middle:* falcon drawing (EG022005); back decoration (EG022008). HU–MFA Expedition drawings. *Bottom:* 3D model views by David Hopkins and Rus Gant. Courtesy of Giza Project, Harvard University.

6.7 *Left:* wireframe polygon editing of engaged statuary in the chapel of Meresankh (G 7530-sub). *Right:* a 3D model superimposed over a Joseph Lindon Smith painting, MFA 28.481. Courtesy of Giza Project, Harvard University.

6.8 *Left:* Menkaure dyad, MFA 11.1738. Photo by author (PDM_IMG_7947). *Right:* an unsatisfactory 3D model created by hand editing.

6.9 *Top:* the replica of the Sphinx built in Hebei Province, China. © CHIEN-YU CHEN/epa/Corbis. *Bottom:* the actual Sphinx at Giza, looking southwest. Jan. 14, 2006. Photo by author (PDM_06094).

6.10 A 3D model of Harvard Camp, Giza. Image by Eli Gershenfeld, courtesy of Giza Project, Harvard University.

6.11 *Top:* a 3D model of the first Khufu boat. *Bottom:* a view of the Giza Plateau from the boat, sailing on the Nile. Courtesy of Dassault Systèmes and Giza Project, Harvard University.

6.12 Casing types, following Reisner's typology for Eastern Cemetery mastabas. Contri-

butions by Jeremy Kisala, Rus Gant, and David Hopkins; courtesy of Giza Project, Harvard University.

6.13 A 3D model of the Giza Plateau, looking west. Image by Rus Gant and David Hopkins, Giza Project, Harvard University, with contributions by Ancient Egypt Research Associates and Dassault Systèmes.

Windows in Chapter 2

W1.1. A popular print of the Battle of the Pyramids, 1830. British Museum 1999,0627.17. Courtesy of the Trustees of the British Museum.

W2.1. Chapel area between the paws of the Sphinx, looking west. Jan. 14, 2006. Photo by author (PDM_06058).

W3.1. Modern painting of the tomb of Merib (G 2100-I), chapel, west wall; after R. Lepsius, *Denkmaeler aus Aegypten und Aethiopien* (Berlin: Nicolai, 1849–1856), 2: pls. 19–20.

W3.2. The chapel of Merib (G 2100-I), reconstructed in the Neues Museum, Berlin; 2009. Courtesy Ägyptisches Museum, Berlin.

W4.1. G 2220 b 1, mummy (wrappings 33–4–22) in wood coffin (33–4–21 = MFA 33.1016), looking south. Jan. 19, 1933. Photo by Dahi Ahmed, (A7041). HU–MFA Expedition, courtesy Museum of Fine Arts, Boston.

W4.2. Object groups from Giza. *Top left:* miniature copper items from the tomb of Impy (G 2381) (CR2275-d1); *top right: pesesh-kef* ritual implement set (E1920CR-d1); *middle left:* selected stone vessels (CR2277-d1); *middle right:* miniature alabaster vessels from Lepsius 52, shaft S 69 (AEOS_8960); *bottom:* ceramics

(CR6523-d1). All images HU–MFA Expedition, courtesy of Museum of Fine Arts, Boston, except for middle right, courtesy of Kunsthistorisches Museum Vienna.

W4.3 Discovery and Harvard Camp photos of the Menkaure dyad, MFA 11.1738. *Top left:* Menkaure Valley Temple. Feb. 9, 1910. Photo by Badawi Ahmed (A327). *Top right:* looking south. Jan. 19, 1910. Photo by Badawi Ahmed (B477). *Bottom left:* looking south. Jan. 19, 1910. Photo by Badawi Ahmed (B481). *Bottom right:* May 1910. Photo by Prosser (A480). HU–MFA Expedition, courtesy of Museum of Fine Arts, Boston.

W5.1.The mastaba of Kaninisut (G 2155). *Top:* packing crates with chapel reliefs, looking north. Mar. 1914 (AEOS_I_5704). *Bottom:* north wall of the chapel in the Kunsthistorisches Museum Vienna, ÄS 8006 (AEOS_8006_35392). Both images courtesy of Kunsthistorisches Museum.

W6.1.*Left:* south side of the Great Pyramid, looking north, showing the Khufu Boat Museum (indicated by the arrow) and, to its left, a temporary structure over the ancient boat pit, in which conservation work on the second boat has been undertaken. Oct. 7, 2011. Courtesy of AirPano. com. *Right:* two views of the Khufu boat in the museum. *Left:* Aug. 11, 2005 (PDM_03400). *Right:* Aug. 1977 (AAW 1615). Photos by author.